INTERCULTURAL COMMUNICATION COMPETENCE

INTERNATIONAL AND INTERCULTURAL COMMUNICATION ANNUAL

Volume XVII **1993**

INTERNATIONAL AND INTERCULTURAL COMMUNICATION ANNUAL
VOLUME XVII 1993

INTERCULTURAL COMMUNICATION COMPETENCE

edited by

Richard L. WISEMAN
Jolene KOESTER

Published in Cooperation with
The Speech Communication Association
Commission on International and Intercultural Communication

SAGE Publications
International Educational and Professional Publisher
Newbury Park London New Delhi

For information address:

SAGE Publications, Inc.
2455 Teller Road
Newbury Park, California 91320

SAGE Publications Ltd.
6 Bonhill Street
London EC2A 4PU
United Kingdom

SAGE Publications India Pvt. Ltd.
M-32 Market
Greater Kailash I
New Delhi 110 048 India

Printed in the United States of America

Library of Congress Cataloging-in-Publication Data

ISBN 0-8039-4719-4
ISBN 0-8039-4720 (pbk.)
ISBN 0270-6075

93 94 95 96 10 9 8 7 6 5 4 3 2 1

Sage Production Editor: Astrid Virding

Contents

Preface

This is the seventeenth volume of the **International and Intercultural Communication Annual,** a series sponsored by the Speech Communication Association's International and Intercultural Communication Division. The series of theme-based publications aims at promoting better understanding of communication processes in international and intercultural contexts. In preparing for this volume, the guiding principle was to bring together current theoretical and research studies focusing on intercultural communication competence. More specifically, *Intercultural Communication Competence* presents state-of-the-art theoretical orientations, methodologies, and research on the nature of communication competence in intercultural and cross-cultural contexts. Theoretical orientations encompass uncertainty reduction, face management, and face negotiation. Recommendations for both quantitative and qualitative research are provided. Exemplary conceptual and empirical studies are also included as models for scholars and students.

The book is developed in three parts. Part I analyzes the conceptual decisions made in intercultural communication competence research. Decisions regarding conceptualization, operationalization, research design, and sampling are examined. Part II presents four different theoretical orientations. Each of these chapters articulates how one's theoretical orientation dictates research foci. Part III examines quantitative and qualitative research in studying intercultural communication competence.

Many people were involved in the completion of this volume. First, I would like to extend my appreciation to all the authors who donated their time and energy. Without their creative thinking, articulate expression, and long hours of work, this book would not exist. Second, I would like to thank Jolene Koester, the coeditor, for her continued support, hard work, and positive attitude throughout the editing process; Judith Sanders, the editorial assistant, for her keen eye for composition and logic; and all the editorial board members for generously offering their time and expertise in reviewing manuscripts. Third, I would like to express my gratitude to Bill Gudykunst and Stella Ting-Toomey, my colleagues and friends, for their constant encouragement and professionalism throughout every phase of the book's preparation. Last, but not least, I extend my appreciation to my special children—Mikey, Michele, and Nicole—for continually reminding me of the joys of life and for the "semi-uninterrupted" time they gave me to work on this book.

Richard L. Wiseman
California State University, Fullerton

I

CONCEPTUAL ISSUES

1

Multiple Perspectives of Intercultural Communication Competence

JOLENE KOESTER • *California State University, Sacramento*

RICHARD L. WISEMAN • *California State University, Fullerton*

JUDITH A. SANDERS • *California State Polytechnic University, Pomona*

The imperative for the scholarly investigation of intercultural communication competence is ubiquitous. Because of the greatest migration of human populations across national boundaries in humankind's history, interactions of people the world over are increasingly intercultural. The traditional goals of the scholar—to describe, to understand, to explain, and to predict—have become critically important to the political, economic, and social vitality of the world's multicultural societies.

Despite widespread agreement about the importance of intercultural communication competence in today's world, there is relatively little consensus among those studying the subject about how best to approach, conceptualize, study, or measure it. Each scholar begins his or her research with different assumptions about how to conceptualize intercultural competence, with different goals about the desired outcomes of research endeavors, and with different methodologies to observe and reach conclusions. Rarely are those starting points clearly explicated, which makes it difficult to coalesce the research findings into a coherent body of knowledge about intercultural communication competence. Just as intercultural communication scholars explicitly recognize that people from different cultures use varying beliefs, values, and norms as the starting points for the construction of "alternative realities" (Stewart & Bennett, 1991), so too must researchers of intercultural communication competence recognize that varying starting points produce alternative realities and multiple truths about competence in intercultural communication.

Our goal in this introductory chapter is to describe the various perspectives from which intercultural communication competence scholars can choose to begin their investigations. In explicating the vantage points, or presuppositions, from which scholars operate, we make explicit the biases and blinders that shape the research literature. In addition, we offer a framework within which the remaining chapters in this volume, and previous and subsequent inquiries about intercultural communication competence, can be placed.

OVERVIEW AND DEVELOPMENT OF RATIONALE

Thomas Kuhn's *The Structure of Scientific Revolutions* (1970) has become a classic work in understanding the consequences of the implicit but pervasive assumptions that serve as the foundation for scientific and social scientific research. Kuhn's argument, which holds that scholarship takes place within accepted paradigms that carry with them accepted truths about the nature of reality and that these are replaced with new truths as new paradigms are accepted, shatters any illusion of total objectivity in the conduct of research. Kuhn argues that an obligation of the scholarly community, or at least of some of its members, is to explicate the assumptions of the prevailing research paradigm.

Every researcher begins the inquiry process with presuppositions or biases about the appropriate motivations for research, the correct methodologies to use, and the relationship between scholarship and everyday human experiences. These presuppositions form blinders, which are worn as the researcher begins a particular study. Most researchers acquire these assumptions gradually, from personal experiences and academic training, and they create their own definitions of reality from them. Such blinders are not evil; rather, they are a necessary and inevitable attribute of all research. Critiques of other scholars' works are often implicitly grounded in a disagreement about the initial presuppositions of the researchers. An understanding, evaluation, and synthesis of intercultural communication competence research requires an explication of the metatheories underlying the epistemology of the research. The researchers' assumptions include issues about basic nomenclature, the domain of inquiry, and the interrelationships among theory, methods, goals, and cultural perspective. In the next section, we explicate the presuppositions commonly underlying research on intercultural communication competence.

STARTING POINTS FOR STUDY

The study of intercultural communication competence has been nurtured in several disciplines over some 40 to 50 years and it is not our intention to provide a summary of the historical record of the study of intercultural communication competence (Hammer, 1989). Rather, our goal is to identify the inevitable choices scholars make, usually implicitly, when they do their research.

In the following discussion of presuppositions, we identify seven common issues researchers typically decide before they begin their research. For each of the *topoi*, we describe the nature of the premise—the range of positions taken by intercultural communication scholars, cite examples of extant work illustrating those choices, and refer the reader to the metatheoretical choices revealed in this volume's contributions.

Nomenclature

All researchers make choices about the nomenclature used to identify their concepts. Succinctly, is the topic of study best conceptualized as intercultural communication competence, intercultural effectiveness, or intercultural success?

Researchers first studying intercultural communication competence used a wide array of labels. Early scholars, using a variety of disciplinary perspectives, studied the problems of individuals working and living in other cultures, labeling what they studied as cross-cultural adjustment, cross-cultural adaptation, cross-cultural success, cross-cultural effectiveness, cross-cultural failure, personal adjustment, personal success, or personal failure (see e.g., Guthrie & Zektick, 1967; Harris, 1975; Lysgaard, 1955; Mischel, 1965).

Within the field of communication, the growth of specialization in intercultural communication produced a similarly heterogeneous list of labels (e.g., substituting *intercultural* for *cross-cultural*). A commonly accepted distinction between cross-cultural and intercultural research is that cross-cultural research involves the comparative study in multiple cultures, whereas intercultural research involves the study of people from differing cultures who are interacting together (Asante & Gudykunst, 1989). Because of this distinction, the adjective *intercultural* has come to be the prevailing modifier, rather than *cross-cultural*.

The two terms most widely used by scholars studying the outcomes of intercultural interaction were *competence* (Hammer, 1984) and *effectiveness* (Hammer, Gudykunst, & Wiseman, 1978; Koester & Olebe,

1988). Within the last decade, the majority of intercultural communication scholars chose to use the term *competence* to identify their subject of study (Bostrum, 1984; McCroskey, 1982; Spitzberg & Cupach, 1984; Wiemann, 1977). Not coincidentally, this development paralleled a growing consensus among communication scholars, who studied the valence and outcomes of interpersonal interactions, to use the nomenclature *competence* to identify what they were studying. The term *competence* has roots in sociolinguistic traditions, as well, giving it increased credibility. By 1989, when the *International Journal of Intercultural Relations* (*IJIR*) published a special issue on this subject (Martin, 1989), there was obviously a growing consensus on the use of *competence* as the preferred term for the outcome under study (see also, Lustig & Koester, 1993). We, in turn, in selecting the title for this volume acknowledged formally the judgments of our colleagues that both *intercultural* and *competence* were the appropriate terms to refer to the phenomenon under study.

While most intercultural communication scholars now consistently use both *intercultural* and *competence*, rarely are explanations offered that explain the coalescing of forces around the choice of *competence* rather than *effectiveness*, *success*, *understanding*, or *adjustment*. Perhaps because communication scholars had previously engaged in the debate about the nomenclature, intercultural scholars have simply accepted the term.

The relative consensus on the use of *competence* was stimulated by methodological innovations in the conceptualization and measurement of the concept (Spitzberg, 1987; Spitzberg & Cupach, 1984). Also, there is general agreement that the two most critical dimensions of competence are effectiveness and appropriateness. Effectiveness is described as a judgment about the ability of the interactants in the intercultural exchange to achieve their goals. Appropriateness refers to what is regarded as proper and suitable in a given situation within a particular culture. Other dimensions of competence that have been considered include ability (knowledge), skill (performance), and clarity (understanding).

Not everyone grappling with the study of intercultural communication competence is willing to settle on the nomenclature represented by either stem of the phrase. The distinction between cross-cultural and intercultural is widely, but not universally, accepted. Even in the special edition of *IJIR* on intercultural communication competence, Ruben (1989) consistently used the term *cross-cultural* to refer to interactions among people from different cultures. A similar choice is made by Kim in this book. Gudykunst, in Chapter 3 of this book, presents a theory for effective interpersonal and intergroup communication. He chooses to define *effectiveness* as "minimizing misunderstandings" (p. 34) and views this as *competence*.

The Domain of Inquiry

Issues about the domain of inquiry require judgments about whether intercultural communication competence resides within an individual, the social context, the culture, or the relationship among individuals, or some combination of these possibilities. Early writing on intercultural communication competence focused on the assessment of the characteristics of individuals and their relationship to the outcomes of intercultural interaction. Attitudes, beliefs, and values, with psychometric measures of how these predispositions were configured in any one person, were employed to predict intercultural success, failure, or adjustment of individuals (e.g., Smith, 1965). Another significant phase of research located intercultural competence in the behaviors of individuals, not in their attitudes, or other self-identified characteristics (Abe & Wiseman, 1983; Hammer, 1987; Hammer, Gudykunst, & Wiseman, 1978; Koester & Olebe, 1988; Ruben, 1976).

Emerging within the study of intercultural communication competence is agreement that competence is a social judgment, which requires an evaluation by one's relational partners of one's communication performance. These judgments are based on perceptions of appropriateness and effectiveness. This view of competence as a social impression also requires recognition that competence is not determined by the knowledge, motivation, or skills of only one of the parties in the interaction, but rather that judgments of competence are relational outcomes. Koester and Olebe (1988) argued that judgments of competence were made by partners in an interaction and could be measured by the description of particular behaviors. Imahori and Lanigan (1989) developed a relational model of intercultural communication competence in which each participant's judgments of the other's intercultural communication competence were measured.

Permeating the chapters in this volume are the authors' judgments about the location of competence. Ting-Toomey, for example, is explicit in placing judgments of intercultural competence as the negotiation of identity "between two or more interactants in a novel communication episode" (p. 73). Likewise, Gudykunst, Cupach and Imahori, and Milhouse (Chapters 3, 5, and 9, respectively) view competence as occurring within a relationship. Alternatively, Nakanishi and Johnson and Kim view competence as primarily based on individual characteristics. In Chapter 8, Carbaugh relies heavily on social context in viewing competence as dependent on what is possible, feasible, appropriate, and actually performed in an interaction.

The Relationship of Theory to Observation

Should the study of intercultural communication competence begin with a well-developed theory that allows for specific predictions, or should researchers begin by documenting observations and then developing theory through carefully presented cases? Tension surrounding the answer to this question ripples through the literature on intercultural communication competence and there are strong advocates on both sides of the debate.

The ethnographer studying competence unequivocally argues for building descriptive cases of competent and incompetent communication to reveal the appropriate and effective patterns of communication within a particular social and cultural situation. Carbaugh, for example, described the manner in which collected ethnographic works "inquire about loci and sources of intercultural asynchrony by examining instances of intercultural contacts" (1990, p. 152). The ethnographer uses this focus on the performance of intercultural communication to highlight "what needs attention theoretically and practically in situations of intercultural contact" (Carbaugh, 1990, p. 153). Collier (1988; 1991) and Collier, Ribeau, and Hecht (1986) provide other examples of researchers who presented detailed and carefully described observations of competence. In these studies, the researchers asked student representatives of diverse U.S. domestic cultural groups to describe the characteristics of competent communicators within their cultural group and about their expectations for competent intercultural communication from other U.S. domestic cultural members. Martin and Hammer (1989) based their work on behavioral categories of intercultural communication competence on perceptions of individuals "grounded in perceptions of everyday communication" (p. 305).

In his critique of the intercultural communication competence research, Spitzberg (1989) offered the other end of the continuum in the debate concerning the proper relationship of theory to observation. He was strident in his plea for the development of a systematic theory from which to make predictions about judgments of competence by intercultural interactants. In this book, both Ting-Toomey and Gudykunst frame their contributions in the form of well-developed theories with theorems and derived axioms, which are testable through specific observations with predicted effects. In contrast, Kim, Nakanishi and Johnson, and

Carbaugh (Chapters 6, 10, and 8, respectively) focus on observations to generate elements of theory.

Goals: Conceptual vs. Practical

Presuppositions about the goals of scholarship can be used also to differentiate among researchers. Some researchers of intercultural communication competence direct their efforts toward the practical application of knowledge in order to improve intercultural interactions. Others argue that the development of conceptual and theoretical excellence must be the primary goal. Much of the original scholarship on intercultural communication competence came directly from individuals engaged in very practical, day-to-day intercultural activities. As Ruben (1989) described this set of circumstances: "Much of the impetus for the study of cross-cultural communication competence arose out of efforts to cope with practical problems encountered by individuals living and working overseas, and by their institutional sponsors" (p. 229).

International education professionals regularly selected students for international exchange programs. In addition, they oriented and counseled those who attended universities and colleges in countries other than their own. Governmental agencies and businesses invested significant resources in selecting and training individuals for international assignments (Ruben & Kealey, 1979). The stimulus for much research was an immediate need to make decisions and choices about whom to send on an overseas assignment and how to train them. Much of this research, when evaluated by the scholar interested in the development of a cogent conceptual framework, has been dismissed for a variety of reasons including lack of methodological rigor and lack of theoretical grounding, and sometimes just because it had a practical goal (Spitzberg, 1989).

Nevertheless, the powerful force of practical need still serves to motivate a significant number of researchers. Koester and Olebe (1988) offered as support for the Behavior Assessment Scale of Intercultural Communication the potential ease with which the scale could be used in practice settings. Dinges and Lieberman (1989) sought to understand the problem of displaying competence in intercultural employment situations. Kealey's (1989) research was directed at the practical goal of improving the selection of personnel who would be involved in international development projects. Hammer and Martin (1992) reported on a training program for Japanese and U.S. managers in one corporation.

Because we believe that theory underlies practical and training applications, this book emphasizes the theoretical end of the goal continuum. Nevertheless, there are threads of practical application weaving their way through the scholarship presented here. The theoretical analyses of face management and negotiation—Ting-Toomey's Chapter 4 and Cupach and Imahori's Chapter 5—provide many heuristic propositions that have practical applications for trainer and educator. Martin gives considerable attention to the contributions of researchers with a practical goal. In Chapter 6, Kim invokes the goal of improving the competence of individuals as a goal for her research.

Methodology: Quantitative to Qualitative

Scholars generally divide on the appropriate choice of methodological tools. Some prefer the precision of quantitative methods, while others want the richness and vitality that qualitative methods provide. Retrospectives of any specialization within the communication discipline acknowledge disagreements about the appropriateness of one methodology over another. Debates on the quantitative-qualitative choice are certainly not unique to the study of intercultural communication competence.

The early history of the study of intercultural communication, however, provides one unique twist to discussions surrounding scholars' choices on this perspective. The founders of the specialization of intercultural communication, working in uncharted territory, depended on numerous anecdotes to develop and direct their ideas. The first decade of research in intercultural communication has often been characterized as "research by anecdote." The growth of doctoral programs that allowed specializations in intercultural communication produced scholars well-trained in the traditional underpinnings of scholarly research, many initially trained to emphasize the collection and evaluation of data through quantitative means. The consequence of this confluence of research history is that qualitative approaches were probably less valued than were quantitative approaches in the study of intercultural communication.

The balance has now shifted, however, toward the center of the methodological continuum, with scholars approaching the study of intercultural communication competence from both the qualitative and quantitative perspectives. Philipsen's (1975) work on the competent communication of men in Teamsterville, along with Carbaugh's (1990) book showcasing numerous studies of competent intra- and intercultural communication, serve as models for those pursuing the study of intercultural communication competence through the use and analysis of qualitative data. Collier (1989) describes an interpretative approach to study cultural competence, which uses primarily qualitative analysis of data.

Discussions on methodology have also shifted beyond arguments for or against a particular methodological approach to arguments establishing judgments about the soundness and rigor with which the methodologies are used. Lustig and Spitzberg in this volume carefully establish the challenges to the researcher when choosing to examine intercultural communication competence through the use of quantitative research methods. They identify concerns in terms of what should be assessed, whom to assess, when to assess, where the assessment is made, why competence should be studied, and with what effects such studies occur. Milhouse (Chapter 9) presents a traditional quantitative study testing the validity of applying quantitative instruments to the measurement of competence. Alternatively, Carbaugh's study demonstrates the logic underlying the analysis of qualitative data about intercultural communication competence between representatives of U.S. and Russian cultures.

Perspective on the Primacy of Culture

Researchers' presuppositions also typically include a judgment about whether to accent the term *intercultural* or the term *communication*. From which theoretical tradition do the researchers of intercultural communication competence draw their inspirations? Does the study of intercultural communication competence begin from an intercultural perspective and investigate the distinctive properties that variations in culture bring to communication? Or is it most appropriate to begin with the study of intracultural communication competence and then extend the results to the intercultural setting?

Again, there are vocal adherents of both points of view among those studying intercultural communication competence. Spitzberg (1989), for instance, is unequivocal in the articulation of his position: "Progress in the study of intercultural communication competence is going to derive mainly from the development of sound interpersonal communication competence theories that can then be applied to the intercultural setting. . . . What is needed is a culture invariant model of communication processes that account for cultural variances" (p. 261).

Martin and Hammer (1989), in contrast, ask their subjects, who are describing intercultural communication competence, to begin with their intercultural experiences and to identify the unique characteristics of their communication in that context. Martin, in Chapter 2 of this book, summarizes the consequences of this debate:

> Researchers investigating interpersonal competence wrestled with the definition and measurement of communication competence, but with little exception . . . largely ignored the cultural constraints of their findings. In contrast, researchers in intercultural communication explored cultural variations in competence, but focused only tangentially on communication behaviors and often ignored the conceptual questions addressed by interpersonal communication research. (p. 16)

Similarly stark representatives of both points of view are included in this book. Milhouse makes a choice similar to that advocated by Spitzberg (1989) and starts with a theory and set of scales developed for the study of interpersonal communication competence. Her purpose is to study the scales' cross-cultural equivalence by using them with individuals from different cultures. Conversely, Kim starts with the dimensions of culture to predict choices of conversational strategy that will be judged competent by representatives from cultures prototypical of the dimensions.

From within the seemingly dichotomous choices on this issue, however, a new approach is beginning to emerge. This approach can best be characterized as the development of theory that recognizes the role of culture in communication. Ting-Toomey's contribution in this volume stands as an excellent illustration. While she develops a theory of identity negotiation as communication competence, the theory itself accounts for the variations in culture as the source for people's interactive images and interactive motivations and meanings. Likewise, Gudykunst's theory considers constructs at the individual, interpersonal, intergroup, and cultural level in explaining communication effectiveness.

Culture General to Culture Specific

Another issue concerns whether it is important to study intercultural communication competence from a culture-general or culture-specific approach. In other words, is intercultural communication competence best understood, theoretically and practically, from the standpoint of specific cultures, with their particular rules, knowledge, and behaviors? Or is it best understood by the identification of more universal concepts, which apply across all cultures? The crux of the choice on this presupposition is a scholar's judgment about whether intercultural competence can be theoretically, conceptually, or even practically identified without reference to the specifics of interaction rules within a particular culture.

Scholars of intercultural communication competence also bring to their research implicit understandings about the generalizability of their research findings beyond those specific individuals studied. Some scholars describe competent communication among members of a particular culture and make no claim about the applicability of their research findings to members of any other culture. Wieder and Pratt, for example, describe the competent communication of Native Americans (1990). Others study competent or incompetent intercultural communication between members from specific cultures, but make no claim beyond these particular interactions. Triandis's (1973) work with the cultural assimilator, which is based in the particular knowledge and interaction rules of two specifically identified cultures, is an example of this approach. Dinges and Lieberman (1989) argue that intercultural competence is not just culture-specific, but also emphasize the importance of context in judgments of competence. Others similarly study intercultural communication competence as it is judged by members of specific cultures, yet use their research findings to generalize to principles of competence that apply to other cultures. Several studies have been conducted using U.S. American and Japanese subjects, for example, with the research findings used to draw some general conclusions about intercultural communication competence (Abe & Wiseman, 1983; Wiseman & Abe, 1986).

Contributors to this volume array themselves at various points along the continuum. Carbaugh describes competent intercultural communication between representatives of the specific cultural groups of the United States and Russia. Cupach and Imahori and Lustig and Spitzberg place themselves at the other end of the continuum with a decidedly culture-general approach, as does Milhouse. In Chapter 10, Nakanishi and Johnson deal specifically with Chinese and U.S. cultural group members, but make claims based on their findings for universal qualities of communication competence.

THE CONSEQUENCES OF CHOICES

The editors of any book, including this one, must make choices about both content and organization. In so doing they provide a frame or filter for understanding the metatheoretic presuppositions embedded within the chapters. Because it is impossible to present ideas in the linear format of a book without an explicit organizational framework, we, too, have followed this protocol. We have chosen a fairly typical organizational framework that segments the book into chapters considering conceptual issues (Koester, Wiseman, & Sanders, and Martin), theoretical perspectives (Gudykunst, Ting-Toomey, Cupach & Imahori, and Kim), and research perspectives in the study of intercultural communication competence (Lustig & Spitzberg, Carbaugh, Milhouse, and Nakanishi & Johnson). This framework represents our understanding of some of the choices the authors have made among the multiple perspectives we have reviewed. The arrangement of the articles into the table of contents also displays our own implicit assumptions about the most desirable vantage points from which to study intercultural communication competence.

It would be possible, however, to organize these chapters to highlight the authors' choices among perspectives differently. Alternative organizational frameworks might have arrayed the chapters based on issues related to the topoi delineated above. For example, similar first and second sections (conceptual and then methodological issues) might be followed by a section on culture-specific approaches to intercultural competence (Carbaugh, Kim, and Nakanishi & Johnson) and then a section on culture-general approaches to competence (Cupach & Imahori, Milhouse, Gudykunst, and Ting-Toomey). Also, with the Koester, Wiseman, and Sanders, Martin, and Lustig and Spitzberg articles serving as conceptual and methodological foundations, a third approach could identify additional chapters focusing on competence as effectiveness and appropriateness (Milhouse, Nakanishi & Johnson, and Carbaugh), competence as relational negotiation (Ting-Toomey and Cupach & Imahori), and competence as prediction and explanation of behavior (Kim and Gudykunst). Other arrangements are likewise possible. Each of the book's chapters, therefore, should be read with an eye toward understanding the choices made by the author(s), not just the choices made by the editors.

It is important for both the beginning and advanced scholar to take stock of the almost unconscious framing of issues in the study of intercultural communication competence. Categorizing any single research contribution on only one perspective or critiquing its approach and findings using only one set of evaluative criteria simplifies the body of research. But dismissing or praising any piece of research because of the scholar's choice on one of the topoi discussed above forces into the background other important considerations. It is necessary to recognize that although the presuppositions of an individual researcher may be correlated with other presuppositions she or he holds, these choices are not necessarily isomorphic.

Finally, it is critical to recognize that too often scholarly orthodoxy about presuppositions produces arguments that scholars *should* or *must* make a particular choice in order to produce excellent research. Arguments about the necessity to conduct research on intercultural communication competence from only a qualitative or only a quantitative point of view, for example, deny the significant contributions of both points of view. Consensus about the choices a scholar makes on any of these perspectives does not necessarily signify that truth has been discovered; it suggests that at a particular point in time members of a portion of the scholarly community have come to share a common understanding on key conceptual and methodological issues. Just as intercultural communication scholarship either implicitly or explicitly acknowledges that different cultures create realities from varying starting points, so too must the intercultural communication scholar interested in studying competence celebrate the diversity in choices made when conducting research.

2

Intercultural Communication Competence

A Review

JUDITH N. MARTIN • *Arizona State University*

The desire to understand and measure communicative competence has produced a substantial body of research and theory (Bostrom, 1984; Spitzberg & Cupach, 1984, 1989). However, there has been less progress made in investigations of intercultural communication competence; scholars have decried the lack of theoretical integration and duplicative efforts of recent research (Hammer, 1989; Kim, 1991; Spitzberg, 1989). This deficit can be traced historically to the research conducted both in intercultural and interpersonal communication. This chapter traces the development of the research, describes current perspectives, and outlines directions for future research in intercultural communication competence.

A review of literature reveals two parallel lines of research conducted by interpersonal communication scholars and intercultural communication scholars in the 1970s and 1980s. Researchers investigating interpersonal competence wrestled with the definition and measurement of communication competence, but with little exception (e.g., Cooley & Roach, 1984) largely ignored the cultural constraints of their findings. In contrast, researchers in intercultural communication explored cultural variations in competence, but focused only tangentially on communication behaviors and often ignored the conceptual questions addressed by interpersonal communication research.

INTERPERSONAL COMMUNICATION COMPETENCE FROM A WESTERN PERSPECTIVE

Early investigations of interpersonal communication competence reveal the applied foundations of the research and the influence of research in related disciplines, including investigations in psychology and social psychology on competence (Athay & Darley, 1981), social competence and social skills (Argyle, 1979, 1980, 1981; McFall, 1982), linguistic competence and performance (Chomsky, 1965; Habermas, 1970a), and sociolinguistic notions of the importance of context in understanding communication competence (Hymes, 1974; Saville-Troike, 1982). In an effort to integrate previous research findings, Wiemann (1977) proposed a model of competence with five components—empathy, affiliation/support, social relaxation, behavioral flexibility, interaction management—and identified specific behaviors within each component. In his model, communicative competence was defined as "the ability of an interactant to choose among available communicative behaviors in order that he [she] may successfully accomplish his [her] own interpersonal goals . . . while maintaining the face and line of his [her] fellow interactants within the constraints of the situation" (p. 198).

Wiemann's conceptualization and most subsequent research in interpersonal communication competence share underlying assumptions. First, individuals hold *cognitive notions* about what comprises competence. Second, individuals form impressions of others' behavior and then use these expectations as guidelines to *judge* their own and others' behaviors. The degree to which the ideal meets the expected is the degree to which behavior is judged competent. Researchers have focused on varying stages of this process. For example, one line of research identified the implicit cognitive prototypes of what the competent or ideal communicator should be (Pavitt, 1981, 1989, 1990; Pavitt & Haight, 1985, 1986), including sets of behaviors (e.g., listens well) and traits (e.g., is friendly) of the ideal communicator. Later research focused on the judgment stage and found a high correlation between impressions and competence evaluations, both from observations of a target individual who was role-playing (Pavitt, 1989) and from reports of more naturally formed impressions of self (Pavitt, 1990).

Spitzberg and Cupach (1984) and Spitzberg and Hecht (1984) proposed a more comprehensive model of competence. In this model, communication competence is also defined as an *impression*, comprising both effectiveness (related to reaching one's goals) and appropriateness (not violating norms), composed of knowledge, motivation, and social skills. The social skills component comprises dimensions similar to those in Wiemann's (1977) model (immediacy, interaction management, social relaxation, expressiveness, and altercentrism) and, again, researchers identified sets of verbal and nonverbal behaviors that demonstrated these and related dimensions of competence (Cegala, 1981, 1984; Coker & Burgoon, 1987; Spitzberg & Cupach, 1984).

Most recently, Spitzberg and Brunner (1991) propose a framework for incorporating context into expectations of competent behavior. They suggest that impressions of competence are based not only on the interactants' motivation, knowledge, and skill but also on the extent to which contextual expectations are met. These expectations are organized along four dimensions: *Cultural* contexts are based on broad group memberships (e.g., national, ethnic, racial); *type* represents situational contexts (e.g., task, social; Cantor, Mischel, & Schwartz, 1982; Hammer, 1989; Wiseman, Hammer, & Nishida, 1989); *relationship* concerns the degree of intimacy; and *function* considers the goals and objectives of the interaction. Spitzberg and Brunner's (1991) research testing this approach confirms the importance of integrating context into a comprehensive theory of interpersonal communication competence. The greater the discrepancy between the expected and the encountered context, the less satisfied the interactants were likely to be. It should be noted, however, that the study was conducted with a primarily Euro-American sample.

To summarize this approach to competence, much of the discussion has revolved around definitions and conceptualizations of communicative competence and related issues: for example, whether emphasis should be placed on the cognitive or on the behavioral aspects of competence (Pavitt & Haight, 1985, 1986; Spitzberg & Cupach, 1984, 1989; Wiemann & Backlund, 1980), whether a distinction between competence and performance was appropriate (Backlund, 1982; McCroskey, 1982; Spitzberg, 1983), whether competence generalizes across situations as a *trait* or is situation-specific (Cupach & Spitzberg, 1983), and whether the judgment of competence varied with the locus of evaluation (the self, the other person in the interaction, or an outside observer; Hecht & Sereno, 1985; Roloff & Kellerman, 1984; Spitzberg & Cupach, 1989).

The research findings are fairly consistent in identifying behaviors and skills that lead to impressions of competence, and thus have contributed much to our understanding of competent behavior. However, this understanding is limited primarily to *a specific speech community* —the Euro-American community, and largely middle-class, college-educated strata within this community. Developing such culture-specific theories of communicative competence, although useful, has inhibited progress toward a general theory of competence because the findings and conclusions from these theories were sometimes inappropriately used to conduct scientific tests whose results were then extrapolated to inferring the universality of general theories (Bormann, 1980, 1989; Craig, 1989). This led to theories and perspectives that were mostly Eurocentric in tradition. For example, the centrality of goal attainment and individual control in Euro-American communicative competence research (Parks, 1985; Wiemann & Kelly, 1981) may not be generalizable to cultural groups where achieving relational harmony may be more important in defining communication competence than achieving individual communicative goals (Gudykunst & Ting-Toomey, 1988; Stewart & Bennett, 1991).

Further, this Eurocentric view of communication competence is reflected not only in research but in teaching. Undergraduate communication texts often instruct students implicitly or explicitly that the behaviors identified as leading to impressions of competence (e.g., those related to expressiveness, interaction management, immediacy) within the Euro-American community generalize to other cultural contexts. It is not clear to what degree the models representing Euro-American communicative competence are applicable to other cultures. As Koester and Lustig (1991) caution:

> The theory and prescriptions taught in . . . communication courses are similarly Anglo-centered. . . . [We do not suggest] that theory, which forms the basis for much of what is taught about communication, be discarded simply because it is informed by an Anglo-U.S. cultural perspective. Instead, we raise these issues to suggest that, at a minimum, instructors of communication should explore the degree to which the content of their courses myopically reflects a set of assumptions and a point of view that may only be appropriate for members of a limited number of cultures. (p. 252)

The Western bias in the research on communicative competence has also led to a reliance on the positivistic research paradigm (Spitzberg, 1989). The limitations of this particular schema have been noted by scholars who advocate more interpretive, subjective research paradigms. Collier (1989), for example, questions the generalizability of culture-specific findings on communication competence and argues that one way to establish representational and cultural validity before developing culture-general theories is by following an ethnographic research tradition. Others have suggested that we view alternative research methodologies as equally useful and complementary (Gudykunst & Nishida, 1989; Hecht, Ribeau, & Alberts, 1989) and that we look "to the great intellectual and cultural traditions of Asia, such as those of China, Japan, and India. . . . Such great civilizations could not have been produced if questions of practical communication and communication metatheory were ignored" (Dissanayake, 1989, p. 168).

In sum, research and theorizing on the notion of interpersonal communication competence from a Western perspective raised and answered important questions about the conceptualization and measurement of the concept of competence, and contributed a great deal to our understanding of knowledge, attitudes, and behaviors that lead to impressions of competence within a specific speech community. However, the research was less successful in confronting the issue of the applicability of findings to a variety of cultural contexts and other research paradigms.

CROSS-CULTURAL COMPARISONS OF INTERPERSONAL COMMUNICATION COMPETENCE

A second area of research investigates (either implicitly or explicitly) how definitions and enactment of communicative competence vary culturally. For example, Barnlund and colleagues' work contrasting communication norms of Japanese and Americans (Barnlund, 1989; Barnlund & Araki, 1985; Barnlund & Yoshioka, 1990) and Kochman's (1981, 1990a, 1990b) descriptions of black and white communication styles are presumably describing patterns of competent communication in these respective cultures.

Similarly, ethnographers of communication (Basso, 1970; Philipsen, 1975, 1986; Saville-Troike, 1982) have been interested in describing competent patterns of communication within specific speech communities. More recently, ethnographers have explicitly investigated variations of speech patterns across cultures, including the communal functions of speech (Philipsen, 1989), terms for talk (Carbaugh, 1989, 1990c), and the uses of silence (Braithwaite, 1990). Collier (1988) and Collier, Ribeau, and Hecht (1986) compared notions of competence in black, Hispanic, and white cultures from a systems/rules perspective. They found that although some rules (e.g., be polite) were shared, the cultural groups varied in rule enactment and outcome. Mexican-Americans emphasized role prescriptions; Afro-Americans emphasized verbal content; and Euro-Americans emphasized politeness behaviors above all other rules.

In order to understand more fully how notions of competence vary from culture to culture, one could take the models developed in the Euro-American community (Pavitt & Haight, 1985, 1986; Wiemann, 1977) and apply them in another cultural context as an imposed etic. Either the framework will hold or modification of categories will be made until it is emically appropriate for both cultural groups without destroying the etic characteristic of the framework. The research approach can be taken into a third and fourth culture as a derived etic (Martin, Hecht, & Larkey, 1992).

These cross-cultural comparisons are useful, but they do not necessarily reveal what happens when interactants from two different cultural backgrounds communicate. One can only infer from the two sets of expectations what competent *intercultural* interaction would look like, and it is more likely that what actually occurs is not based exclusively on one or the other cultural group's norms, but rather an amalgam—related to the notion of third culture perspective (Casmir & Asuncione-Lande, 1988; Olebe & Koester, 1989), depending on the particular context.

INTERCULTURAL COMMUNICATION COMPETENCE

Many intercultural researchers recognized the cultural variability in the notion of competence and to some extent have been more open to alternative research methodologies (Asante & Vora, 1983; Casmir & Asuncione-Lande, 1988; Kincaid, 1987). However, most early research investigating intercultural competence was characterized by little attention to conceptual and metatheoretical considerations and little attention to the concurrent work in interpersonal communication competence.

In a way similar to investigations of interpersonal competence, the interest in intercultural competence arose from practical concerns, those experienced by overseas sojourners such as American diplomatic personnel (Leeds-Hurwitz, 1990) as well as Peace Corps and technical assistance workers overseas (Ruben, 1976, 1977, 1989; Ruben & Kealey, 1979). The conceptualizations and measurement of competence usually focused on sojourners' attitudes, skills, and general ability to function in an intercultural setting, encompassing more than communicative dimensions (Barna, 1979; Dinges, 1983; Martin, 1987).

There were two early research efforts focused on intercultural *communication* competence. Ruben (1976) identified seven categories in evaluating effective intercultural communication, similar to those identified in the interpersonal literature: display of respect, interaction posture, orientation to knowledge, empathy, role behavior, interaction management, and tolerance for ambiguity. He developed operational definitions and a one-item scale for each dimension. The original scale was intended for use by trained observers. Later researchers, using both self-report and observer ratings, applied these same dimensions to evaluate the effectiveness of overseas technical assistance personnel (Kealey, 1989; Ruben & Kealey, 1979), Japanese student sojourners (Nishida, 1985), and intercultural communication workshop participants (Hammer, 1984).

Koester and Olebe (1988) argued that the approach was theoretically sound, and could be operationalized to a multicultural population. They reworded the scales to be used by nontrained observers and evaluated the effectiveness of intercultural roommates. Later, they attempted to establish equivalence of the scale (conceptual/functional, construct operationalization, and item levels) with some success (Olebe & Koester, 1989). Although they provide evidence to suggest that the categories may be culture-general and the scale may be used by nontrained peers to evaluate intercultural communication effectiveness, there has been little empirical research demonstrating precisely how these dimensions were enacted behaviorally.

Hammer, Gudykunst, and Wiseman (1978) derived three basic factors from their review of literature and self-report data from successful overseas sojourners: ability to deal with psychological stress, ability to communicate effectively, and ability to establish interpersonal relationships. Subsequent investigations (Abe & Wiseman, 1983; Gudykunst & Hammer, 1984; Hammer, 1987; Wiseman & Abe, 1984) focused on the question of the generalizability of these factors and findings to other cultural groups beyond North America, rather than addressing the conceptual and measurement issues posed by the interpersonal competence researchers.

CURRENT APPROACHES

Only recently have scholars tried to integrate these disparate research efforts by attempting to answer the conceptual questions of the interpersonal researchers and to develop theoretical frameworks of competence that are applicable to intercultural contexts. The problems and challenges of this endeavor have been well described. Theoretical and empirical research efforts should develop culture-general models that apply to a range of intra- and intercultural interaction. Perhaps the foremost challenge is understanding the relationship between culture-specific and culture-general aspects of communicative competence: the identification of elements that apply to specific intercultural interaction between members of specific groups (e.g., between Afro-American and white-American), and elements that apply to all intercultural interaction. As Koester and Olebe (1988) describe the dilemma: "A difficulty in the measurement of intercultural communication effectiveness is that this universal construct necessarily occurs within the context of particular cultures. As cultures vary, so do the specific behaviors which represent the more universal, underlying component of effectiveness" (p. 237).

Before developing a culture-general model, we need to understand more about perceptions of intercultural communication competence from other cultural group's perspectives. At this point we know that models developed from Eurocentric data may not be generalizable, however, we do not know enough about the universality of competence to develop a general model. Therefore, much of the current research aims to develop culture-general models by first understanding specific patterns of intercultural communication competence.

Empirical research should also attempt to be integrative, and a number of integrative foci are possible. Empirical research should (a) strive for a clear conceptualization that is theoretically integrated with previous work, that is, connecting previous research to new theory and findings in order to discover underlying abilities and constructs (Chen, 1989; Collier, 1989; Spitzberg, 1989); (b) incorporate situational dynamics into the explanation of competence (Hammer, 1989; Spitzberg & Brunner, 1991; Wiseman et al., 1989); (c) represent communicators' realities by incorporating emic perspectives that represent the intersubjectivity of the communicators (Collier, 1989; Martin & Hammer, 1989); and (d) address the issue of the locus of competence or the vantage point from which it should be conceptualized or measured (Ruben, 1989; Spitzberg & Cupach, 1989).

Finally, theory development and empirical research should be clear about the level of conceptualization and analysis. As noted by Spitzberg (1989) and Spitzberg and Cupach (1989), and shown in Figure 2.1, a distinction can be made among at least three levels in the processes of competence: (a) high order cognitive and behavioral processes (global encoding and decoding skills, e.g., understanding cultural, social, and relational rules governing interaction); (b) mid-range constructs, which have been investigated and identified by many researchers as molar constellations of specific behaviors (e.g., interaction management, social relaxation), traits (e.g., empathy, assertiveness), functions (e.g., be friendly, be polite) (Martin & Hammer, 1989), or rules (e.g., be polite, follow role prescriptions) (Collier et al., 1986; Collier & Thomas, 1988); and (c) molecular overt behaviors (e.g., head nods, eye gaze, interruptions) (Coker & Burgoon, 1987; Spitzberg & Cupach, 1984). The confusion of these levels has made theoretical integration very difficult. For example, Wiemann's (1977) list includes behaviors at both the molar and molecular level, as does Ruben's (1976) early list (e.g., turn taking, empathy).

Current research approaches these challenges from various theoretical perspectives. Several examples are outlined below. Although they vary somewhat in focus and conceptualization, they are similar in that

High order cognitive processes (Spitzberg & Cupach, 1989)	
Encoding skills	*Decoding skills*
ability to translate goals into action	receptive skills
linguistic competence	perceptual
	interpretation
Mid range (molar) constructs	
Traits (Spitzberg & Cupach, 1989)	*Situational* (Wiemann, 1977)
assertiveness	interaction management
empathy	social relaxation
cognitive complexity	expressiveness
self-monitoring	other-orientation
self-esteem	
Functions (Martin & Hammer, 1989)	*Rules* (Collier, 1988)
be polite	politeness rules (e.g., behave politely)
be friendly	role prescription rules
show interest, etc.	content rules
	expression rules (e.g., assertiveness)
	relational climate rules
Molecular behaviors (Martin & Hammer, 1989)	
smiling	
head nods	
eye gaze	
interruptions, etc.	

Figure 2.1: Examples of Three Levels of Analysis in Interpersonal Communication Competence Research

they extend previous research, are grounded in perceptions of communicators, try to integrate conceptualizations of intra- and intercultural interaction, and focus on different cultural groups' conceptualization of intercultural communication competence. The first approach is founded on an interpretive, ethnographic approach and attempts to understand the dynamics of interaction between members of several groups and extract general principles from these specific themes.

Cultural Identity Model

Collier (1989) suggests that one way to establish representational and cultural validity before developing culture-general theories is by following an ethnographic research tradition (Hymes, 1972a, 1974; Philipsen, 1975, 1986; Saville-Troike, 1982). Using this general approach, Collier and others emphasize the notion of cultural identity in communicative competence (Collier & Thomas, 1988; Hecht & Ribeau, 1991). Cultural identities are identifications with and perceived acceptance into a group with shared systems of symbols and meanings as well as rules for conduct (Collier, 1989).

Intercultural communication competence then is defined as the mutual avowing/confirmation of the interactants' cultural identities where both interactants engage in behavior perceived to be appropriate and effective in advancing both cultural identities (Collier, 1989). Research efforts identify rules and outcomes for communicatively competent interactions of specific cultural groups. For example, Collier (1988) and Collier et al. (1986) investigated and identified rules in intercultural interaction between Afro-Americans and Euro-Americans and Euro-Americans and Hispanics, and extrapolated general rules for competent behavior (e.g., politeness) that appear to apply to diverse ethnic group members in the United States. However, the particular behaviors defined as polite may vary from group to group. Although cultural membership is conceptualized as being negotiated in interactions and saliency of membership changes from one conversation to another, membership still seems to be determined a priori and research findings represent a static slice of conversational life, not the negotiated aspects of communication the perspective purports to describe.

An alternative and related research effort is that proposed by Hecht and colleagues. In an effort to build models of intercultural communication that extend beyond the Eurocentric framework, Hecht and Ribeau (1984) and Hecht, Ribeau, and Sedano (1990) explored Hispanic perceptions of successful (satisfying) interethnic interaction. Further, Hecht, Ribeau, and Alberts (1989) and Hecht, Larkey, Johnson, and Reinard (1991) explored Afro-American perceptions of successful interethnic interaction. Findings from these studies suggest that models of effective interethnic communication vary for these cultural groups. The models comprise the same components: cultural identity, communication issues important to each cultural group, and conversational improvement strategies associated with communication issues. However, the Afro-American model is more clearly focused on issues of powerlessness, understanding, and worldview; the Euro-Americans seem more focused on goal attainment and relational solidarity.

This research provides a complementary approach to the competence research. Rather than focusing on communication as competent or incompetent, interaction is viewed as sometimes problematic, requiring moment-to-moment strategies to correct or adjust the conversation to keep it running smoothly. Identifying characteristics or prototypes of competent communication is very useful but does not explain how individuals go about the task of improving conversations that are not meeting expectations or not proceeding smoothly. The preliminary findings suggest that Afro-Americans and Euro-Americans differ in the kinds of strategies and issues identified as salient (Martin, Hecht, & Larkey, 1992). These results taken together suggest one way of ensuring cultural validity (emic) before extending the frameworks to other cultural groups, and also confirm the speculation that previously established models of interpersonal competence may not be generalizable beyond the Euro-American community.

Even this research based on the cultural identity model is limited by the problem of equivalence and lack of integration with previous research. Although there is a great deal of similarity among the issues and strategies identified by Hecht and colleagues, the rules identified by Collier, the prototypical characteristics identified by Pavitt and Haight (1986), the behaviors and social skills identified by Spitzberg and Cupach (1984), and Wiemann (1977), no comprehensive model has been elucidated.

Behavioral Expectations Model

The second approach is based on the general assumptions of the interpersonal communication competence literature outlined earlier: that individuals hold cognitive notions of competencies and use these notions to make judgments about the behavioral competence of others, and that these expectancies vary depending on the cultural and situational context. The approach is based on previous work, but at the same time remains theoretically flexible (grounded in communicators' perceptions) in order to be culturally appropriate. This extends the cognitive prototype approach of Pavitt and Haight (1985, 1986) and the contextual approach suggested by Spitzberg and Brunner (1991) to notions of intercultural communication. It identifies cognitive expectations of competent intercultural communication held by various cultural groups within particular contexts.

Previous research identified a very general framework with which to investigate diverse groups' notions of intercultural competence at the microbehavioral level (Martin & Hammer, 1989). Research in progress (Martin, Hammer, & Bradford, 1992) tests the framework in various cultural and situational contexts. The framework comprises three dimensions (nonverbal, topic, and conversational management). Given scenarios of intercultural interaction, respondents are asked to identify the relative importance of behaviors in creating impressions of competent communication. Results so far demonstrate that judgments of competence depend on both situational (task and social) and cultural (inter/intra) contexts for both Anglo and Hispanic respondents. After important molecular behaviors are identified, one can investigate the relationship between the molecular and the molar (behavioral clusters) levels. In this way it will be possible to integrate current findings with previous research findings.

A second focus of the behavioral expectations approach investigates how the more molar level of clusters of skills dimensions are related to microbehaviors in actual intercultural interaction. The objective of this research is to determine whether the molar dimensions proposed in interpersonal communication research (interaction management, expressiveness, and social relaxation—see Figure 2.1) can be extended appropriately to measure intercultural communication competence. Preliminary research investigating Japanese-American interaction in task contexts seems promising. Hammer, Martin, Otani, and Koyama (1990) used dimensions identified in previous studies (e.g., involvement, immediacy, and other-orientation) as a framework for analyzing the intercultural communication competence of Japanese and Euro-American managers in videotaped discussions at the beginning and end of a cross-cultural training program. Impressions of competence were assumed to depend on the mutual accommodation of interactants to the others' communication system, and competence was measured from outside observers' perspectives. Japanese raters evaluated the Americans' competence and American raters evaluated Japanese competence. The results confirmed the utility of the framework in understanding intercultural competence, and could be applied to other intercultural interactions.

However, some modification of the framework was necessary. For example, involvement seemed to overlap conceptually with the immediacy dimensions and might be better labeled expressiveness. It was also possible to infer cross-cultural comparisons. There seemed to be cultural differences in emphases (e.g., Americans placed more emphasis on involvement behaviors and less on other-orientation, while Japanese were the converse) and cultural differences in behaviors that express or enact the dimensions (e.g., Japanese and Americans placed same emphasis on social relaxation, but demonstrated through different behaviors).

The strengths of this approach are that it extends research and theory on interpersonal communication competence, builds on previous culture-specific findings, incorporates context, and focuses on actual interaction. More important, it begins to address the question of the relationship between levels of competence dimensions, and the issue of equivalence. This could be extended to other intercultural interactions. As we know more about verbal and nonverbal behaviors that constitute competent communication within the Euro-American community (Burgoon & Hale, 1988; Coker & Burgoon, 1987; Pavitt & Haight, 1985, 1986), and identify dimensions/clusters of competent behavior in intercultural interactions (Martin & Hammer, 1989), we are provided with a framework and methodology for investigating actual intercultural interaction.

There are some limitations to this approach. First, it still rests on the comparative model, assuming that competence involves mutual accommodation. The approach is not as grounded in communicators' perceptions of intercultural communication competence and does not allow for a creative, third-culture perspective. Second, although interview information was gathered from the interactants regarding their perceptions of their communicative competence, the only systematic evaluation was from outside observers' perspectives. Each of three foci (self, other, and outside observer) is useful and may provide complementary information (Hecht & Sereno, 1985; Imahori & Lanigan, 1989; Spitzberg & Hecht, 1984). Last, cultural membership is determined a priori by the researchers and is not as useful to explain interaction between members of all levels of culture (gender, socioeconomic status, age, etc.).

FUTURE RESEARCH

The requisites for research efforts have been identified and current efforts have been reviewed in light of these requisites. The current perspectives described are more theoretically integrated and conceptually grounded in communicators' perceptions than previous research and account for contextual expectations. However, there are several criteria that continue to be elusive. The first is being able to distinguish between culture-general and culture-specific notions. The eventual goal is an integrated theory of communicative competence—one that is emically appropriate to any one particular cultural context, and that provides a framework allowing for meaningful comparisons (Berry, 1980).

Second, the notion of culture needs to be extended. Conceptualizations of competence should incorporate cultural membership beyond national culture, such as racial, ethnic, or gender groups—what Singer (1987) describes as *identity groups* (groups that share a common perception, both voluntary and involuntary). Although the cultural identity approach deals with this issue conceptually, it is not implemented clearly in the research.

Third, the type of relationship between interactants should also be considered. To this point, most investigations have not examined the differences in impressions of competence in varying levels of intimacy. Most have focused on initial interaction between strangers or acquaintances. However, the degree of intimacy (Altman & Taylor, 1973) and perceived group membership (Gallois, Franklyn-Stokes, Giles, & Coupland, 1988; Leung & Bond, 1984; Tajfel, 1981) are important in influencing communicative expectations and interaction (Martin, Hecht, & Larkey, 1992). Related to this is the notion of incorporating differential power relationships in investigations of competence (Singer, 1987). Research based on communication accommodation theory has underscored the importance of power differential in intergroup communication (Gallois et al., 1988; Giles & Smith, 1979).

Finally, research efforts should focus more on actual behavior. Although it seems useful to understand the cognitive prototypes and expectations related to competence, as well as respondents' self-reporting of imagined and recalled conversations within specific contexts, it is also important to understand how those expectations and self-reports are manifested in everyday conversations, in real interaction. It is time to take the frameworks, prototypes, expectations, and rules and see how they are manifested in actual interaction. This focus would also enable us to deal with a final criterion—the issue of the vantage point of the evaluation of the criteria, to see more clearly the congruence (or incongruities) of perception of self/other/outside observers' judgments of competence.

II

THEORETICAL PERSPECTIVES

3

Toward a Theory of Effective Interpersonal and Intergroup Communication

An Anxiety/Uncertainty Management (AUM) Perspective

WILLIAM B. GUDYKUNST • *California State University, Fullerton*

> Theories . . . are nets cast to catch what we call "the world": to rationalize, to explain, to master it. We endeavor to make the mesh ever finer and finer.
>
> *Karl Popper*

> A good theory is one that holds together to get you to a better one.
>
> *Anonymous*

> There is nothing so practical as a good theory.
>
> *Kurt Lewin*

Over the past several years, I have been working with several colleagues[1] on developing a theoretical research program (Lakatos, 1970) on interpersonal and intergroup communication. A theoretical research program is a set of interrelated theories, including theoretically based research designed to test the theories, as well as action research that applies the theories to individual or social change (Berger, Conner, & Fisek, 1974). At the present time, the program includes three interrelated theories: a theory of effective communication, a theory of communication and the development of social bonds, and a theory of intercultural adaptation.[2] The purpose of this chapter is to *outline* the theory of effective interpersonal and intergroup communication.[3] The theory is

AUTHOR'S NOTE: *I want to thank Stella Ting-Toomey and Lea Stewart for their comments on an earlier version of this chapter. I also want to thank Seiichi Morisaki for his help with the figure.*

in the process of being constructed and is not finalized at this writing, but it is sufficiently developed to be presented publicly.

Within the theoretical framework presented, effective communication refers to minimizing misunderstandings.[4] "To say that meaning in communication is never totally the same for all communicators is not to say that communication is impossible or even difficult—only that it is imperfect" (Fisher, 1978, p. 257). Minimizing misunderstandings, in part, involves accurately predicting and explaining our own and others' behavior within the context of the communication that is occurring. Effective communication does *not* imply clarity, intimacy, positiveness, or control (see Montgomery, 1988, for a discussion of ideological positions on quality of communication). Effective communication can occur through univocal and/or ambiguous messages (e.g., Eisenberg, 1984; Levine, 1985). It also can be intimate or nonintimate, positive or negative, controlling or noncontrolling.

It is not possible to present the complete rationale for the theory of effective interpersonal and intergroup communication in this chapter. Given the theme of this volume, the focus here is on those aspects of the theory traditionally associated with communication competence. The goal is to outline the basic rationale for and present the axioms of the theory (the rationale for many of the axioms is summarized in Gudykunst, 1988, 1991; Gudykunst & Hall, in press; and Gudykunst & Kim, 1992). Beginning with a brief discussion of the assumptions of the theory, I then discuss the processes underlying the theory, managing uncertainty and anxiety, and mindfulness. Following this, I examine the roles of motivation, knowledge, and skills (i.e., the components of competence isolated by Spitzberg & Cupach, 1984) in effective communication, and then link the management of uncertainty and anxiety to effective communication. In conclusion, I examine the role of cultural variability in uncertainty and anxiety reduction.

THEORETICAL ASSUMPTIONS

The goal of theory is to provide an explanation of the phenomenon being studied. In my view, theories should (a) be logically consistent (no particular form of logic is better than another), (b) provide a plausible explanation of the phenomenon under investigation,[5] (c) address all levels of analysis, and (d) be stated in such a way that they can be applied. In this section, the metatheoretical assumptions and the procedures used in generating the theory are briefly outlined.

Metatheoretical Assumptions

There are at least three metatheoretical issues about which any theorist must make assumptions: ontology (e.g., the nature of reality), epistemology (e.g., how we gain knowledge), and human nature (e.g., the basis of human behavior). In making metatheoretical assumptions, I have tried to avoid extreme "objectivist" and "subjectivist" assumptions (see Gudykunst & Nishida, 1989, for an overview of the positions; the position taken is compatible with Hooker's, 1987, realistic approach to science).

With respect to ontology, I assume that names, concepts, and labels are artificial constructs we use to create our "subjective" realities. Because of our socialization into a culture and ethnic group, we share a large portion of our intersubjective realities with other people in our culture or ethnic group. Our shared intersubjective realities are sufficiently stable that we consider the shared portion as an "objective" reality. I assume that the basic process of communication is the same across cultures, but that cultures provide rules for how to interpret the content of communication. This assumption is similar to Hamill's (1990) argument that humans are endowed with innate logical structures, but cultures create unique meanings out of this innate knowledge.

Epistemologically, I assume that our interpretations of our communication *and* external observations of our communication provide useful data for generating and testing theories. Meanings are not simply in the person, but are constructed in discourse (Gergen, 1985). As researchers, we need to search for underlying regularities in communication and, at the same time, recognize that our explanations will never be perfect because our subjective realities are different.

With respect to human nature, I assume that our communication is influenced by our culture and group memberships, as well as structural, situational, and environmental factors. We nevertheless have the ability to choose how we communicate. Following Fisher and Brown (1988), I believe that one person can change a relationship based on how she or he chooses to communicate with her or his partner. One person, therefore, can increase the effectiveness of communication that occurs in a relationship.

Theory Construction

Two types of theoretical statements are used in the theory: axioms and theorems. Axioms are "propositions that involve variables that are taken to be directly linked causally; axioms should therefore be statements that imply direct causal links among variables" (Blalock, 1969,

p. 18, italics omitted). The axioms are combined to derive theorems for a theory of effective communication (theorems are not presented). When combined, the axioms and theorems form a "causal process" theory (Reynolds, 1971) that explains effective communication. It should be noted, however, that I believe that many of the relationships are reciprocal and that dialectical processes influence much of our communication (Altman, Vinsel, & Brown, 1981; Baxter, 1988; Vanlear, 1991). In the present version of the theory, dialectics are incorporated as boundary conditions for the axioms. This is not the ideal; rather it is a compromise in developing the working version of the theory. To date, the fundamental problem of combining reciprocal, dialectical, and linear statements in one theory has not been solved.

I believe that a theory should specify axioms about what is occurring at all levels of analysis and "articulate" how the levels are interrelated (Doise, 1986). Four levels of analysis can be isolated: individual, interpersonal, intergroup, and cultural. The individual level involves those factors that motivate us to communicate and influence the way we create and interpret messages. The interpersonal level includes those factors that influence our exchange of messages when we are acting as unique persons. The intergroup level involves the factors that influence our exchange of messages when we are acting as representative of the groups of which we are members and the relations between the groups themselves. The cultural level involves those factors that lead people in one culture to communicate similarly to or differently from people in other cultures.

In isolating axioms, I have drawn on theoretical work in communication (Berger, 1988; Berger & Calabrese, 1975; Berger & Gudykunst, 1991; Burgoon, 1992; Gallois, Franklyn-Stokes, Giles, & Coupland, 1988), sociology (Giddens, 1979; Scheff, 1990; J. H. Turner, 1988), social psychology (Brewer, 1991; Greenberg, Pyszczynski, & Solomon, 1986; Hamilton, Sherman, & Ruvolo, 1990; Johnstone & Hewstone, 1991; Langer, 1989; Linville, Fisher, & Salovey, 1989; Stephan & Stephan, 1985; Tajfel, 1978; J. C. Turner, 1987), cross-cultural psychology (Hofstede, 1980; Schwartz, 1990; Triandis, 1988) and anthropology (Fiske, 1991; Hall, 1976). There are a large number of axioms in the working version of the theory, but they are not excessive. Reynolds (1971) points out that "in dealing with logical systems that are completely abstract . . . a common criteri[on] is to select the smallest number of axioms from which all other statements can be derived, reflecting a preference for simplicity and elegance. There is reason to think that this is inappropriate for a substantive theory, particularly when it makes it more difficult to understand the theory" (p. 95). Since one of my concerns is applying the theory, I have included a sufficient number of statements to make it clear to practitioners and have stated the axioms informally to make applications easier.[6]

Lieberson (1985) suggests that in our theorizing we need to isolate the basic causes of the phenomenon under investigation. In generating the axioms for the theories, I assumed that uncertainty and anxiety are basic causes influencing effective communication. Other variables (which are organized under the components of communication competence, e.g., motivation, knowledge, skills), therefore, are treated as superficial causes of effective communication. The influence of these superficial causes on effective communication is mediated through uncertainty and anxiety. Mindfulness of our communication is posited to be a moderating process affecting the influence of uncertainty and anxiety reduction on effective communication.

A schematic summary of the theory is presented in Figure 3.1. The figure involves only one person to emphasize the underlying processes and to make the application of the theory as straightforward as possible.[7] I believe that the processes diagrammed in the figure generalize across cultures and across types of interaction (e.g., intracultural and intercultural communication). There is, however, variability in the content of the processes (e.g., what constitutes uncertainty and how it is reduced) across cultures and ethnic groups. This issue is discussed in more detail in the concluding section.

In earlier work (Gudykunst, 1988, 1991; Gudykunst & Kim, 1992), I have argued that the process underlying communication between people from different groups (including cultures and ethnicities) is the same as the process underlying communication between members of the same group. I refer to the common process underlying our communication with people who are unknown and unfamiliar in an environment unfamiliar to them as "communicating with strangers" (using Simmel's, 1950/1908, notion of the stranger; see Gudykunst & Kim, 1992, for a complete description of the concept). Since the stranger-ingroup relationship is a figure-ground phenomenon, it is necessary to take one perspective in stating the axioms. Arbitrarily, the perspective of the member of the ingroup being approached by the stranger is used for the general theory of effectiveness.[8] The theory, however, also is applicable from the perspective of the stranger approaching the ingroup.[9]

UNDERLYING PROCESSES

The purpose of this section is to describe the processes underlying the theory presented. I believe that effective communication is moderated

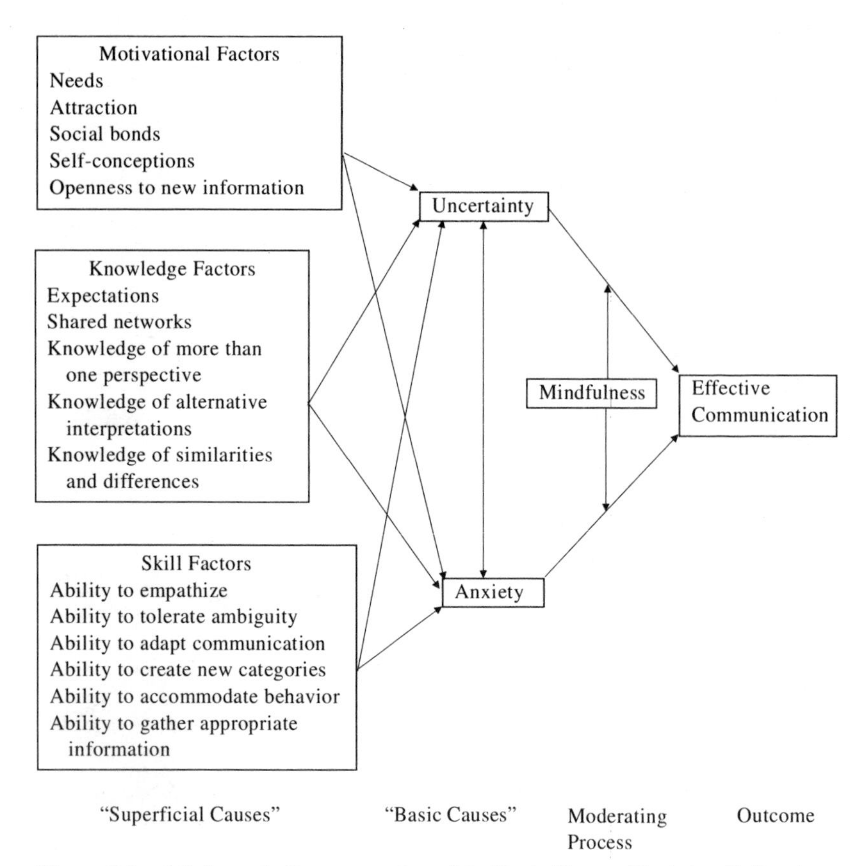

Figure 3.1: A Schematic Representation of the Basic Theory (Omitting Cultural Variability)

by our ability to mindfully manage our anxiety and reduce our uncertainty about ourselves and the people with whom we are communicating. For this reason, I refer to the theory as an *anxiety/uncertainty management (AUM) perspective*.

Uncertainty and Anxiety

Interacting with people from other cultures and/or ethnic groups is a novel situation for most people. Novel situations are characterized by high levels of uncertainty and anxiety. "The immediate psychological result of being in a new situation is lack of security. Ignorance of the potentialities inherent in the situation, of the means to reach a goal, and of the probable outcomes of an intended action causes insecurity"

(Herman & Schield, 1961, p. 165). Attempts to deal with the ambiguity of new situations involve a pattern of information seeking (uncertainty reduction) and tension (anxiety) reduction (Ball-Rokeach, 1973).

Uncertainty refers to our inability to predict and explain our own and others' behavior (Berger & Calabrese, 1975). *Predictive uncertainty* involves the degree to which we can predict strangers' attitudes, beliefs, feelings, values, and behavior. *Explanatory uncertainty*, in contrast, involves the degree to which we can accurately explain why they behave the way they do.

Anxiety refers to the feeling of being uneasy, tense, worried, or apprehensive about what might happen (Stephan & Stephan, 1985).[10] It is an affective (e.g., emotional) response, not a cognitive response like uncertainty. Whereas uncertainty results from our inability to predict others' behavior, "anxiety stems from the anticipation of negative consequences. People fear at least four types of negative consequences: psychological or behavioral consequences for the self, and negative evaluations by members of the outgroup and the ingroup" (Stephan & Stephan, 1985, p. 159). Many writers (e.g., Lazarus, 1991; May, 1977) argue that anxiety is the fundamental problem with which all humans must cope.

In general, our uncertainty and anxiety decrease the better we get to know strangers. Uncertainty and anxiety, however, do not increase or decrease consistently over time. Uncertainty, for example, is not reduced every time we communicate with strangers. We may reduce our uncertainty the first time we communicate, but something may occur the second time we communicate (e.g., the other person does something we did not expect) and our uncertainty might increase (see Planalp & Honeycutt, 1985; Planalp, Rutherford, & Honeycutt, 1988). Once we have established a relationship with another person, we can expect our uncertainty and anxiety regarding the other person to fluctuate over time. Baxter (1988) talks about this phenomenon as a dialectic between predictability and novelty. As the relationship becomes more intimate, nevertheless, there should be a general pattern for uncertainty and anxiety to decrease. To illustrate, there tends to be less uncertainty and anxiety in acquaintance relationships than in relationships with strangers, and there is less uncertainty and anxiety in friendships than in acquaintance relationships. At the same time, within any stage (e.g., acquaintance, friend) of a particular relationship and within particular conversations, uncertainty and anxiety fluctuate. The process is similar to the openness-closedness dialectical process Vanlear (1991) describes.

We do not want to totally reduce our anxiety and uncertainty. At the same time, we cannot communicate effectively if our uncertainty and anxiety are too high. If uncertainty and anxiety are too high, we cannot accurately interpret strangers' messages or make accurate predictions about strangers' behavior. This line of thinking suggests that there are minimum and maximum thresholds for uncertainty and anxiety.

If uncertainty and anxiety are above our maximum thresholds, as they often are when we first meet strangers, we are too anxious and uncertain to communicate effectively. When uncertainty and anxiety are too high and we communicate mindlessly (e.g., on automatic pilot; discussed in next section), we interpret strangers' behavior using our own cultural frame of reference. In many situations, however, there are sufficiently clear norms and rules for communication that our uncertainty and anxiety are reduced below our maximum thresholds. Even if our uncertainty and anxiety are below the maximum threshold, either or both may still be too high for us to communicate effectively. To communicate effectively our anxiety needs to be sufficiently low so that we can accurately interpret and predict strangers' behavior.

If uncertainty and anxiety are too low we may not be motivated to communicate. If both uncertainty and anxiety are consistently below our minimum threshold in a particular relationship, for example, the relationship becomes boring. Kruglanski (1989) points out that we all have a need to avoid closure on topics or people to allow for "mystery" to be maintained. To communicate effectively, our uncertainty and anxiety must be above our minimum threshold.

Uncertainty and anxiety do not necessarily increase and decrease at the same time. We may reduce our uncertainty and be highly anxious. Consider, for example, a situation in which we predict very confidently that something negative is going to happen. We also may reduce our anxiety and have high uncertainty. To communicate effectively, our anxiety must be sufficiently low (well below maximum threshold, but above minimum) so that we can reduce our explanatory uncertainty.[11] If our anxiety is high, we must cognitively manage our anxiety (i.e., become mindful) if we are to communicate effectively.

Mindfulness

Our communication behavior is based on one of three sources (Triandis, 1977). First, we engage in much of our communication behavior out of habit. When we are communicating habitually, we are following *scripts* —"a coherent sequence of events expected by the individual involving him [or her] either as a participant or an observer" (Abelson, 1976, p. 33). According to Langer (1978), when we first encounter a new situation, we consciously seek cues to guide our behavior. As we have repeated experiences with the same event, we have less need to consciously think about our behavior. "The more often we engage in the activity, the more likely it is that we rely on scripts for the completion of the activity and the less likely there will be any correspondence between our actions and those thoughts of ours that occur simultaneously" (Langer, 1978, p. 39).

The greeting ritual is one example of a script. The ritual for greeting others reduces the vast amount of uncertainty and anxiety present in initial interactions to manageable portions and allows us to interact with others in a coordinated fashion. The norms and rules for the ritual provide us with predictions about how others will respond in the situation. When someone deviates from a script or we enter a situation for which we do not have a script, we cannot fall back on the ritual's implicit predictions. Under these circumstances, we have to actively manage our uncertainty and anxiety to make accurate predictions and communicate effectively.

The second basis for our communication is the intentions we form. Intentions are "instructions" we give ourselves about how to communicate (Triandis, 1977). When we think about what we want to do in a particular situation, we form intentions.[12] Intention, therefore, is a cognitive construct—it is part of our thought processes. When our behavior is based on intentions we are, at least implicitly, reducing our uncertainty by trying to predict our own and others' behavior.

The final factor on which our communication may be based is our affect, feelings, or emotions. We often react to others on a strictly emotional basis. If we feel anxious, for example, we may avoid interacting with strangers. We can, however, cognitively manage our emotional reactions. When we are engaging in scripted behavior or are basing our behavior on our emotional reactions, we are not highly aware of what we are doing or saying. Stated differently, we are "mindless" (Langer, 1978, 1989).[13] The mindfulness construct is used widely, but it often is referred to in different terms. Bellah et al. (1991) and Csikszentmihalyi (1990), for example, use "paying attention." Cognitive therapists (Beck, 1988; Burns, 1989) refer to it as "cognitive management" of emotions.

Another condition that contributes to being mindless is the use of categories. Categorization often is based on physical (e.g., gender, race) or cultural (e.g., ethnic background) characteristics, but we also can categorize others in terms of their attitudes (e.g., liberal, conservative) or approaches to life (e.g., Christian, Buddhist; Trungpa, 1973). In order to communicate effectively in nonscripted situations, we must become "mindful" of our thought processes.[14] Langer (1989) isolates three qualities of mindfulness: "(1) creation of new categories; (2) openness to new information; and (3) awareness of more than one perspective" (p. 62). She points out that "categorizing is a fundamental and natural human activity. It is the way we come to know the world. Any attempt to eliminate bias by attempting to eliminate the perception of differences is doomed to failure" (p. 154).

Langer (1989) argues that being mindful involves making more, not fewer, distinctions. To illustrate, Langer uses an example of people who are in the category "cripple." If we see all people in this category as the same, we start treating the category in which we place them as their identity—cripple. If we draw additional distinctions within this category (e.g., create new categories), however, it stops us from identifying the person as a category. If we draw an additional distinction and see a person with a "lame leg," we do not necessarily regard her or him as a member of the category "cripple," thereby making it possible to see the person as an individual. The finer our categories, the more our communication is based on the specific person with whom we are interacting.

Berger and Douglas (1982) isolate five conditions under which we are highly cognizant of our behavior:

> (1) in novel situations where, by definition, no appropriate script exists, (2) where external factors prevent completion of a script, (3) when scripted behavior becomes effortful because substantially more of the behavior is required than is usual, (4) when a discrepant outcome is experienced, or (5) where multiple scripts come into conflict so that involvement in any one script is suspended. (pp. 46-47)

From Berger and Douglas's summary of these conditions, it can be inferred we are more aware of our behavior when communicating with strangers (e.g., when communication is mainly intergroup) than we are when communicating with people who are familiar (e.g., when communication is mainly interpersonal).

Improving the effectiveness of our communication with strangers requires that we become aware of how we communicate. Howell (1982) argues that awareness and competence can be thought of as a four-stage process: (a) *unconscious incompetence*, in which we misinterpret others' behavior, but are not aware of it; (b) *conscious incompetence*, in which we are aware that we misinterpret others' behavior, but we do not do anything about it; (c) *conscious competence*, in which we think about our communication behavior and consciously modify it to improve our effectiveness (mindfulness); and (d) *unconscious competence*, in which we have practiced the skills for effective communication to the extent that we no longer have to think about them to use them.[15]

Langer (1989) argues that for our effectiveness to increase when we are mindful, we must focus on the process of communication, not the outcome. More specifically, she contends that

> an outcome orientation in social situations can induce mindlessness. If we think we know how to handle a situation, we don't feel a need to pay attention. If we respond to the situation as very familiar (as a result, for example, of overlearning), we notice only minimal cues necessary to carry out the proper scenarios. If, on the other hand, the situation is strange, we might be so preoccupied with the thought of failure ("what if I make a fool of myself?") that we miss nuances of our own and others' behavior. In this sense, we are mindless with respect to the immediate situation, although we may be thinking quite actively about outcome related issues. (p. 34)

Langer believes that focusing on the process (e.g., how we do something) forces us to be mindful of our behavior and pay attention to the situations in which we find ourselves. It is only when we are mindful of the process of our communication that we can determine how our interpretations of messages differ from others' interpretations of those messages. Recent research also suggests that when individuals are mindful, they can break the automatic negative prejudicial response associated with negative stereotypes (Devine, 1989).

Organizing Framework

Mindfully managing our uncertainty and anxiety is necessary for effective communication with strangers. As indicated earlier, uncertainty and anxiety are the basic causes of effective communication. For this version of the theory, the superficial causes of effective communication are linked to uncertainty and anxiety using the components of communication competence as the organizing framework.

Spitzberg and Cupach (1984) isolate three components of competence: motivation, knowledge, and skills. *Motivation* refers to our desire to communicate appropriately and effectively with others. Of particular importance to the present analysis is our motivation to communicate with strangers. *Knowledge* refers to our awareness or understanding of what needs to be done in order to communicate appropriately and effectively. *Skills* are our abilities to engage in the behaviors necessary to communicate appropriately and effectively. Langer's (1989) three components of mindfulness can be integrated with the three components of competence: openness to new information (motivation), awareness of more than one perspective (knowledge), and the ability to create new categories (skill). Each of these components must be taken into consideration in explaining effective communication with strangers.

We may be highly motivated and lack the knowledge and/or the skills necessary to communicate appropriately and effectively. We also may be motivated and have the knowledge necessary, but not the skills. If we are motivated and have the knowledge and skills, this does not ensure that we will communicate appropriately or effectively. It is also possible that we may act appropriately and effectively without actually having the knowledge necessary to engage in the behaviors by imitating the behavior of strangers. Although this can work when communicating with strangers when we do not have sufficient knowledge of the strangers' groups, it is not the best strategy. As Wiemann and Kelly (1981) point out, "knowledge without skill is socially useless, and skill cannot be obtained without the cognitive ability to diagnose situational demands and constraints" (p. 290).

Following Spitzberg and Cupach (1984), I believe that competence resides within the dyad. The specific motivation, knowledge, and skills we possess do not ensure that we will be competent in any particular interaction. Our skills, however, do increase the likelihood that we are able to adapt our behavior so that others will perceive us as competent (Wiemann & Bradac, 1989). The following sections are organized around the three components of perceived competence.

MOTIVATION

Motivation refers to our desire to communicate appropriately and effectively. For the purpose of generating the theory of effective communication, I discuss the needs that motivate our behavior; self-conceptions; the component of mindfulness directly related to motivation, openness to new information; motivation to form social bonds; and attraction to strangers.

Needs

J. H. Turner (1988) suggests that certain basic needs motivate us to interact with others. Needs are "fundamental states of being in humans which, if unsatisfied, generate feelings of deprivation" (p. 23). The needs that serve as motivating factors in communicating with strangers are (a) our need for a sense of security as human beings, (b) our need for a sense of predictability (or trust), (c) our need for a sense of group inclusion, (d) our need to avoid diffuse anxiety, (e) our need for a sense of a common shared world, (f) our need for symbolic/material gratification, and (g) our need to sustain our self-conception. These needs vary in the degree to which we are conscious of them. We are the least conscious of the first three, moderately conscious of the fourth, and the most conscious of the last three.

Each of the needs, separately and in combination, influences how we want to present ourselves to others, the intentions we form, and the habits or scripts we choose to follow. The needs also influence each other. Anxiety, for example, can result from not meeting our needs for group inclusion, trust, security, and/or sustaining our self-concept.

Although avoiding anxiety is an important motivating factor in our communication with people who are similar, it is critical in our communication with strangers. Intergroup anxiety is largely a function of our fear of negative consequences when we interact with people who are different (Stephan & Stephan, 1985). As our anxiety becomes high, our need for group inclusion, our need for a sense of a common shared world, and our need to sustain our self-conception become central (J. H. Turner, 1988). Having a sense of a common shared world and sustaining our self-concept are much more difficult when we communicate with strangers than when we communicate with people who are similar. High anxiety leads us to avoid communicating with strangers.

The combination of our need to avoid anxiety and our need to sustain our self-concept leads to an approach-avoidance orientation toward intergroup encounters. Most of us want to see ourselves as nonprejudiced and caring people and we therefore may want to interact with strangers to sustain our self-concept. At the same time, however, our need to avoid anxiety leads us to want to avoid interactions that are not predictable. Holding both attitudes at the same time is not unusual.

Most of us spend the vast majority of our time interacting with people who are relatively similar to us. Our actual contact with people who are different is limited; it is a novel form of interaction (Rose, 1981). If our attempts to communicate with strangers are not successful and we can not easily get out of the situations in which we find ourselves, then our unconscious need for group inclusion becomes unsatisfied. This leads to anxiety about ourselves and our standing in a group context (J. H. Turner, 1988). The net result is that we retreat into known territory and limit our interactions to people who are similar.[16]

Six axioms in the theory of effective communication are based on J. H. Turner's theory of motivation:

Axiom 1: An increase in our need for a sense of group inclusion will produce an increase in our anxiety.

Axiom 2: An increase in our need to sustain our self-conceptions will produce an increase in our anxiety.

Axiom 3: An increase in the degree to which strangers confirm our self-conceptions will produce a decrease in our anxiety.

Axiom 4: An increase in the predictability of others' behavior will produce a decrease in our anxiety.[17]

Axiom 5: An increase in our sense of security will produce a decrease in our anxiety.

Axiom 6: An increase in our motivation to interact with strangers will produce a decrease in our anxiety.

Self-Conceptions

Maintaining our self-conceptions is one of the major needs J. H. Turner (1987) isolates. The relative emphasis we place on the components of our self-conceptions also influences our motivation to communicate with strangers. J. C. Turner (1987) defines the self-concept as "the set of cognitive representations of self available to a person" (p. 44). He argues that cognitive representations of the self take the form of self-categorizations in which individuals group themselves into categories with others that they see as similar to themselves on some dimension and different from others on that dimension. J. C. Turner goes on to point out that

> there are at least three levels of abstraction of self-categorization important in the self-concept: (a) the superordinate level of the self as a human being, the common features shared with other members of the human species in contrast to other forms of life, (b) the intermediate level of ingroup-outgroup categorizations based on similarities and differences between human beings that define one as a member of certain social groups and not others (e.g., "American", "female", "black", "student", "working class"), and (c) the subordinate level of personal categorizations based on differences between oneself as a unique individual and other ingroup [or outgroup] members that define one as a specific individual person (e.g., in terms of one's personality or other kinds of individual differences). (p. 45)

The three levels define our human, social, and personal identities. Social identity is the major generative mechanism for intergroup behavior, whereas personal identity is the major generative mechanism for interpersonal behavior. Both forms of identity, however, influence behavior in virtually all interactions (see Gudykunst & Kim, 1992). We, therefore, cannot theorize about interpersonal or intergroup communication in isolation.

Following Tajfel (1978), J. C. Turner (1987) argues that the process of evaluating our self-conceptions is one of social comparison. To illustrate, we compare the groups of which we are members with others on value-laden attributes and characteristics. Positive comparisons of the ingroup with an outgroup lead to high prestige and negative comparisons lead to low prestige (Tajfel & Turner, 1979).[18] The social comparison process also affects how self-conceptions are formed. In the self-categorization theory, Turner also assumes that the self and others are evaluated positively when they are seen as prototypical members of positively valued groups. Gallois et al. (1988) argue that the more we rely on our group memberships for self-esteem, the more we will define encounters in intergroup terms. This results in anxiety when we communicate with strangers.

Schlenker (1986) argues that "self-identification constructs and expresses an identity" (p. 23). Identity, as Schlenker uses the concept, is a person's theory of him or herself:

> Identity, like any theory, is both a *structure*, containing the organized contents of experience, and an active *process* that guides and regulates one's thoughts, feelings, and actions. . . . It influences how information is perceived, processed, and recalled . . . it acts as a script to guide behavior . . . and it contains the standards against which one's behavior can be compared and evaluated. (p. 24)

Our self-conceptions, therefore, influence how we communicate with others and our choices (conscious and unconscious) of those with whom we form relations.

Gudykunst (1988) argues that the stronger our social identities (e.g., the more important our group memberships are to how we define ourselves), the greater our ability to reduce our uncertainty and anxiety regarding strangers' behavior. This claim, however, has to be qualified. Gudykunst and Hammer (1988) discovered that strength of social identity reduces uncertainty only when we recognize that the strangers are from another group and when the strangers with whom we are communicating are perceived to be typical members of their group. When the strangers are perceived to be atypical members of their group, we do not treat them based on their group membership—we see them as "exceptions to the rule." In this case, our communication is influenced by our personal identities, not by our social identities. When communication is based on our personal identities, we use information about the individual stranger with whom we are communicating to reduce uncertainty. Gudykunst, Nishida, and Morisaki's (1992) research, however, suggests that the influence of personal identity is limited to individualistic cultures such as that in the United States (discussed in the final section).

Three axioms in the theory focus on personal and social identity:

Axiom 7: An increase in the strength of our social identities will produce an increase in our ability to manage our anxiety and reduce our predictive and explanatory uncertainty. Scope condition: This axiom holds only if strangers are perceived to be members of another group and they are perceived to be typical members of the group.[19]

Axiom 8: An increase in our dependence on our ingroups for our self-esteem will produce an increase in our anxiety.

Axiom 9: An increase in the degree to which our personal identities influence our behavior will produce an increase in our ability to reduce our anxiety and our predictive and explanatory uncertainty. Boundary condition: This axiom only holds in individualistic cultures.

Social Bonds

Scheff (1990) argues that our need for secure social bonds with others is one of the major factors motivating our behavior. He contends that we need to balance our closeness and distance to others (e.g., this is similar to Bowen's, 1978, concept of differentiation). Scheff claims that "optimal differentiation defines an intact social bond, a bond which balances the needs of the individual and the needs of the group" (p. 4).[20] Scheff goes on to suggest that attunement, "mutual understanding that is not only mental but also emotional" (p. 7), is necessary for a social bond to exist.[21]

Scheff (1990) believes that *pride* and *shame* are the primary emotions that influence our social bonds with others. Pride is a sign of an intact social bond; shame is a sign of a threatened social bond.[22] He argues that "shame is the primary social emotion in that it is generated by the virtually constant monitoring of the self in relation to others. Such monitoring . . . is not rare but almost continuous in social interaction and, more covertly, in solitary thought" (p. 79). Scheff defines self-esteem as "freedom from chronic shame" (p. 168). Several researchers have related self-esteem to managing anxiety (e.g., Becker, 1971; Epstein, 1976).

When our social bonds are not intact and/or we feel unconnected to others, we feel shame (Scheff, 1990) and may act in a morally exclusive manner (Optow, 1990). Optow points out that "moral exclusion occurs when individuals or groups are perceived as *outside the boundary in which moral values, rules, and considerations of fairness apply*. Those who are morally excluded are perceived as nonentities, expendable, or undeserving; consequently, harming them appears acceptable, appropriate, or just" (p. 1). When we are morally exclusive, we may think that it is justified, but it will form what Lewis (1971) calls "unacknowledged shame."

To communicate effectively with strangers, we must consciously work toward *attunement* in our social bonds with them. Attunement does not imply that our social bonds are highly intimate, but rather that they involve mutual understanding (Scheff, 1990). If we achieve attunement, then the bonds will be intact and we will feel pride not shame.[23]

Three axioms are based on Scheff's (1990) work on social bonds:

Axiom 10: An increase in our self-esteem (pride) will produce an increase in our ability to manage our anxiety.

Axiom 11: An increase in our shame will produce an increase in our anxiety and a decrease in our ability to reduce our predictive and explanatory uncertainty.

Axiom 12: An increase in our attunement with strangers will produce a decrease in our anxiety and an increase in our ability to reduce our predictive and explanatory uncertainty.

Attraction

The degree to which we are attracted to others and want to establish an interpersonal relationship with the specific strangers also contributes to the reduction of uncertainty (Gudykunst, 1988). If we are physically or socially attracted to the strangers with whom we are communicating, our predictive uncertainty will be reduced (Berger & Calabrese, 1975). This conclusion is supported by extensive research (Gudykunst, Chua, & Gray, 1987). Stephan and Stephan's (1985) work also suggests that attraction should reduce anxiety as well. Attraction, however, does not necessarily increase the *accuracy* of our explanatory certainty regarding strangers' behavior. The following axiom, therefore, is posited:

Axiom 13: An increase in our attraction to strangers will produce an increase in our ability to decrease our anxiety and in our ability to reduce our predictive and explanatory uncertainty.

Openness to New Information

Openness to new information involves the degree to which we willingly seek out new information. The cognitive style that influences our openness to new information is our orientation toward uncertainty. Sorrentino and Short (1986) point out that

> there are many people who simply are not interested in finding out information about themselves or the world, who do not conduct causal searches, who could not care less about comparing themselves with others, and who "don't give a hoot" for resolving discrepancies or inconsistencies about the self. Indeed, such people (we call them certainty oriented) will go out of their way not to perform activities such as these (we call people who *do* go out of their way to do such things uncertainty oriented). (pp. 379-380)

Uncertainty-oriented people integrate new and old ideas and change their belief systems accordingly. They evaluate ideas and thoughts on their own merit and do not necessarily compare them with others. Uncertainty-oriented people want to understand themselves and their environment. *Certainty-oriented* people, in contrast, like to hold on to traditional beliefs and have a tendency to reject ideas that are different. Certainty-oriented people maintain a sense of self by not examining themselves or their behavior. Uncertainty-oriented people will recognize that their expectations of strangers' behavior are not necessarily accurate and, therefore, are more likely to reduce their explanatory uncertainty about strangers than are certainty-oriented people. This line of reasoning suggests:

> *Axiom 14*: An increase in our uncertainty orientation will produce an increase in our ability to reduce our predictive and explanatory uncertainty.

Another cognitive style closely related to uncertainty orientation is *need for closure*. In his theory of lay epistemics, Kruglanski (1989) argues that we need to seek and avoid (specific and nonspecific forms of) cognitive closure. Stated differently, we have the need to reduce uncertainty *and* the need to avoid reducing uncertainty at the same time. Kruglanski goes on to point out that we differ in our cognitive need for closure. If our need to seek closure is high and our need to avoid closure is low, for example, we may prefer any type of closure to the uncertainty that exists. This would lead us to use any information we have about strangers (e.g., their group memberships; discussed below) to predict or explain their behavior. Kruglanski's theory, therefore, implies:

> *Axiom 15*: A decrease in our need for closure and/or an increase in our need to avoid closure will produce an increase in our ability to reduce our predictive and explanatory uncertainty.

KNOWLEDGE

Knowledge refers to our awareness and understanding of what needs to be done to communicate effectively. For purposes of generating the theory of effective communication I focus on knowledge of more than one perspective (i.e., the knowledge component of mindfulness); understanding differences between descriptions, interpretations, and evaluations of others' behavior; our expectations; knowledge of similarities and differences between our group and the others' groups; and shared networks.

Knowledge of More Than One Perspective

Knowledge of more than one perspective involves recognizing that different people interpret behavior in different ways. One cognitive style that appears to influence our knowledge of more than one perspective is *category width*. "Category width refers to the range of instances included in a cognitive category" (Pettigrew, 1982, p. 200). Pettigrew suggests that individual differences in category width are related to more general information processing strategies. Broad categorizers, for example, tend to perform better than narrow categorizers on tasks that require holistic, integrated information processing. Narrow categorizers, in comparison, tend to perform better than broad categorizers on tasks that require detailed, analytic information processing.

Detweiler (1975) studied how category width influences the attributions whites in the United States make about people who are culturally similar (another white from the United States) or culturally dissimilar (a person from Haiti) and who engage in either positive or negative behavior. His findings indicate that narrow categorizers

> assume that the effects of behavior of a person from another culture tell all about the person, even though he [or she] in fact knows nothing about the actor's [or actress's] cultural background. He [or she] seems to make strong judgments based on the positivity or negativity of the effects of the behavior as evaluated from his [or her] own cultural viewpoint. Contrarily, when making attributions to a person who is culturally similar, the narrow [categorizer] seems to view the similarity as overshadowing the behavior. Thus, positive effects are seen as intended, and negative effects are confidently seen as unintended. (p. 600)

This suggests that narrow categorizers may have trouble making accurate attributions about messages from both people who are culturally similar and people who are culturally dissimilar.

The wide categorizers in Detweiler's (1975) study had a very different orientation. When making attributions about a culturally dissimilar person, a wide categorizer

> seems to assume that he [or she] in fact doesn't know enough to make "usual" attributions. Thus, behaviors with negative effect result in less confident and generally more neutral attributions when judgments are made about a person from a different culture. Conversely, the culturally similar person who causes a negative outcome is rated relatively more negatively with greater confidence by the wide [categorizer], since the behavior from one's own cultural background is meaningful. (p. 600)

Wide categorizing, therefore, is necessary to see that there is more than one perspective and to make isomorphic attributions. Detweiler's findings suggest the following axiom:

> *Axiom 16*: An increase in our category width will produce an increase in our ability to reduce our predictive and explanatory uncertainty.

Knowledge of Alternative Interpretations

There are at least three interrelated cognitive processes involved when we communicate with strangers: description, interpretation, and evaluation. *Description* refers to an actual report of what we have taken in with our senses with minimal distortion and without attributing social significance to the behavior. *Interpretation* involves attaching meaning or social significance to social stimuli. *Evaluation* involves our judgments of social stimuli.

If we are unable to distinguish among these three cognitive processes, it is likely that we will skip the descriptive process and jump immediately to either interpretation or evaluation when communicating with strangers. This leads to misattributions of meaning and, therefore, to ineffective communication. If we mindfully distinguish among the three processes, however, we are able to see alternative interpretations that are used by strangers, thereby increasing our effectiveness. Differentiating among the three processes also increases the likelihood of our making more accurate predictions and explanations of strangers' behavior.

To decrease the chance of misinterpretations of others' messages based on our unconscious interpretations, we must be aware of our "normal" tendencies. Beck (1988) outlines five principles of cognitive therapy that are useful in understanding how misinterpretations occur:

1. We can never know the state of mind—the attitudes, thoughts, and feelings —of other people.
2. We depend on signals, which are frequently ambiguous, to inform us about the attitudes and wishes of other people.
3. We use our own coding system, which may be defective, to decipher these signals.
4. Depending on our own state of mind at a particular time, we may be biased in our method of interpreting other people's behavior, that is, how we decode.
5. The degree to which we believe that we are correct in divining another person's motives and attitudes is not related to the actual accuracy of our belief. (p. 18)

When we are not mindful of the process of our communication, we assume others interpret stimuli the same as we do. When we cognitively manage our anxiety, or are mindful, we can separate descriptions from interpretations and evaluations. Being mindful of the process of communication is necessary if we are to manage our anxiety and make isomorphic attributions. This line of reasoning suggests:

Axiom 17: An increase in our ability to describe others' behavior and search for alternative interpretations of their behavior will produce an increase in our ability to accurately predict and explain strangers' behavior. Boundary condition: This is only possible if we are mindful of the process of communication.

One factor that influences our ability to search for alternative interpretations of strangers' behavior is our level of *cognitive complexity*. Werner (1957) points out that "whenever development occurs it proceeds from a state of relative globality and lack of differentiation to a state of increasing differentiation, articulation and hierarchic integration" (p. 126). The more differentiations we make in an area, the more complex our cognitive systems.

Cognitively complex people form impressions of others that are more extensive and differentiated, and better represent the behavioral variability of others, than cognitively simple people (O'Keefe & Sypher, 1981). Honess (1976) also points out that cognitively complex people seek out unique features of their environments more than cognitively simple people. Downey, Hellriegel, and Slocum (1977) found that there is a negative association between cognitive complexity and perceived uncertainty. Davidson (1975) argued

> the relation between cognitive complexity and cross-cultural effectiveness is assumed to exist because a cognitively simple person has a single frame-

> work within which to evaluate the observed behavior of others in the target culture. Thus, when a behavior which he [or she] does understand takes place, he [or she] is likely to evaluate it ethnocentrically. A complex person, on the other hand, has several frameworks for the perception of the same behavior. (p. 80)

Detweiler's (1980) research supports this speculation. This suggests:

> *Axiom 18*: An increase in our cognitive complexity will produce an increase in our ability to reduce our predictive and explanatory uncertainty.

Expectations

Expectations involve our anticipations and predictions about how others will communicate with us.[24] Our expectations are derived from social norms, communication rules, scripts, and strangers' personal characteristics of which we are aware. There is a "should" component to most of our expectations. "People who interact develop expectations about each others' behavior, not only in the sense that they are able to predict the regularities, but also in the sense that they develop preferences about how others *should* behave under certain circumstances" (Jackson, 1964, p. 225).

Our culture and ethnicity provide guidelines for appropriate behavior and the expectations we use in judging competent communication. To illustrate, Burgoon and Hale (1988) point out that in the white middle-class subculture[25]

> one expects normal speakers to be reasonably fluent and coherent in their discourse, to refrain from erratic movements or emotional outbursts, and to adhere to politeness norms. Generally, normative behaviors are positively valued. If one keeps a polite distance and shows an appropriate level of interest in one's conversational partner, for instance, such behavior should be favorably received. (p. 61)

It must be recognized, however, that norms for what is a "polite" distance and what constitutes an "emotional" outburst vary across cultures and across subcultures within a culture.

In addition to cultural norms and rules, intergroup cognitions create expectations and influence our preconscious or automatic thoughts regarding our affective reactions to strangers. The important intergroup cognitions, according to Stephan and Stephan (1985), are our knowledge of the stranger's culture, our stereotypes, our prejudice, our ethnocentrism, and our perceptions of ingroup-outgroup differences. The less knowledge we have of strangers' groups, the more anxiety we will experience. Negative cognitive expectations (e.g., ethnocentrism, negative stereotypes, prejudice) lead to uncertainty and intergroup anxiety. Positive expectations (e.g., positive stereotypes), in contrast, help us reduce uncertainty and anxiety (Gudykunst, 1988). Positive expectations lead us to behave in a positive manner toward strangers (Hamilton et al., 1990, for a discussion of expectancy-confirming processes). Positive expectations alone, however, do not necessarily increase our explanatory certainty. To reduce our explanatory uncertainty we need to have accurate information regarding the stranger's culture, group memberships, and the individual stranger with whom we are communicating.

In addition to our expectations of strangers, strangers' violations of our expectations influence our ability to reduce our uncertainty and anxiety. If one person violates another's expectations to a sufficient degree that the violation is recognized, the person recognizing the violation becomes aroused and has to assess the situation (Burgoon & Hale, 1988). In other words, the violation of expectations leads to some degree of mindfulness. Burgoon (1992) further points out that violations of expectations by communicators with low reward valence tend to lead to negative outcomes. Since strangers have low reward valence, the more strangers violate our positive expectations and we are aware of the violations, the greater our uncertainty and anxiety. Stephan (1985) points out that strangers' disconfirmations of positive expectations and their confirmations of negative expectations lead to negative affect.

Two axioms on expectations are included in the theory:

Axiom 19: An increase in our positive expectations regarding strangers' behavior will produce a decrease in our anxiety and an increase in our ability to reduce our predictive uncertainty.

Axiom 20: An increase in our awareness of strangers' violations of our positive expectations or their confirmation of our negative expectations will produce an increase in our anxiety and a decrease in our ability to reduce our predictive and explanatory uncertainty.

Spitzberg and Brunner (1991) argue that our expectations regarding contexts influence our perceptions of strangers' competence and their perceptions of our competence. They go on to suggest that "contexts are perceptually organized according to culture, type, relationship, and function" (p. 29, italics omitted). The cultural component refers to the communication rule systems of national cultures and ethnic groups. Type involves the setting and social situations in which interaction occurs (Forgas, 1988). Relationship involves the specific relationship we have formed with strangers (e.g., in terms of the intimacy), and function refers to our goals and objectives in the context.

One important aspect of our perceptions of the contexts in which we come into contact with strangers is the complexity of our scripts. As indicated earlier, most of us do not have complex scripts for communicating with strangers. The complexity of our scripts should influence our ability to reduce our anxiety and uncertainty.

Research on the contact hypothesis (e.g., Stephan, 1987) also indicates that situational constraints influence the outcomes of our interactions with strangers. Research suggests, for example, that informal interaction between members of different groups leads to a greater reduction in prejudice than formal interaction. Similarly, working on cooperative goals (as opposed to competitive goals) and having normative/institutional support for intergroup contact lead to reductions in prejudice.[26]

Four axioms on situational expectations are included in the theory:

Axiom 21: An increase in the complexity of our scripts for communicating with strangers will produce a decrease in our anxiety and an increase in our ability to reduce our predictive and explanatory uncertainty.

Axiom 22: An increase in the informality of the situation in which we are communicating with strangers will produce a decrease in our anxiety and an increase in our ability to reduce our predictive and explanatory uncertainty.

Axiom 23: An increase in the cooperative structure of the goals on which we work with strangers will produce a decrease in our anxiety and an increase in our ability to reduce our predictive and explanatory uncertainty.

Axiom 24: An increase in the normative and institutional support for communicating with strangers will produce a decrease in our anxiety and an increase in our ability to reduce our predictive and explanatory uncertainty.

Knowledge of Similarities and Differences

As indicated in the previous section, making accurate attributions about others' behavior requires that we be able to determine how they are interpreting their own and our messages. To make accurate predictions and explanations, we must understand the "stocks of knowledge" (Scheff, 1990) being used to interpret the messages.[27] Stated differently, we need knowledge of strangers' cultures and group memberships. The focus here is on how group memberships (e.g., culture, ethnicity, gender) influence the way we interpret stimuli. This suggests:

Axiom 25: When we are mindful, an increase in our understanding the stocks of knowledge of the groups of which strangers are members will produce an increase in our ability to manage our anxiety and our ability to reduce our predictive and explanatory uncertainty.

In addition to understanding of strangers' stocks of knowledge, knowledge of their language and/or dialect facilitates the reduction of our uncertainty and anxiety. Research, for example, indicates that second-language competence increases individuals' ability to cope with uncertainty (Naiman, Frohlich, Stern, & Todesco, 1978). Stephan and Stephan (1985) also point out that this finding extends to anxiety. This implies:

Axiom 26: An increase in our understanding of strangers' language (or dialect) will produce a decrease in our anxiety and an increase in our ability to decrease our predictive and explanatory uncertainty.

To communicate effectively with strangers, we also must seek out commonalities between ourselves and others. Bellah, Madsen, Sullivan, Swidler, and Tipton (1985), for example, point out that we need to seek out commonalities because "with a more explicit understanding of what we have in common and the goals we seek to attain together, the differences between us that remain would be less threatening" (p. 287). Finding commonalities requires that we be mindful of our prejudices.

The position that Bellah and his associates advocate vis-à-vis cultural and/or ethnic differences is consistent with Langer's (1989) contention that

> because most of us grow up and spend our time with people like ourselves, we tend to assume uniformities and commonalities. When confronted with someone who is clearly different in one specific way, we drop that assumption and look for differences. . . . The mindful curiosity generated by an encounter with someone who is different, which can lead to exaggerated perceptions of strangeness, can also bring us closer to that person if channeled differently. (p. 156)

Langer suggests that once individuals satisfy their curiosity about differences, understanding can occur. This, however, requires that we be mindful. This line of reasoning suggests the following axiom:

Axiom 27: An increase in our understanding of similarities and differences between our groups and strangers' groups will produce an increase in our ability to reduce our predictive and explanatory uncertainty.

Extensive research suggests that perceived similarity is one of the major factors we use in deciding who to approach (see Berscheid, 1985, for a review of this research). Self-related factors underlie many of the explanations as to why similarity affects social relations. Swann (1983), for example, suggests that similarity is important because we assume that people who are similar to us are more likely to verify our self-conceptions than people who are different. Perceived similarity has been related to reducing uncertainty (Gudykunst, Chua, & Gray, 1987) and anxiety (Stephan & Stephan, 1985). Research on perceived similarity suggests:

Axiom 28: An increase in the similarity we perceive between ourselves and strangers will produce a decrease in our anxiety and an increase in our ability to reduce our predictive uncertainty.

The degree to which we monitor our behavior (e.g., Snyder's, 1974, self-monitoring construct)[28] influences the nature of information we seek out about strangers. In comparison to low self-monitors, high self-monitors are better able to discover appropriate behavior in new situations, have more control over emotional reactions and create the impressions they wish (Snyder, 1974), modify their behavior to changes in situations more (Snyder & Monson, 1975), make more confident and extreme attributions (Berscheid, Graziano, Monson, & Dermer, 1976), and seek more information about others with whom they anticipate interacting (Elliott, 1979). This suggests the following axiom:

Axiom 29: An increase in our self-monitoring will produce an increase in our ability to manage our anxiety and our ability to reduce our predictive and explanatory uncertainty.

Shared Networks

Blau and Schwartz (1984) argue that group memberships provide structural constraints on our establishing relationships with strangers. They point out that as the size of our ingroup increases, we are less likely to form communication networks with strangers. If there are few strangers in our environment, we do not have the opportunity to gather information about them.

The amount of uncertainty we experience when we communicate with strangers is influenced by the degree to which we share communication networks with the strangers (Gudykunst, 1988). This conclusion is supported by extensive research (e.g., Gudykunst, Chua, & Gray, 1987; Parks & Adelman, 1983; see Albrecht & Adelman, 1984, for a review). Research also links shared networks to reducing anxiety (e.g.,

Dyal & Dyal, 1981). The more we know the same people that the strangers with whom we are communicating know, the more we can reduce uncertainty and anxiety. This suggests:

> *Axiom 30*: An increase in our shared networks will produce a decrease in our anxiety and an increase in our ability to reduce our predictive and explanatory uncertainty.

SKILLS

As indicated earlier, skills involve our abilities to engage in the behaviors necessary to communicate appropriately and effectively. For the purpose of the theory of effective communication, I focus on those skills directly related to managing anxiety and reducing uncertainty: ability to create new categories (i.e., the skill component of mindfulness), ability to tolerate ambiguity, ability to empathize, ability to adapt communication, ability to gather and use appropriate information about others, and ability to accommodate our behavior.[29]

Ability to Create New Categories

Langer (1989) argues that we need to learn to make more, not fewer, distinctions. She argues that when we create new categories it forces us to pay attention to the communication process that is occurring and the context in which our communication is taking place. If we reduce uncertainty using our regular categories, we will be using our own frame of reference and, therefore, probably make inaccurate attributions about others' behavior. Creating new categories is necessary to make accurate attributions of others' behavior.[30] This suggests:

> *Axiom 31*: An increase in our ability to create new categories will produce an increase in our ability to manage our anxiety and an increase in our ability to reduce our predictive and explanatory uncertainty.

Ability to Tolerate Ambiguity

The second skill necessary to manage our anxiety is tolerance for ambiguity. Tolerance for ambiguity implies the ability to deal successfully with situations, even when a great deal of information needed to interact effectively is unknown. According to Ruben and Kealey (1979),

> the ability to react to new and ambiguous situations with minimal discomfort has long been thought to be an important asset when adjusting to a new

> culture. . . . Excessive discomfort resulting from being placed in a new or different environment—or from finding the familiar environment altered in some critical ways—can lead to confusion, frustration, and interpersonal hostility. Some people seem better able to adapt well in new environments and adjust quickly to the demands of a changing milieu. (p. 19)

Ruben and Kealey suggest that people who have a higher tolerance for ambiguity are more effective in completing task assignments in other cultures than are people with lower tolerances. This implies the following axiom:

> *Axiom 32*: An increase in our ability to tolerate ambiguity will produce an increase in our ability to manage our anxiety.

Ability to Empathize

Sympathy refers to "the imaginative placing of ourselves in another person's position" (Bennett, 1979, p. 411). Sympathy, like ethnocentrism, uses our own frame of reference to interpret incoming stimuli. According to Bennett, if we apply the Golden Rule ("Do unto others as you would have them do unto you") in interactions with strangers, we are being sympathetic because the referent is our own standard of appropriate behavior. Empathy, however, is "the imaginative intellectual and emotional participation in another person's experience" (p. 418). The referent for empathy is not our own experience, but that of the stranger. Bennett proposes an alternative to the Golden Rule, the "Platinum Rule," which he argues involves empathy rather than sympathy: "Do unto others as they themselves would have done unto them" (p. 422). To summarize, the use of sympathy in our interactions with strangers invariably leads to misunderstanding rather than understanding. The use of empathy, in contrast, increases the likelihood that understanding occurs. This line of reasoning leads to the following axiom:

> *Axiom 33*: An increase in our ability to empathize will produce an increase in our ability to reduce our predictive and explanatory uncertainty.

Ability to Adapt Our Communication

To gather appropriate information about strangers requires that we be able to adapt our behavior. We also must be able to adapt and accommodate our behavior to people from other groups if we are going to be successful in our interactions with them. Duran's (1983) conceptualization of communicative adaptability is consistent with the perspective used in the theory. He argues that communication adaptability involves "(1) the requirement of both cognitive (ability to perceive) and behavioral (ability to adapt) skills; (2) adaptation not only of behaviors but also interaction goals; (3) the ability to adapt to the requirements posed by different communication contexts; and (4) the assumption that perceptions of communicative competence reside in the dyad" (p. 320). One axiom on communication adaptability is included:

Axiom 34: An increase in our ability to adapt our communication will produce an increase in our ability to manage our anxiety and an increase in our ability to reduce our predictive and explanatory uncertainty.

Ability to Gather and Use Appropriate Information

Reducing uncertainty requires that we be able to describe others' behavior, select accurate interpretations of their messages, accurately predict their behavior, and be able to explain their behavior. To accomplish these objectives, we must be able to gather appropriate information about others. Wilder and Shapiro's (1989) research, however, indicates that when anxiety is too high we are not able to gather accurate information about others. We, therefore, will not be able to make accurate predictions or explanations of strangers' behavior. This implies:

Axiom 35: An increase in the anxiety we experience above our maximum threshold will produce a decrease in our ability to make accurate predictions and explanations of strangers' behavior.

Linville et al.'s (1989) research suggests that we view our ingroups as more differentiated than outgroups. They also suggest that the more familiar we are with outgroups, the greater our perceived differentiation of the group. Johnstone and Hewstone (1991) argue that the more variability we perceive in outgroups, the less our tendency to treat all members in a similar negative fashion. Increases in the variability we perceive in outgroups provide additional information about the strangers with whom we are communicating and, therefore, should decrease our uncertainty and anxiety.

Pettigrew (1979) combines the "fundamental attribution error" and the "principle of negativity" to propose the "ultimate" attribution error, "a systematic patterning of intergroup misattributions shaped in part by prejudice" (p. 464). He points out that our tendency to attribute behavior to dispositional characteristics, rather than situational characteristics, is enhanced when a member of an outgroup is perceived to engage in negative behavior. When members of an outgroup engage in what is perceived to be positive behavior, in contrast, our tendency is to treat the person as an exception to the rule and we discount dispositional explanations for the behavior. We, therefore, attribute the behavior to situational factors.

Two axioms regarding the use of group memberships in explaining others' behavior are included in the theory:

Axiom 36: An increase in the degree to which we attribute others' behaviors to their group memberships will produce a decrease in our ability to reduce our anxiety and a decrease in our ability to reduce our predictive and explanatory uncertainty.

Axiom 37: An increase in the variability we perceive in strangers' groups will produce an increase in our ability to reduce our anxiety and an increase in our ability to reduce our predictive and explanatory uncertainty.

Ability to Accommodate Our Behavior

There is a tendency for members of ingroups to react favorably to outgroup members who linguistically converge toward them (Giles & Smith, 1979). This, however, is not always the case. Giles and Byrne (1982) point out that as outgroup members begin to learn the speech style of the ingroup, ingroup members may diverge in some way to maintain linguistic distinctiveness. Reaction to outgroup members' speech convergence depends on the intent ingroup members attribute to the outgroup members (Simard, Taylor, & Giles, 1976).

Giles, Mulac, Bradac, and Johnson (1987) argue that communication convergence is a function of a speaker's desire for (a) social approval, (b) high communication efficiency, (c) shared self- or group-presentation, and (d) an appropriate identity definition. For communication convergence to occur, there also needs to be a match between the speaker's view of the recipient's speech style and the actual style used, and the specific speech style used must be appropriate for both speaker and recipient. Divergence, in contrast, is a function of the speaker's desire (a) for a "contrastive" self-image, (b) to dissociate from the recipient, (c) to change the recipient's speech behavior, and (d) to define an encounter in intergroup terms. Divergence also occurs when recipients use a speech style that deviates from a norm that is valued and consistent with the speaker's expectations regarding the recipient's performance. If strangers accommodate to our communication style and we perceive their intent to be positive, it will reduce our uncertainty and anxiety in communicating with them.

One axiom on accommodation is included in the theory:

Axiom 38: An increase in the degree to which strangers accommodate to our behavior will produce a decrease in our anxiety and an increase in our ability to reduce our predictive uncertainty.

UNCERTAINTY, ANXIETY, AND EFFECTIVE COMMUNICATION

To communicate effectively we must be able to make isomorphic attributions regarding others' behavior (Triandis, 1977). As indicated earlier, we cannot make accurate attributions regarding others' behavior if uncertainty and anxiety are either too low or too high. This claim is supported by research on social support (Albrecht & Adelman, 1984) and test anxiety (Byrne & Kelley, 1981), as well as research on perceived uncertainty and effectiveness (Downey & Slocum, 1979). When uncertainty is too high (i.e., above our maximum threshold), we cannot predict and/or explain others' behavior. When uncertainty is too low (i.e., below our minimum threshold), we lose interest. When anxiety is too high, our behavior is based on our affective responses and we interpret others' behavior based only on our own frame of reference. When anxiety is too low, we are not motivated to communicate with others.

Cognitively, intergroup anxiety leads to biases in information processing (Stephan & Stephan, 1985). The more anxious we are, the more likely we will attune to the behaviors we expected to see (e.g., those based on our stereotypes) and the more likely we are to confirm these expectations (i.e., we will not attune to behavior that is inconsistent with our expectations) (Stephan & Stephan, 1985). The greater our anxiety, the more we will be self-aware and concerned with our self-esteem. When we are highly anxious we, therefore, try to make our own group look good in comparison to other groups.

The intergroup anxiety we experience when communicating with strangers transfers to other emotions we experience in the situation. "Positive interactions will produce strong positive emotions, while negative interactions will have the opposite effect. Among the positive emotions are relief, joy, or even love; negative emotions frequently include fear, hate, resentment, guilt, disgust, or righteous indignation" (Stephan & Stephan, 1985, p. 169). Finally, intergroup anxiety amplifies our evaluative reactions to strangers; for example, the more anxious we are, the more likely we are to evaluate strangers negatively.

When anxiety is too high, we must cognitively manage our affective reaction (i.e., be mindful) in order to communicate effectively. When mindful we need to overcome our propensity to interpret others' behavior using our own frame of reference. This is only possible when we focus on the process of communication and separate descriptions, interpretations, and evaluations of others' behavior. This line of reasoning suggests the following axiom:

> *Axiom 39*: When we are mindful of the process of communication, a decrease in our anxiety about interacting with others *and* an increase in the accuracy of predictive and explanatory certainty regarding others' behavior will produce an increase in the effectiveness of our communication. Boundary condition: Anxiety and uncertainty below our minimum threshold will not produce increases in our effectiveness; anxiety and uncertainty above our maximum threshold will produce decreases in effectiveness.

Before proceeding there are several issues that need to be clarified. Mindfulness is not a mediating variable between uncertainty and anxiety and effective communication. Rather, it *moderates* the relationship. If we are not mindful, managing anxiety and reducing uncertainty do not necessarily lead to effective communication. To illustrate: When we are not mindful, we reduce our uncertainty using our own frame of reference. Our predictions and explanations of others' behavior, therefore, may not be accurate. When we are mindful, we can choose to compare alternative interpretations for messages, select the interpretations others are most likely using, and, therefore, increase the likelihood that we make accurate predictions and explanations.

I do not take a specific position on the degree to which individuals should be mindful of their communication behavior. Howell (1982) suggests that unconscious competence is a higher form than conscious competence (which involves mindfulness). Buddhist scholars (e.g., Hanh, 1976), in contrast, suggest that we should be mindful in all of our behavior. I believe that the degree to which we are mindful of our communication is a choice each of us must make. I do believe, however, that we each have a responsibility to communicate as effectively as we can with others in order to build community and create peace in the world.[31]

As indicated earlier, effective communication involves minimizing misunderstandings. What is perceived as effective, however, is relative (Knapp & Vangelisti, 1992). We make judgments of the effectiveness of specific communication messages and episodes. Knapp and Vangelisti point out that our perceptions of whether a particular message or episode is effective depends on when we are making the judgment, our relationship with the other person, where we make the judgment (e.g., the context), and so forth. Individually, we must decide how much of a difference in meanings being attached to stimuli is problematic in specific contexts. This is based in part on cultural expectations for clarity (discussed below), our idiosyncratic expectations, and the unique criteria for effective communication that may have been negotiated in our relationship with the other person (see Montgomery, 1988, for a discussion of relationship standards for effective communication).

As indicated earlier, the theory is presented from the perspective of the members of the ingroup being approached by a stranger, but it also is applicable to strangers approaching ingroups. Although one person can change a relationship (Fisher & Brown, 1988), the ideal is if both partners are mindful of their communication, manage their anxiety, and try to make accurate interpretations of their own and their partners' messages.

The perspective presented here does *not* presuppose a particular form that our messages must take for us to be effective. Messages may be univocal or ambiguous (Levine, 1985), based on elaborated or restricted codes (Bernstein, 1981), or based on syntactic or pragmatic codes (Ellis, 1992).[32] Eisenberg (1984), for example, demonstrates that ambiguous messages can lead to effective communication in organizational contexts. Individuals choose the type of messages that they think will work best in specific situations.

CULTURAL VARIABILITY

The theory would be incomplete if the cultural level of analysis was not included. In order to understand similarities and differences in communication across cultures, it is necessary to have a way of talking about how cultures differ. It does not make sense to say that "Yuko communicates indirectly because she is a Japanese" or that "Ruth communicates directly because she is from the United States." This does not tell us why there are differences between the way people communicate in the United States and Japan. There has to be some aspects of the cultures in Japan and the United States that are different and this difference, in turn, explains why Japanese communicate indirectly and people from the United States communicate directly. In other words, there are variables on which cultures can be different or similar that can be used to explain communication across cultures.

Individualism-collectivism is the major dimension of cultural variability used to explain cross-cultural differences in behavior across disciplines and cultures (Gudykunst & Ting-Toomey, 1988). Emphasis is placed on individuals' goals in individualistic cultures, whereas group goals have precedence over individuals' goals in collectivistic cultures. In individualistic cultures, "people are supposed to look after themselves and their immediate family only," whereas in collectivistic cultures, "people belong to ingroups or collectivities which are supposed to look after them in exchange for loyalty" (Hofstede & Bond, 1984, p. 419). The "I" identity has precedence in individualistic cultures over the "we" identity, which takes precedence in collectivistic cultures. Gudykunst and Nishida (1986) argue that people in individualistic and collectivistic cultures use different types of information to reduce uncertainty. In individualistic cultures, individuals seek person-based information (e.g., others' attitudes, feelings, values) to reduce uncertainty. In collectivistic cultures, in contrast, individuals seek out group-based information (e.g., group memberships, status, age) to reduce uncertainty.

Power distance is defined as "the extent to which the less powerful members of institutions and organizations accept that power is distributed unequally" (Hofstede & Bond, 1984, p. 419). People in high power distance cultures see power as a basic fact in society, and stress coercive or referent power, whereas people in low power distance cultures believe power should be used only when it is legitimate and prefer expert or legitimate power. People in high power distance cultures should experience greater uncertainty and anxiety when communicating with people higher in status (in comparison to people of equal status) than members of low power distance cultures.

In comparison to members of low uncertainty avoidance cultures, members of high uncertainty avoidance cultures have a lower tolerance "for uncertainty and ambiguity, which expresses itself in higher levels of anxiety and energy release, greater need for formal rules and absolute truth, and less tolerance for people or groups with deviant ideas or behavior" (Hofstede, 1979, p. 395). There is a strong desire for consensus in cultures high in uncertainty avoidance and, therefore, deviant behavior is not acceptable. Hofstede (1991) summarizes the view of people in strong uncertainty avoidance cultures as "what is different, is dangerous," (p. 119) and the credo of people in low uncertainty avoidance cultures as "what is different, is curious" (p. 119). Gudykunst, Nishida, and Morisaki (1992) argue that since high uncertainty avoidance cultures provide rules for dealing with members of other groups, individuals in high uncertainty avoidance cultures do not see intergroup encounters as abrasive as individuals in low uncertainty avoidance cultures. Individuals in high uncertainty avoidance cultures, therefore, should experience less anxiety than individuals in low uncertainty avoidance cultures in interacting with strangers in situations where there are clear rules.

In high masculinity cultures, people place a high value on things, power, and assertiveness (Hofstede, 1980). Systems in which people, quality of life, and nurturance prevail are low on masculinity or high on femininity. Cultural systems high on the masculinity dimension emphasize differentiated sex roles, performance, ambition, and independence. Conversely, systems low on masculinity value fluid sex roles, quality of life, service, and interdependence. In comparison to members of low masculinity cultures, members of high masculinity cultures should experience greater differences in uncertainty and anxiety when interacting with members of the opposite and same sex (Gudykunst & Ting-Toomey, 1988).

Eight axioms relate the dimensions of cultural variability to the basic and superficial causes in the theory:

Axiom 40: Members of individualistic cultures use person-based information (e.g., attitudes, feelings, beliefs) to reduce uncertainty more than members of collectivistic cultures, whereas members of collectivistic cultures use group-based information (e.g., background, age, status) to reduce uncertainty more than members of individualistic cultures.

Axiom 41: Members of low uncertainty-avoidance cultures experience more anxiety in communicating with strangers than members of high uncertainty-avoidance cultures.

Axiom 42: Members of high masculine cultures experience greater uncertainty and anxiety when communicating with members of the opposite sex (in comparison to communicating with members of the same sex) than members of low masculine cultures.

Axiom 43: Members of high power distance cultures experience greater uncertainty and anxiety when interacting with someone higher in status (in comparison to people equal in status) than members of low power distance cultures.

Axiom 44: Members of individualistic cultures emphasize personal identity more than social identity; members of collectivistic cultures emphasize social identity more than personal identity.

Axiom 45: Members of collectivistic cultures share more networks with members of their ingroups than members of individualistic cultures.

Axiom 46: Members of collectivistic cultures accommodate and adapt their behavior more than members of individualistic cultures.

Axiom 47: Members of high uncertainty avoidance cultures are more certainty oriented and have more need for closure than members of low uncertainty avoidance cultures.

At least two personality-level equivalents of the dimensions of cultural variability also will influence our ability to manage our anxiety and uncertainty.[33] Triandis and his associates (1986), for example, isolate the personality equivalent for individualism-collectivism—idiocentrism-allocentrism, respectively. Egalitarianism (e.g., belief in human equality) is the personality equivalent of power distance. High egalitarianism (the equivalent of low power distance) should lead to low levels of anxiety about interacting with strangers. The two final axioms link these constructs to managing uncertainty and anxiety:

Axiom 48: An increase in our idiocentrism will produce an increase in our reliance on person-based information when reducing uncertainty; an increase in our allocentrism will produce an increase in our reliance on group-based information in reducing uncertainty.

Axiom 49: An increase in our egalitarianism will produce a decrease in our anxiety.

CONCLUSION

The AUM theory proffered in this chapter is an initial attempt to formally state a general theory of effective interpersonal and intergroup communication. The version of the theory presented here should be considered a preliminary working version that is in the process of being reformulated to increase parsimony and clarity.

Theorems can be generated from the axioms by logically combining the axioms. To illustrate, if Axioms 1 and 2 are combined, Theorem 1 can be generated: There is a positive association between our need for group inclusion and sustaining our self-conceptions. This theorem is consistent with J. H. Turner's (1987) theory of motivation. Some theorems generated will be consistent with previous research and some will form hypotheses for future research.[34]

The AUM theory incorporates constructs at all levels of analysis. Motivation (e.g., needs), uncertainty orientation, need for closure, category width, tolerance for ambiguity, and empathy, for example, are the individual-level phenomena. Interpersonal constructs include, but are not limited to, self-conceptions, attraction, attunement, social bonds, and accommodation. Social identities, stereotypes, intergroup expectations, and social networks are examples of the intergroup phenomena included in the theory. The dimensions of cultural variability (e.g., individualism-collectivism) are the cultural-level phenomena. These constructs are linked directly to managing anxiety and/or reducing uncertainty in the theory.

It is important to point out that the general processes included in the AUM theory should generalize across cultures. There will be differences, however, in what constitutes uncertainty and anxiety across cultures. As indicated earlier, Gudykunst and Nishida (1986) found that uncertainty is more person-based in individualistic cultures than in collectivistic cultures, and more group-based in collectivistic cultures than in individualistic cultures. This position is compatible with Hamill's (1990) argument that humans are endowed with innate logical structures, but cultures create unique meanings out of the innate knowledge.

Although the AUM theory is complex and involves a large number of theoretical statements, most, but not all, statements are empirically testable. As with any theory, however, the present theory includes some statements that are not testable. The theory is logically consistent; it explains effective communication; it involves all levels of analysis; and it can be applied in practical settings. The theory presented has been used to design and implement general cultural awareness training programs, cultural adjustment training programs, and training programs designed to help participants manage conflict between members of different groups. More important, when presented to students the theory makes intuitive sense to them and they are able to use it to improve their communication with others.

To conclude, application of the AUM theory will lead us to act in a way consistent with the Vulcan salutation: "Greetings. I see that you are different. May we together become greater than the sum of both of us" (*Star Trek*). The quest, however, often is similar to novice students' responses to the Zen Master Haukin (1686-1769) when he asked for their answer to the Zen koan: "In clapping both hands a sound is heard; what is the sound of one hand?"

NOTES

1. A number of colleagues have been involved in various aspects of developing the theoretical research program. I want to especially thank Gao Ge, Mitch Hammer, Tsukasa Nishida, and Stella Ting-Toomey for their contributions. I also want to thank the numerous students who have used earlier versions of the theory to design training programs, helping to demonstrate its usefulness. I also owe an intellectual debt to those whose work I have used in developing the theory. These scholars include Georg Simmel, Charles Berger, Harry Triandis, Walter Stephan, Cookie Stephan, Henri Tajfel, John C. Turner, Johnathan H. Turner, Howard Giles, and Thomas Scheff.

2. Earlier versions of these theories have been presented in Gudykunst (1988, 1991), Gudykunst and Hammer (1988), and Gudykunst and Kim (1992).

3. I view intercultural communication as a special case of intergroup communication (see Gudykunst, 1988). I also believe that *all* human communication involves both interpersonal and intergroup components. To theorize about one without including the other leads to an incomplete theory.

4. This view is consistent with Triandis's (1977) position that effectiveness involves making "isomorphic attributions." It also is compatible with Powers and Lowrey's (1984)

conceptualization of "basic communication fidelity"—"the degree of congruence between the cognitions [or thoughts] of two or more individuals following a communication event" (p. 58). Rogers and Kincaid (1981) use the term *mutual understanding* and McLeod and Chaffee (1973) use the term *accuracy* for what I am calling *effective communication*. This may sound like what Eisenberg and Phillips (1991) call a "classical-structuralist" approach, but it is not. My focus is not on the sender, but both the sender and receiver, as well as the context. This is discussed in more detail below.

5. By suggesting that theories involve explanation, I am taking a more objectivist than subjectivist position on the nature of theory (see Gudykunst & Nishida, 1989, for an overview of the two approaches). Although the goal of theory is objectivist in nature, I have used the work of subjectivists (e.g., Scheff, 1990) in constructing the theory.

6. One reason people often do not see theories as "practical" (to use Kurt Lewin's term) is that the theoretical statements are highly abstract with no connection to everyday life. I have stated the axioms at a lower level to make them easier to apply. This, however, necessitates an increase in the number of statements needed.

7. If two people were included in the figure, the second person would be a mirror image of the first with effective communication in the middle.

8. The rationale for the use of the concept of the stranger is presented in Gudykunst and Kim (1992). This orientation treats the member of the ingroup as a sender or receiver in different axioms or theorems. I believe that we simultaneously send and receive messages. The separation is used for purpose of clarity in the theoretical statements and for ease of application.

9. From the perspective of the stranger the theory also forms the foundation for a theory of intercultural adaptation. A few additional axioms are needed to complete the theory. An earlier version of this theory was presented by Gudykunst and Hammer (1988b) and tested by Gao and Gudykunst (1990).

10. Stephan and Stephan include *uncertainty* in their anxiety construct. I see them as separate processes—one cognitive (uncertainty) and one affective (anxiety).

11. There probably are "optimal" levels of uncertainty and anxiety. This concept, however, is beyond the scope of this chapter.

12. See Motley (1990, 1991) and Andersen (1991) for a recent debate on the role of intentions in communication. I tend to side with Andersen (see Gudykunst, 1991, for a rationale).

13. Recent research, however, suggests that we do not communicate totally on automatic pilot. Rather, we pay sufficient attention so that we can recall key words in the conversations we have (Kitayama & Burnstein, 1988).

14. Billig (1987) argues that social thought involves a dialectic between categorization and particularization. Langer (1989) argues we cannot stop categorizing, but that we can create new categories that are finer and finer. I see these two theorists as essentially making the same argument, but using different constructs.

15. Howell includes a fifth stage, unconscious super competence, which is not discussed here.

16. Confronting the anxiety we experience strengthens the self (e.g., May, 1977).

17. This axiom assumes a relationship between uncertainty and anxiety. In the 1988 version of the theory, I argued that they are not necessarily related. In J. H. Turner's theory, however, they are related.

18. There are individual and collective forms of self-esteem that must be taken into consideration (see Luhtanen & Crocker, 1992). When group comparisons are being made collective self-esteem is the issue.

19. This axiom is slightly different than presented in the 1988 version of the theory. I have modified the axiom to suggest the same relationship between social identity and uncertainty and anxiety. There probably is an optimal strength of social identity for facilitating the management of uncertainty and anxiety. This, however, is beyond the scope of this chapter.

20. Brewer (1991) uses a similar idea in her discussion of optimal distinctiveness, which involves balancing personal and social identities to maximize distinctiveness.

21. Scheff also argues that there can be attunement between groups and to the extent that this exists, society can be said to exist.

22. Following Lewis (1971), Scheff includes embarrassment, guilt, and other related emotions as part of the shame construct.

23. On the surface, this claim appears inconsistent with Tajfel's (1978) social comparison process. Tajfel's conceptualization, however, does not take into consideration the existence of unacknowledged shame.

24. I believe that Sunnafrank's (1986) notion of predicted outcome value is part of our expectations and can easily be incorporated into the current theory.

25. Burgoon and Hale do not limit their statement to this group, I do.

26. There are numerous other variables that could be included. I have selected those that I believe are most critical. See Stephan (1987) for a full discussion of the contact hypothesis.

27. This use is consistent with Keesing's (1974) definition of culture, which I have used in most recent writings (see Gudykunst, 1991; Gudykunst & Kim, 1992).

28. Snyder's conceptualization of self-monitoring is biased toward individualistic cultures. Gudykunst et al. (1992) present a derived etic conceptualization and measurement.

29. Obviously these six skills are not the only ones I could isolate. For the purpose of the initial version of the theory, however, they appear to be a reasonable first approximation.

30. This is similar to Billig's (1987) notion of particularization. Particularizing stimuli could be substituted for creating new categories in the following axiom (Axiom 31).

31. The position I am taking here is consistent with a communitarian perspective (see Etzioni, 1990).

32. Ellis argues that the chance for misunderstanding is high when only syntactic codes are used, but this does not mean that they necessarily lead to ineffective communication.

33. Uncertainty orientation (discussed earlier) could be considered the personality-level equivalent of uncertainty avoidance. Sex roles would be the equivalent to masculinity-femininity.

34. Not all axioms should be combined to form theorems. Some will involve the fallacy of the excluded middle and should not be generated.

4

Communicative Resourcefulness

An Identity Negotiation Perspective

STELLA TING-TOOMEY • *California State University, Fullerton*

Although past intercultural communication competence studies have investigated trait-like, behavioral, and outcome-specific characteristics, many studies are atheoretical and unfocused. For example, for each intercultural communication competence study, one can pose the following questions: What are the boundary parameters of competence in the study? What are the antecedent, process, and outcome conditions of the competence perspective? How is communication competence being defined in the study? What is the role of "culture" in competence? What is the role of "communication"? What are the end goals of competence stemming from this particular perspective? From whose viewpoints is competence defined and measured? Past competence studies have provided rich indicators of what sensitizing concepts should be included in a research design or training program, but it is critical now to move beyond the descriptive stage of competence research into the explanatory stage of theory building.

A coherent theory on communication competence can help unveil hidden assumptions, generate testable propositions, and uncover salient constructs for research and training purposes. In addition, a sound theory can help put the various components of communication competence into a more meaningful perspective. Finally, a working theory on communication competence can, at the minimum, offer a common starting point to accumulate knowledge and refine a set of common constructs for cross-comparative purposes either within or across cultures.

AUTHOR'S NOTE: *I want to thank William Gudykunst for his helpful comments on an earlier version of this chapter. I also wish to express appreciation to Seiichi Morisaki for his help in the preparation of the figure.*

The purpose of this chapter is to present a working theory of intercultural communication competence. The chapter is developed in three sections. The basic assumptions of an identity negotiation perspective for the study of communication competence are presented in the first section. The specific domains of communicative resourcefulness are delineated in the second section. Theoretical propositions derived from the identity negotiation perspective are presented in the last section. *Effective identity negotiation* refers to the smooth coordination between interactants concerning salient identity issues, and the process of engaging in responsive identity confirmation and positive identity enhancement. Effective identity negotiation requires an individual to draw on a wide range of cognitive, affective, and behavioral resources to deal with novel, identity-improvisation situations.

AN IDENTITY NEGOTIATION PERSPECTIVE

Intercultural communication competence is viewed in this chapter as the effective identity negotiation process between two or more interactants in a novel communication episode. Every communication episode, to a certain degree, can be framed or reframed by the interactants as carrying some elements of novelty. Novel episodes can include strangers meeting for the first time or encounters in a new environment, or refer to interactants holding the desire to reframe their relationship in new ways. Novelty is viewed in this context as containing both unpredictability and challenge. It is how one manages a novel situation that shapes anxiety-provoking encounters into identity-strengthening experiences. Thus, while unpredictability can create identity insecurity, it also stretches one's identity resilience. It is within this orientation that the word *intercultural* is defined here as connoting a certain degree of newness, novelty, or dissimilarity.

Each communication episode, in essence, always carries some elements of strangeness or novelty because of the reconfiguration of persons, situations, and spatial-temporal and cultural contexts. Whether the strangers are from similar cultural backgrounds or different cultural backgrounds, all individuals enter into a novel communication episode with culturally grounded and culturally framed identity images. Individuals also enter an unfamiliar situation with a certain degree of identity vulnerability and apprehension. Although the substance of the identity negotiation perspective applies to all types of relationships, the focus of this chapter emphasizes identity negotiation in novel, unfamiliar situations.

The identity negotiation perspective draws heavily from the ideas of identity cultural variability (Ting-Toomey, 1985, 1986, 1988, 1989a, in press a), symbolic interaction (Blumer, 1969; Mead, 1934; McCall & Simmons, 1978), identity theory (Stryker, 1981, 1991; R. Turner, 1987), social identity theory (Tajfel, 1978; Tajfel & Turner, 1979), and optimal distinctiveness theory (Brewer, 1991). There are eight basic assumptions to the identity negotiation perspective: (a) Individuals in all cultures hold multiple images concerning the sense of *self*—this sense of self can be both unarticulated (i.e., unconscious) and articulated (i.e., conscious); (b) cultural variability influences the *locus* of self-identification; (c) an individual's self-identification involves both structure and process—while the structure of one's sense of self-identification confers existential security, the change process of self-identification promotes existential vulnerability; (d) the motivations to human communication are to reinforce existential security and diffuse existential vulnerability via identity boundary regulation; (e) identity boundary regulation processes are expressed through the dialectical management of inclusion and differentiation; (f) the dialectic of inclusion and differentiation rests on an optimal balance of self, other, and group membership; (g) the effective management of inclusion-differentiation dialectic influences our sense of coherence level and our global self-esteem level; and (h) a coherent sense of self-conception enhances cognitive, affective, and behavioral resourcefulness and these resources contribute to both knowledge and predispositions to effective identity negotiation process. *Communicative resourcefulness* is defined as the knowledge and the ability to apply cognitive, affective, and behavioral resources appropriately, effectively, and creatively in diverse interactive situations.

The identity negotiation process framework is presented in Figure 4.1. The framework presents only person A's orientation to effective identity negotiation—readers should add person B's orientation (from right to left on the model) to the identity negotiation process.

Identity is defined as the mosaic sense of self-identification that incorporates the interplay of human, cultural, social, and personal images as consciously or unconsciously experienced and enacted by the individual. Although there is a sense of structure or stability to an individual's sense of generalized self, each communication episode produces an inevitable change in this mosaic sense of self-identification. The following sections explain the various theoretical assumptions in more detail.

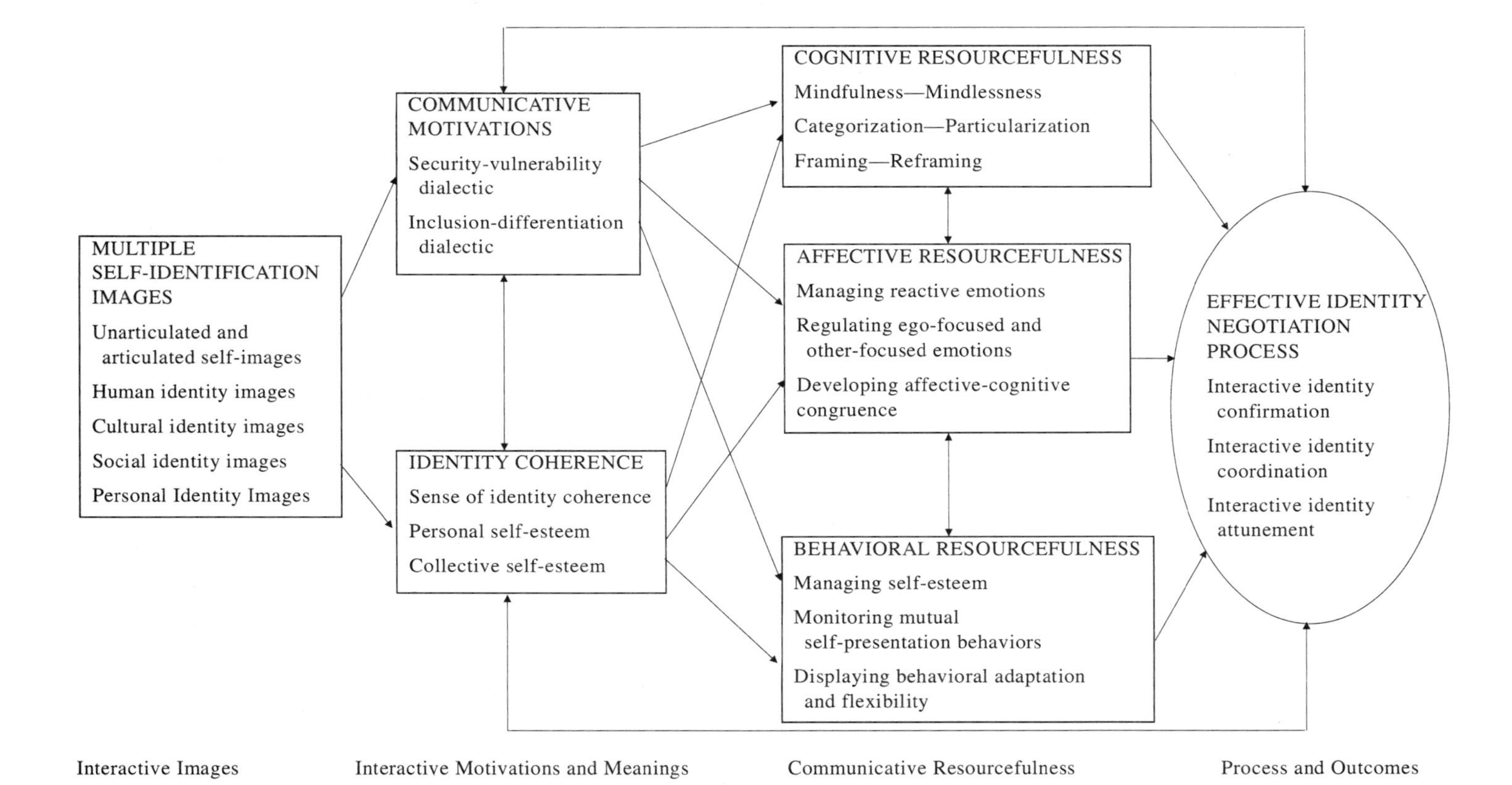

Figure 4.1: Identity Negotiation Process Model: Composite Constructs

Self-Identification: Content and Locus

The first assumption is that human beings in all cultures carry with them images of themselves that are both unarticulated and articulated (R. Turner, 1987). The unarticulated images are the unconscious, taken-for-granted images that we carry around in our habituated, everyday interaction. The articulated images are the images, in contrast, that surface into our consciousness when they are called into question by others or ourselves in a particular communication episode. Unarticulated and articulated images exist on a continuum of difference. They can be self-labels, adjectives, nouns, or visual metaphors that we associate with our self-identifications. They can also cover ethnic/cultural identity images, social/gender identity images, and personal/moral identity images.

J. C. Turner (1987) argues that a person's self-conception takes the form of self-categorizations on the superordinate human image level, on the intermediate ingroup-outgroup level as based on perceived differences and similarities between human beings, and on the subordinate level of uniqueness as defined by personality or individual differences. Of course, how relevant others interact with us, and the larger context in which the question of self-identification arises, create a profound impact on how we give priority to these identity images and how we translate them into communicative actions.

Self-identification provides the motivational key to communicative actions. How we conceive our sense of self and how we want to be perceived by others are fundamental communicative questions. In each interaction episode, the implicit or explicit messages express our underlying self-views and, concurrently, our appraisals of the other's self-views. How we want to be defined by others and how our conversational partners want us to define them are expressed in and through communication processes. In addition, it is through communication that we can reframe and modify our self-views. Thus, self-identification is maintained, re-created, and changed through mutual affirmation or mutual enhancement processes.

Three fundamental assumptions of the symbolic interactionist school (Blumer, 1969; Blumstein, 1991; Cooley, 1902; Howard & Callero, 1991; McCall & Simmons, 1978; Mead, 1934; Stryker, 1981, 1991; R. Turner, 1987) guide the development of the identity negotiation perspective. First, individual and society are mutually interdependent and supportive of one another; second, society is sustained in the dynamic processes of interaction; third, cognition, emotion, and action are sometimes modified or changed by the individual or by forces greater than the individual (Callero, 1991, p. 324; R. Turner, 1987). *Society*, on the basic level, is defined as (a) recurring patterns of interaction, (b) a system of beliefs and norms, (c) a system of positions and identities, (d) situated identities, and (e) a change agent (Callero, 1991). Through symbolic interaction, these systems of norms and positional identities are tested and confronted. Thus, effective identity negotiation rests on how we maintain existential security in our self-views and at the same time are responsive to the self-views of the conversational partner in the interaction episode.

To briefly summarize, symbolic interactionists view social life as a process of interaction between and among individuals who use symbolic means (i.e., verbal and nonverbal interaction) to maintain, establish, and modify certain systems of beliefs and conventions, and to uphold certain positions and identities in particular encounters or episodes. Human beings are viewed as capable of reflexivity—at the same time we are in the process of negotiating our identities, we can also be reflexive of our identities-in-context. Human interaction is viewed as leading to or reinforcing shared identity meanings that are bounded by rules, norms, and conventions in the society.

More specifically, Stryker's (1981, 1987, 1991) identity theory emphasizes the internal hierarchical organization of the self and stresses self-society consistency and order. R. Turner's (1968, 1987) identity theory, in contrast, acknowledges the dialectic interplay between articulated and unarticulated selves. R. Turner (1968) views generalized self-conception as consisting of "a selective organization of values and standards, edited to form a workable anchorage of social interaction" (p. 105). For R. Turner (1987), an individual can have competing multiple selves or identities because of competing role demands and constraints. Because of the resourceful nature of the human mind, for most of the time, individuals can hold diverse and even conflicting images of the self. In addition, Stryker's (1987) identity theory emphasizes the importance of identity salient motivation in influencing interaction opportunities on an identity reward basis. R. Turner's (1987) identity theory emphasizes the importance of identity self-affirmation and self-discovery process in novel situations.

Overall, the degree of interdependence between self and society, the value priorities on identity salience and commitment levels, and the meanings and interpretations associated with self-change and self-discovery processes are grounded in the cultural folk models of personhood (DeVos & Suarez-Orozco, 1990; Holland & Quinn, 1987; Marsella, DeVos, & Hsu, 1985; Ochs, 1988; Rosaldo, 1984; Shweder & LeVine, 1984). In addition, the degree of felt consciousness concerning different facets of self-identification also takes on cultural variations. Finally, the degree of identity choices and behavioral options are also bounded by the cultural variability level and the social role variability level. While cultures with loose social structures (Boldt, 1978) tend to afford the individuals with multiple behavioral choices and options, cultures with tight social structures tend to emphasize cultural norms and social scripts of appropriate and inappropriate role enactments. While cultures with loose social structures are more lenient in accepting a wide range of role-deviant behaviors, cultures with tight social structures are much more stringent in their rewards and punishments. Loose and tight social structures also influence our identity expectation demand level and identity negotiation latitude level.

The second assumption in the identity negotiation perspective states that cultural variability influences the locus of self-identification. Whether we are discussing personal identity, social identity, or ethnic/cultural identity, the meanings and logic we attach to these images are culturally grounded. As LeVine (1982) observes, "cultures vary in the attributes of the ideal self over the life course, in the actions with which pride and shame are associated and in expectancies for autonomy or interdependence in the domains of social action" (p. 295). Culture influences the perceived discrepancy between the actual self and the ideal self, and lends the criteria in which self-esteem is appraised and evaluated. The cultural variability perspective is concerned primarily with how definable dimensions of a culture affect identity location and identity enactment.

Although there are many dimensions in which cultures differ, one dimension that has received consistent attention from both cross-cultural communication researchers and psychologists around the world is individualism-collectivism. Countless cross-cultural studies (Chinese Culture Connection, 1987; Gudykunst & Ting-Toomey, 1988; Hofstede, 1980, 1991; Hui & Triandis, 1986; Schwartz & Bilsky, 1990; Ting-Toomey, 1991; Triandis, 1988, 1990; Triandis, Brislin, & Hui, 1988b; Wheeler, Reis, & Bond, 1989) have provided theoretical and empirical evidence that the value orientations of individualism and collectivism are pervasive in a wide range of cultures.

Basically, *individualism* refers to the broad value tendencies of a system in emphasizing the importance of individual identity over group identity, individual rights over group rights, and individual needs over group needs. In contrast, *collectivism* refers to the broad value tendencies of a system in emphasizing the importance of the *we* identity over the *I* identity, group rights over individual rights, and ingroup-oriented needs over individual wants and desires. An *ingroup* is a group whose values, norms, and rules are internalized by its members. In contrast, an *outgroup* is a group whose values, norms, and rules are inconsistent with those of the ingroup. Macro-level factors such as ecology, affluence, social and geographic mobility, migration, cultural background of parents, socialization, rural/urban environment, mass media exposure, education, and social change have been identified by Triandis (1990) as some of the underlying factors that contribute to the development of individualistic and collectivistic value tendencies in different cultures.

High individualistic index values have been found in the United States, Australia, Great Britain, Canada, Netherlands, and New Zealand. High collectivistic index values have been uncovered in Indonesia, Columbia, Venezuela, Panama, Ecuador, and Guatemala (Hofstede, 1991, p. 53). In intercultural communication research (Gudykunst & Ting-Toomey, 1988), the United States and Canada have been identified consistently as cultures high in individualistic tendencies, while strong empirical evidence has supported that China, Taiwan, Korea, Japan, and Mexico can be identified clearly as collectivistic cultures. Within each culture, different ethnic communities can also display distinctive individualistic and collectivistic value tendencies. In trying to "locate" the sense of self-identification in individualistic and collectivistic cultures, the basic building block of individualism-collectivism is its relative emphasis on the importance of *autonomous self* or *connected self* in the culture. In individualistic cultures, members are influenced by the moral codes of an internalized, *freewheeling* self. In collectivistic cultures, members are governed by the implicit and explicit moral standards of a "self in connection with group" phenomenon. In individualistic cultures, the right to think, feel, and act based on the autonomous-self level is critical. In collectivistic cultures, the self is embedded in some form of relational context and in the larger sociocultural context. In individualistic cultures, the recognition of self is based on personal achievements and the self-actualization process. In collectivistic cultures, the recognition of self is based on ascribed status, role relationships, family reputation, and/or workgroup reputation. According to Triandis et al. (1988b), when respondents were asked to give 20 descriptions of themselves by completing 20 sentences that started with "I am . . . ," people from individualistic cultures used only 15% group-related attributes to define themselves, while people from collectivistic cultures used 35%-45% group-related attributes (e.g., "I am the third daughter of my family") to describe their sense of personhood.

In managing identity security and identity vulnerability issues, the sense of identity threat for members of individualistic cultures exists on either the personal or the interindividual level. Comparatively speaking, the sense of identity threat for members of collectivistic cultures exists on either the ingroup or intergroup comparative level. While the sense of individual guilt or personal shame can accompany identity loss for individualists, the sense of group shame or relational shame usually accompanies "face loss" for collectivists. While individualists emphasize individual self-esteem protection, collectivists emphasize social/ situated face protection (Ting-Toomey, 1988, in press b; Ting-Toomey, Gao, Trubisky, Yang, Kim, Lin, & Nishida, 1991).

In using the terms *independent construal of self* and *interdependent construal of self* to represent individualistic self versus collectivistic self, Markus and Kitayama (1991) argue that how one locates one's sense of self-identification in different cultures has a profound impact on the self-system's information processing field. For them, the sense of individuality that accompanies this independent construal of self includes a sense of

> oneself as an agent, as a producer of one's actions. One is conscious of being in control over the surrounding situation, and of the need to express one's own thoughts, feelings, and actions to others. Such acts of standing out are often intrinsically rewarding because they elicit pleasant, ego-focused emotions (e.g., pride) and also reduce unpleasant ones (e.g., frustration). Furthermore, the acts of standing out, themselves, form an important basis of self-esteem. (p. 246)

Conversely, the sense of self-conception that accompanies an interdependent construal of self includes an

> attentiveness and responsiveness to others that one either explicitly or implicitly assumes will be reciprocated by these others, as well as the willful management of one's other-focused feelings and desires so as to maintain and further the reciprocal interpersonal relationship. One is conscious of where one belongs with respect to others and assumes a receptive stance toward these others, continually adjusting and accommodating to these others in many aspects of behavior. Such acts of fitting in and accommodating are often intrinsically rewarding, because they give rise to pleasant, other-focused emotions (e.g., feeling of connection) while diminishing unpleasant ones (e.g., shame) and, furthermore, because the self-restraint required in doing so forms an important basis of self-esteem. (p. 246)

Thus, the cultural variability of independent versus interdependent construal of self frames our existential experience and serves as an anchoring point in terms of how we process self-views, and by what criteria we evaluate others' self-presentation performance. The cultural variability dimension of individualism-collectivism and the symbolic interactionist school guide the rest of the development of the assumptions in the identity negotiation perspective.

Identity Security-Vulnerability Dialectic

The third assumption in the identity negotiation perspective is that our self-identifications involve both structure and process, and that while the structure of our self-identifications reinforces our sense of existential security, the change process of our self-identifications promotes existential vulnerability. In the context of the identity negotiation perspective, identity security-vulnerability is viewed as the primary dialectic of human existence. Human beings need security in their sense of self-conception; too much security can bring boredom and inertia, but too much insecurity or unpredictability can exhaust the self-system in question. An individual can only learn to balance this primary dialectic in the presence of others. Family/peer support system provides the basic role model in which individuals learn to balance identity security-vulnerability issues, and to regulate differentiation-inclusion needs. The family socialization process, however, is moderated by individual and sociocultural factors. In addition, the threshold levels of the security-vulnerability dialectic also vary in accordance with individual, social, cultural, and structural factors.

According to Baxter (1988; Altman, Vinsel, & Brown, 1981), two basic principles are involved in dialectics: the dialectical principle of unity and the dialectical principle of contradiction. The first principle emphasizes mutual interdependence of two opposing forces; the second principle emphasizes mutual negation of tendencies. It is probably because of this push-and-pull factor that identity evolves, stabilizes, and develops. This dual sense of existential security and change also profoundly affects the way we communicate, with whom we communicate, and how we communicate in our everyday environment.

Cultural variability asserts a strong influence on what constitutes identity security or identity threat. For the individualists, existential security means identity security that reinforces a sense of self-reliance and maintaining an unencumbered sense of self. For the collectivists, existential security means security in the knowledge of ingroup interdependence, maintaining ingroup membership identities, and knowing that their socially connected identities are being respected. Effective identity negotiation rests on the dynamic management of the primary need for identity security on one hand, and the inevitable move of identity change and vulnerability on the other.

Communicative Motivations

Assumption four posits that the basic motivations to human communication are to reinforce existential security and diffuse identity vulnerability via identity boundary regulation. Assumption five states that identity boundary regulation gives rise to the specific communicative motivations of inclusion need and differentiation need. Identity boundary regulation helps to create self-identification and other-identification distinctiveness. It also creates a protective zone and distancing space between ingroups and outgroups. Human beings in all cultures regulate visible and invisible boundaries to strengthen identity security and diffuse identity vulnerability—where they place their identity boundaries, and the meanings they attach to these boundaries, are culturally-grounded. Depending on the cultural variability of individualism-collectivism, individuals can vary in the locus of their identity-protection boundaries. For example, for individualists, the identity boundary protection is likely to be associated with individual attributes, traits, abilities, and competence. It also extends more to voluntary relationships than prescribed relationships. For collectivists, identity boundary regulation is likely to be associated with ingroup commitment, loyalty, and mutual face protection. It also extends more to obligatory reciprocal relationships than spontaneous individual-based relationships.

If existential security-vulnerability serves as the primary motivational dialectic for human interaction, inclusion-differentiation serves as the secondary motivational dialectic in social interaction. Too much inclusion or connection can stifle one's personal/group space or privacy, but too much differentiation or deindividuation can lead to alienation and loneliness. Again, the secondary dialectic of inclusion-differentiation is subject to individual and cultural variations. On the normative level, while members of individualistic cultures tend to invest more time and energy in cultivating individual space and personal privacy, members of collectivistic cultures tend to spend more resources in managing the group inclusion need.

Overall, the gatekeeping process of selecting whom to include or whom to exclude, whom to turn to for self-affirmation and self-other connections, and on whom to impose or not to impose varies by self-conception constructions, goal functions, situational type, and cultural context. Research (Howard, 1991; Pelham & Swann, 1989) on self-conceptions suggests that most individuals do operate with a positivity bias: Most people have positive self-conceptions and wish to enhance or verify these self-conceptions with supportive others. Thus, an individual tends to associate with people who provide affirmative feedback on positive self-views while avoiding people who engage in negative appraisals of one's self-identification. According to Swann, Pelham, and Krull (1989), even people who have very low self-esteem tend to be able to articulate positive self-attributes within the network of negative attributes, and they prefer, foremost, positive enhancement feedback before negative verification. More important, the ways people frame their different aspects of self-views (e.g., positively or negatively, salient or nonsalient) have been found to profoundly influence their feedback levels with their peers.

Assumption six of the identity negotiation perspective posits that the dialectic of inclusion and differentiation rests on an optimal balance of self, other, and group membership. Effective identity negotiation depends heavily on how an individual can maintain an optimal degree of balance between inclusion and differentiation, and how self/other and group membership can each occupy a functional role. Whereas the inclusion need idea echoes that of J. H. Turner's (1987) theory of motivation, the boundary differentiation idea echoes both Tajfel's (1978) social identity theory and Brewer's (1991) optimal distinctiveness theory. For J. H. Turner (1987), maintaining the "substance, esteem, and coherence of self is not only dependent upon an individual's capacity to confirm self directly through self-presentations, but also to achieve a sense of inclusion, trust, and security, thereby avoiding more deep-seated sources of diffuse anxiety which cause self-doubt" (p. 25). His motivational model emphasizes that "the intensity of needs for sustaining self and the visibility of self-presentations" (p. 25) are a joint function of both interactants successfully achieving the needs for inclusion, trust, and security in the social interaction level. Of these three needs, inclusion is viewed as the most critical here because it is via relational or group inclusion that personal trust and security can be established.

In relating J. H. Turner's (1987, 1988) motivation model with social identity, social identity confers a sense of inclusion, trust, and security on an individual. Tajfel (1978) defined social identity as "that part of an individual's self-concept which derives from his [or her] knowledge of his [or her] membership of a social group (or groups) together with the value and emotional significance attached to the membership" (p. 63). By social categorization, an individual orders the social environment based on similarity groupings and strength of associations. These various group memberships can also affect the valence of our self-conception via social comparison. To the extent that our salient ingroup compares favorably with other relevant social/cultural groups, we achieve a positive social identity. Conversely, to the extent that our salient ingroup compares unfavorably, we would attempt different options such as changing the identity group if possible, changing the comparative criteria dimensions, or downgrading the comparative group via intergroup aggression. Social comparison, however, rests on how we frame the comparative group and whether we use positive or negative appraisal strategies.

Drawing on the social identity theory, Brewer (1991) argues that:

> social identity derives from a fundamental tension between human needs for validation and similarity to others (on the one hand) and a countervailing need for uniqueness and individuation (on the other). The idea that individuals need a certain level of both similarity to and differentiation from others is not novel. . . . In general, these [individuation] models assume that individuals meet these needs by maintaining some intermediate degree of similarity between the self and relevant others. . . . Social identity can be viewed as a compromise between assimilation and differentiation from others, where the need for deindividuation is satisfied within in-groups, while the need for distinctiveness is met through intergroup comparisons. . . . Instead of a bipolar continuum of similarity-dissimilarity, needs for assimilation and differentiation are represented as opposing forces. (p. 477)

The proposed dialectics in this chapter, namely, identity security-vulnerability and inclusion-differentiation need, closely reflect Brewer's (1991) theoretical point. The one key difference, however, concerns the nature of viewing dialectic as composed of opposite forces or complementary tendencies. While Western, Cartesian tradition tends to view self-conception in opposing, dualistic terms, the Eastern tradition typically tends to approach dualistic concepts from a complementary, relational whole perspective. Again, how one frames the two dialectics—whether they consist of opposing, tension-filled poles or whether they contain complementary elements—would have a profound influence on how one deals with identity negotiation and relationship development issues.

Overall, a balanced degree of inclusion and differentiation is critical to the functional well-being of the individual and provides the appropriate motivational energy to social interaction. As Brewer (1991) notes,

> at either extreme along the inclusiveness dimension, the person's sense of security and self-worth is threatened. Being highly individuated leaves one vulnerable to isolation and stigmatization. . . . However, total deindividuation provides no basis for comparative appraisal or self-definition. As a consequence, we are uncomfortable in social contexts in which we are either too distinctive or too undistinctive. (p. 478)

How individuals frame a communication episode, how they frame their sense of inclusion or distinctiveness, and how surrounding others help to alleviate such sense of distinctiveness or undistinctiveness can have a dramatic influence on the actual interaction. Effective identity negotiation takes place through the mutual acknowledgments and the mutual responsive behaviors concerning inclusion and differentiation thresholds. These threshold levels, furthermore, are influenced by interactive goal functions, relationship levels, and cultural/structural constraints. As assumption four in Brewer's (1991) optimal distinctiveness theory states, "the optimal level of category distinctiveness or inclusiveness is a function of the relative strength . . . of the opposing drives for assimilation and differentiation. For any individual, the relative strength of the two needs is determined by cultural norms, individual socialization, and recent experience" (p. 478).

While norms of individualistic cultures emphasize the opposing nature of the two poles, norms of collectivistic cultures emphasize the complementary nature of the opposing tendencies. In addition, the locus of inclusion and differentiation needs depends heavily on whether one operates from an independent construal of self or interdependent construal of self. From an independent construal of self perspective, an optimal balance point of inclusion and differentiation is to feel the security of relational belonging and protection but at the same time be able to stand apart freely from the voluntary relationship or the group. From an interdependent construal of self perspective, an ideal balance point of inclusion and differentiation rests on the secure feelings of long-term ingroup-based harmony and protection, with differentiation on the ingroup/outgroup comparative level.

While individualists embrace inclusion need more readily (especially via voluntary relationship) before personal differentiation need arises, collectivists seek out opportunity to screen off constant ingroup demands before the ingroup inclusive pressures resurface. While independent construal of self, recursively, promotes a deep level of inclusion need, interdependent construal of self, reflexively, promotes a complex level of differentiation need. More important, however, the resilience sense of self-conception does adapt, change, and transform itself based on situational fit and cultural context demands. The more resourceful we are in dealing with the inclusion-differentiation dialectic, the more we can engage in effective identity negotiation with others. The more we are sensitive to cultural framing of inclusion-differentiation dialectic, the more we are equipped to negotiate identity with culturally dissimilar others. On the more basic human level, however, both group membership inclusion and personal relationship connection do serve critical roles in most human beings' sense of coherence and self-worth in most cultures.

Sense of Coherence and Global Self-Esteem

Assumptions seven and eight state that the effective management of the inclusion-differentiation dialectic influences an individual's sense of coherence and self-esteem and these, in turn, advance one's cognitive, affective, and behavioral resourcefulness. According to Antonovsky (1987), the sense of coherence refers to a

> global orientation that expresses the extent to which one has a pervasive, enduring though dynamic feeling of confidence that (1) the stimuli deriving from one's internal and external environments in the course of living are structured, predictable, and explicable; (2) the resources are available to one to meet the demands posed by the stimuli; and (3) these demands are challenges, worthy of investment and engagement. (p. 19)

The sense of coherence has three components: comprehensibility, manageability, and meaningfulness. Casting these terms in the context of effective identity negotiation: *Identity comprehensibility* refers to the extent to which one perceives one's sense of self-identification as making cognitive sense, and as having relative order and consistency rather than constant identity chaos. *Identity manageability* refers to the extent to which one perceives that resources are at one's disposal and that they are adequate to meet the demands posed by the environment. Finally, *identity meaningfulness*, which is the most important component in Antonovsky's (1987) conceptualization of the sense of coherence, refers to the extent to which one feels that "life makes sense emotionally, that at least some of the problems and demands posed by living are worth investing energy in, are worthy of commitment and engagement, are challenges that are 'welcome' rather than burdens that one would much rather do without" (p. 18). In essence, Antonovsky (1979, 1987) views the sense of coherence concept from the salutogenic model perspective. This model emphasizes the movements and positive coping mechanisms that enable an individual to move along a continuum from a dysfunctional end to a functional end, from insecurity to security, and from not knowing to knowing.

Complementing Antonovsky's (1987) sense of coherence concept is Kobasa's (1979, 1982) "hardiness" construct. Kobasa uses the tripartite variables of commitment, control, and challenge to define the hardiness construct. Individuals who are high in *challenge* regard life changes to be the norm rather than the exception, and they anticipate these changes as a stimulus to growth rather than a threat to security. In addition, individuals who welcome challenge are characterized by cognitive flexibility and tolerance of ambiguity. Individuals who are high in *control* believe they can influence the events of their experience and perceive different choices and alternative options in handling the situation. They also tend to emphasize their own responsibility for self-change and situational self-regulation. Finally, individuals who are high in *commitment* tend to engage themselves fully in the many situations of life, including, work, family, interpersonal relationships, and social institutions, and they carry an overall sense of purpose and meaningfulness in their actions. In short, Kobasa's (1982) challenge, control, and commitment correspond closely to Antonovsky's (1987) comprehensibility, manageability, and meaningfulness. Cultural variability of individualism-collectivism influences the way individuals manage, monitor, or make sense of such identity change situations. For individualists, personal control can indeed be a major way of dealing with novel experiences. For collectivists, existing support networks can help to serve as the buffering cushions to the identity change experiences.

Overall, the key difference between the two approaches rests on the concept of challenge—while Kobasa (1982) emphasizes a novel situation as an opportunity and incentive for identity testing and growth, Antonovsky (1987) emphasizes the importance of constructing a sense of order and consistency out of the identity testing experience. Kobasa also emphasizes the search for identity meaning in the ever-changing environment, but Antonovsky emphasizes the importance of identity structure and coherence (Orr & Westman, 1990). Both approaches, however, emphasize the importance of maintaining optimistic cognitive appraisals and the mobilization of constructive resources to deal with the novel, unfamiliar situation.

Finally, countless studies in social psychology, mental health, behavioral medicine, human services, cultural/ethnic studies, communication, sociology, and self/identity literature since the 1950s have testified to the enduring role of self-esteem in human interaction. After an exhaustive review of existing literature on individual need for self-esteem, Greenberg, Pyszczynski, and Solomon (1986) propose a culturally grounded self-esteem perspective along the following points:

> Humans are not unique because they are social animals, but because they are *cultural animals*. Humans live within a shared symbolic conception of the universe that is ultimately determined by culture, and yet is believed to be an absolutely accurate representation of reality by individuals within the culture. As the source of meaning and value, the culture provides the

> individual with a basis for valuing himself or herself. The individual can have a sense of worth to the extent that she or he satisfies the cultural criteria for being good (valuable). Thus, self-esteem consists of viewing oneself as valuable within the context of the universal drama conveyed by the culture. (pp. 196-197)

Self-esteem is, in essence, a cultural creation. Protective self-esteem serves as a cultural anxiety-buffer for both children and adults. Children learn to be "good" children or "bad" children by engaging in "good" behavior or "bad" behavior as endorsed or sanctioned by the culture and as rewarded or punished by the parents. The cultural family system, in essence, provides the anchoring foundation for self-esteem appraisal and interpretation. According to Greenberg et al. (1986), children learn the contingency value of positive self-esteem as associated with warmth and security, and negative self-esteem as associated with terror and exclusion. Thus, affective feelings stemming from the learned self-esteem level also profoundly influence internalized self-conception. Supportive family, peer, or institutional environments strengthen the development of global self-esteem in the child. The baseline issue is, in order to attenuate feelings of identity-threat terror, individuals must believe they are valuable or worthy of everyday existence. Therefore, "individuals need [positive] self-esteem to function with minimal anxiety" (Greenberg et al., 1986, p. 197).

An individual's global sense of self-esteem can consist of personal self-esteem and collective self-esteem. Personal self-esteem can refer to (a) one's tendencies to experience positive and negative affective states, (b) one's specific self-views (i.e., one's conceptions of one's strengths and weaknesses), and (c) the way one frames one's self-views (Pelham & Swann, 1989, p. 672). Framing factors include the relative certainty and importance of an individual's positive versus negative self-views and the discrepancy between an individual's actual and ideal self-views (Pelham & Swann, 1989, p. 672). Research indicates that healthy, secure individuals maintain positive personal self-evaluations. In addition, how one frames one's specific self-views in a manner that is favorable to oneself has positive implications for one's global self-esteem level. Finally, positive or negative self-worth is, in large part, derived from social experience and pieced together by the individual to form a meaningful self-worth structure. Personal self-esteem, in essence, refers to an individual's sense of emotional well-being or self-worth.

Beyond personal self-esteem level, collective self-esteem also plays a critical role in the management of inclusion-differentiation dialectic.

Collective self-esteem connotes "those aspects of identity that have to do with memberships in social groups and the value placed on one's social groups" (Luhtanen & Crocker, 1992, p. 302). Collective self-esteem has been found to include four components: membership esteem, private collective self-esteem, public collective self-esteem, and importance of identity. Both membership esteem and personal self-esteem have been found to be highly correlated. Thus, individuals' positive or negative appraisal of the self in their social groups strongly influences their personal self-views. The degree to which individuals appraise their sense of worthiness or value as group members in different social/ethnic/cultural groups has a profound impact on their perceived collective self-esteem level. The more secure the individuals are in their selective membership self-conceptions, the more likely they maintain a high sense of collective membership self-esteem. In addition, the higher the collective self-esteem level, the more secure and resourceful the individuals are in dealing with membership boundary issues. The works of Luhtanen and Crocker (1992) and Phinney (1990; 1991; Phinney & Alipuria, 1990) on social/ethnic identity memberships provide some initial evidence for the relationship between strengthened membership identity and positive self-esteem, especially when the particular identity is viewed as a salient dimension of one's self-conception.

Drawing from the identity negotiation perspective, a person's overall sense of self-worth is heavily dependent on the effective regulation of identity/boundary issues and the satisfaction derived out of the appropriate management of the security-vulnerability dialectic and the inclusion-differentiation dialectic. Effective identity negotiation depends on the cumulative communicative resources learned in interaction with other individuals and the ability to apply them appropriately, effectively, and creatively. The more we approach novel situations as a learning experience, the more likely we learn to be resourceful. By approaching strangers from different cultures, ethnic groups, social classes, and gender orientations, their diverse perspectives and culturally grounded assumptions can potentially enhance our sense of resourcefulness on multiple levels. Our monitored openness to their diverse sense of self-conceptions can also potentially enrich our self-construal process and widen our cognitive and emotional identity scope. The last assumption of the identity negotiation perspective concerning communicative resourcefulness is explicated more fully in the following section.

Overall, the more effective individuals are in managing both security-vulnerability dialectic and inclusion-differentiation dialectic, the more likely they would have a high regard for the sense of self on both the collective and personal self-esteem levels. In sum, individuals who have reconciled the different self-conception images into a functional whole and who have developed a strong sense of identity coherence would also be more likely to have a global, positive self-esteem level. In addition, the more resourcefully we manage our self-identifications and other-identifications, the more likely we would develop a global, positive self-view. Finally, the more meaningful we perceive our self-identifications in relationship to other self-identifications, the more likely we would develop an interactive, positive self-esteem level.

COMMUNICATIVE RESOURCEFULNESS

To summarize briefly, the identity negotiation perspective emphasizes the importance of managing the identity security-vulnerability and the inclusion-differentiation dialectics. Effective management of the security-vulnerability and inclusion-differentiation dialectics can enhance both our sense of identity coherence and our sense of global self-esteem. With a secure sense of identity coherence and an enhanced sense of positive self-esteem, we are better prepared to approach novel and unpredictable situations. The more secure our sense of self-conception, the more likely we will approach stranger interactions openly and responsively, and the more we will be able to apply and practice the communication resources available to us.

Communicative resourcefulness is defined here as the cognitive knowledge and the affective and behavioral predispositions to act appropriately, effectively, and creatively in any novel situation. A resourceful intercultural communicator should be able to apply the knowledge of identity negotiation to validate, to redefine, and to reframe her or his identity-in-context. One of the major objectives in any intercultural encounter is to manage identities effectively and to regulate self/relational/group membership boundaries resourcefully. The specific objectives in a distinct communication episode can include mutual identity confirmation, mutual identity coordination, and mutual identity attunement (Scheff, 1990).

In short, a resourceful intercultural communicator knows how to negotiate self-other identities effectively, knows when to follow situational rules and cultural scripts, and knows when to transcend or transform conventions to obtain maximum relational and situational outcomes. An individual who is high on communicative resourcefulness has acquired a diverse range of cognitive tools, a rich spectrum of emotional repertoires, and a flexible behavioral set, and is able to apply them effectively, appropriately, and creatively in different novel settings. Communicative resourcefulness is a learned concept and knowledge is viewed as the core underlying construct across all three resourcefulness domains. Rachman (1990) defines learned resourcefulness as "the ability to apply one's personal and social resources successfully to deal with novel problems" (p. 178). There are three basic assumptions of communicative resourcefulness. First, interaction is a relational system—both interactants have an interdependent effect on the identity negotiation and identity construction process. Second, perception and behavioral interaction are inseparable—individuals formulate their impressions of a resourceful communicator based on their global perceptions inferred from observable behavioral actions. Competence is located in the conjoint perceptions and the communicative process of effective identity negotiation between the interactants. Third, the general outcomes of identity negotiation are accomplishing mutual goal functions and identity protection and enhancement. Competent identity negotiation involves utilizing the knowledge and resources in the cognitive, affective, and behavioral domains to attain identity confirmation, identity coordination, and identity attunement. Specific intercultural/relational outcomes can include the interactive goals of maximizing mutual understanding, developing an effective working relationship, and/or invoking reciprocal respect, trust, and relational acceptance. There are four domains of communicative resourcefulness: cognitive, affective, behavioral, and ethical resourcefulness.

Cognitive Resourcefulness

Cognitive resourcefulness refers to an individual's knowledge capacity and predispositional ability to deal with novel situations. Concepts in the cognitive resourcefulness domain include the dialectics of mindfulness-mindlessness, particularization-categorization, and framing-reframing.

Mindfulness-Mindlessness

Langer's (1989) concept of mindfulness is a critical cognitive construct that helps individuals to tune-in conscientiously to their habituated mental scripts. According to Langer, if mindlessness is the "rigid reliance on old categories, mindfulness means the continual creation of new ones. Categorization and recategorization, labeling and relabeling as one masters the world are processes natural to children" (p. 63). Mindlessness and mindfulness appear to be dialectical poles of a continuum. Acting mindlessly all the time can create a sense of noncaring, and acting mindfully all the time can create a sense of monitored constraint. An optimal point of mindlessness and mindfulness rests on the creative mixing of the two poles. Whereas mindlessness is built upon habituated identity security, mindfulness is based on identity openness, and hence, carries a certain degree of existential vulnerability. One can act mindlessly based on one's customary self-views in a scripted situation, but encountering a stranger can be a mindful, anxiety-provoking event. In order to protect one's sense of identity vulnerability, one typically glosses over such encounter anxiety by mapping familiar attributions or cognitive schema onto the novel situation. Familiar labels and attributions can create a temporary sense of security. Stated more precisely, being mindful requires cognitive energy, time, and, most important, putting one's sense of self-conception on hold. According to Langer (1989), to engage in a mindfulness state, an individual needs to learn to (a) create new categories, (b) be open to new information, and (c) be aware that multiple perspectives typically exist in viewing a basic event (Langer, 1989, p. 62). Creating new categories, openness to new information, and awareness of the existence of more than one perspective demand opening up the sense of familiar self-conception to internal and external threat or challenge.

In the context of the identity negotiation perspective, this identity suspending process works on two levels. On the first level, the identity suspending process can revolve around the reflexivity level of self-identification. In stranger encounters, we typically experiences identity anxiety or identity fear (Gudykunst, 1988). This sense of identity anxiety or fear can lead us to reappraise our familiar worldviews/assumptions/values and ways of being. How we mindfully handle the self-appraisal process coupled with our positive or negative past experiences with strangers would lead us to approach the novel situation constructively or reluctantly. On the second level, the identity suspending process can center around our acquisition of information concerning how our conversational interactants identify themselves and what constitutes their salient identity images in the particular interaction episode. Finding out the salient dimensions of other's self-conceptions is a mindful, responsive process that involves thoughtful observations and interactive feedback. Mindful observation requires patience, energy, and time. Of course, the process of seeking and expressing identity-relevant information also varies greatly from low-context communication to high-context communication systems (Hall, 1976, 1983; Ting-Toomey, 1985, 1988).

Low-context communication emphasizes direct questioning, explicit verbal styles, outcome-orientation, and a linear approach in information exchange; high-context communication stresses indirect subtle questioning, nonverbal contextual nuances, process-orientation, and a spiral approach in information presentation. Thus, if an encounter takes place in a low-context environment, one has to learn to be mindful of the direct verbal message level and the goal-oriented communication outcome level. If an encounter takes place in a high-context environment, one has to learn to be mindful of the implicit nonverbal message level and the contextual nuances that frame the identity negotiation encounter.

Categorization-Particularization

The second dialectic in the cognitive resourcefulness domain is categorization-particularization. This dialectic overlaps somewhat with mindfulness-mindlessness and is a natural extension of the mindfulness state. Categorization occurs when a perceiver, often implicitly, makes a mental association between a pattern of features and the category in question, and particularization occurs when a perceiver adds additional features to cognitive generalization labels (Billig, 1987). The categorization process reinforces our sense of security and perceptual familiarity; particularization enriches our perceptual set via finer, distinctive categories. Thus, it is possible that in effective identity negotiation, we can broadly categorize or locate ourselves and other in certain identity categories for predictable interaction to occur, and concurrently, anticipate room for identity change and recategorization. In addition, we can meta-monitor our perceptual set. Such meta-monitoring includes whether we are mindful of the open-ended versus closed-ended stereotyping process, whether we are cognizant of our own ethnocentric attitudes or deny such attitudes, and whether we are conscientious about our cognitive biases or are likely to suppress such self-knowledge.

A flexible attitude in categorization and particularization that incorporates divergent categorization and hierarchical particularization would lead to an effective, creative identity negotiation process. As Langer (1989) comments on creative uncertainty:

> We can look at the world and ask how things differ (make distinctions) or how they are the same (make analogies). The first approach results in the creation of new categories, the second usually involves shifting contexts. . . . In making an analogy, we apply a concept learned in one context to another one. Such a mental operation is in itself mindful. . . . Intentionally mixing metaphors with an eye toward finding similarities can spark new insights. Comparing people, businesses, and religions, across and within categories, for example, can lead to a greater understanding of both sides of the comparison. (pp. 130-131)

Thus, a cognitively creative individual is one who knows how to mobilize diverse communication resources by utilizing the dialectical interplay of categorization-particularization—to maintain cognitive stability and to flex its elasticity, and ultimately to mark identity boundaries and to transform identity boundaries when necessary.

Framing and Reframing

Drawing from both Antonovsky's (1987) concept of coherence and Kobasa's (1982) hardiness concept, how one frames novel interaction with a stranger—whether one views the encounter episode as an identity challenge opportunity or as an anxiety-ridden event—has a profound influence on how one approaches stranger interaction and beyond. If one frames stranger interaction as a potentially identity-strengthening experience, one would be more eager to learn alternative worldviews and alternative perspectives. In addition, if one realizes that identity security and identity change can be reframed as complementary dialectical tendencies, one can be motivated to be more eager to deal with stranger encounter episodes. Through a circular causality loop, one's conveyed sense of identity security also evokes the sense of security in the other. One's conveyed sense of identity anxiety also reinforces the stranger's sense of anxiety and fear. Finally, one can learn to reframe one's self-identification and the other's self-identification from the ethnic/cultural difference level to the universal human identity level. Perhaps it is in learning to reach that ethnocentric-free human identity-conception level (as opposed to the ethnocentric-laden "every human being is the same as me" level) that intercultural bridges can be built and the larger human community can be emphasized.

Framing and reframing influence the interaction posture we hold toward approaching strangers' interaction episodes. Interaction posture includes the underlying motivations, interaction attitudes, and interactive goal orientations for approaching strangers or host nationals in the new culture. An interaction posture reflecting a mutual win-win orientation, a collaborative attitude, and a genuine responsiveness level enhances the supportive climate of the interaction and develops bilateral trust. Beyond identity reframing, power resources, affective orientations, and attribution processes can be actively reframed and transformed via the resourceful minds of the interactants—basically, by acting creatively, dynamically, and flexibly.

On the individual cognitive style level, uncertainty orientation (Sorrentino & Short, 1986), tolerance for ambiguity (McPherson, 1983; Ruben & Kealey, 1979), category width (Detweiler, 1975; Pettigrew,

1982), and cognitive complexity (Applegate & Sypher, 1988; Wiseman & Abe, 1986) can be linked with perceived self-complexity, high individual resourcefulness (Rosenbaum, 1990), and high individual flexibility (Kim, 1991). The higher the uncertainty orientation, the higher the tolerance of ambiguity, the greater the cognitive width, and the greater the cognitive complexity, the more likely the individual can use framing-reframing ability effectively in identity negotiation process. In addition, such an individual would function more resourcefully in a new culture (especially in terms of long-term operation) than an individual whose cognitive style reflects low uncertainty orientation, low tolerance for ambiguity, and narrow categorization, and who is cognitively simple. Finally, a person who is highly resourceful is able to use the framing-reframing cognitive skill creatively to balance relationship dialectics effectively with strangers or relational partners.

In sum, in order to engage in effective identity negotiation in stranger interaction, a mindful-of-the-moment habit, an open categorization-particularization posture, and a creative reframing attitude can contribute to the smooth coordination of identities and mutual affirmation process of identities in interaction.

Affective Resourcefulness

Affective resourcefulness refers to an individual's predispositional ability to regulate identity-driven emotional reactions, develop a sensitivity to culturally grounded ego-focused and other-focused emotions, and develop a sense of congruence between affect and cognition. Concepts in the affective resourcefulness domain include managing reactive emotions, regulating ego-focused and other-focused emotions, and developing a sense of congruence between affect and cognition.

Reactive Emotions

Typically, when one encounters strangers or loved ones in unpredictable situations, feelings of existential anxiety are inevitable. According to Lazarus (1991), anxiety is generated by an uncertain, existential threat. Anxiety always entails existential vulnerability and insecurity, and also provokes gut-level (but culturally grounded) emotional responses. To be a resourceful communicator, one has to learn to manage such reactive emotions and appraise the relational and contextual appropriateness for expressing or containing such emotions. In addition, one also needs to recognize how these reactive emotions give rise to biased cognitive attributions of the stranger's behavior. Typically, an individual uses preconceived, familiar cognitive categories to evaluate a stranger's behavior. These preconceived cognitive categories serve as buffering mechanisms to diffuse the affective vulnerability response.

The emotional reaction level, however, depends on whether one comes from an independent construal of self or an interdependent construal of self perspective (Markus & Kitayama, 1991). From an independent construal of self perspective, spontaneous emotional reactions and expressions can be the normative ways of behaving. From an interdependent construal of self perspective, emotional self-restraints and maskings can serve as the culturally grounded emotional reactions. Thus, cultural construction of self-conception shapes the interactive rules of emotional displays and emotional maskings. On the most universal human level, deep-seated feelings such as anxiety, fear, ambiguity, and attachment need are commonly experienced by all individuals in all cultures, but how such feelings and needs are being expressed or retained is deeply ingrained in the primary socialization process of one's culture.

Ego-Focused and Other-Focused Emotions

Culture plays a major role concerning the emotional meanings and reactions that are attached to the fundamental identity protection-threat dialectic. According to Lutz (1988), although most emotions are viewed as universally experienced, they can be viewed as "cultural and interpersonal products of naming, justifying, and persuading by people in relationship to each other. Emotional meaning is then a social rather than an individual achievement—an emergent product of social life" (p. 5). To be affectively resourceful, an individual has to learn to regulate both ego-focused emotions and other-focused emotions (Markus & Kitayama, 1991). Ego-focused emotions (e.g., guilt, pride, frustration) stem from the independent construal of self perspective; other-focused emotions (e.g., relational shame, honor, deference) stem from the interdependent construal of self viewpoint. For example, although individuals coming from either perspective experience the emotional arousals of pride and shame, the emotional locus and meanings for such feelings can differ from one culture to the next. According to Scheff (1990), "pride and shame serve as instinctive signals, both to self and other, to communicate the state of the bond. We react automatically to affirmations of, and threats to, our bonds. However, if a culture is sufficiently insistent, it can teach us to disguise and deny these signals" (p. 15). *Bonds*, in this context, refers to webs of social connection.

Pride and shame serve as the primary emotions that are associated with self-appraisal and social-bonding connection. Pride and shame basically revolve around the issue of "self's perception of the evaluation of self by other(s)" (Scheff, 1990, p. 72). Although either pride or shame can be experienced continuously by all individuals, the degree of emotional consciousness experienced by individuals varies from one cultural system to the next. In general, one can predict that in individualistic cultures, individual pride is more likely to be overtly expressed while individual shame is more likely to be channeled via other ego-based emotional reactions (e.g., anger, frustration, guilt). In collectivistic cultures, relational shame or face loss is more likely to be experienced (e.g., face embarrassment, face humiliation) while individual-based pride is more likely to be suppressed. Overall, individualistic cultures emphasize ego-based emotional expressions and individual self-esteem protection, and collectivistic cultures value other-focused emotions' management and collective self-esteem protection and assertion.

Ego-based emotions tend to generate the "morality of justice," whereas other-focused emotions tend to give rise to the "morality of caring" (Belenky, Clinchy, Goldberg, & Tarule, 1986; Gilligan, 1982; Gilligan, Ward, & Taylor, 1988; Lyons, 1988). According to Gilligan (1988), these two moral voices signal "different ways of thinking about what constitutes a moral problem and how such problems can be addressed or solved. In addition, the two voices draw attention to the fact that a story can be told from two different angles and a situation seen in different lights" (p. xvii). She (1988) concludes that

> self, others, and the relationship between them—can be organized in different ways, depending on how "relationship" is imagined and constructed. From the perspective of someone seeking or loving justice, relationships are organized in terms of equality. . . . Moral concerns focus on problems of oppression, problems stemming from inequality, and the moral ideal is one of . . . equal respect. From the perspective of someone seeking or valuing care, relationship connotes responsiveness or engagement, a resiliency of connection that is symbolized by a network or web. Moral concerns focus on problems of detachment, on disconnection or abandonment or indifference, and the moral ideal is one of attention and response. Since all relationships can be characterized both in terms of equality and in terms of attachment or connection, all relationships—public and private—can be seen in two ways and spoken of in two sets of terms. (pp. xvii-xviii)

Morality problems as framed in the morality of justice revolve around conflicting claims between self and others, and can be resolved by invoking impartial rules, principles, or standards. Conversely, morality problems as cast in the morality of caring revolve around issues of relationships, and they can be approached through the activities of caring (Lyons, 1988). Thus, the morality of justice is grounded in the independent construal of self perspective, and the relational-based morality of caring is grounded in the interdependent construal of self point of view. According to gender-related research studies (Gilligan et al., 1988), Euro-American males tend to engage in the morality of justice, while Euro-American females tend to engage in the morality of caring. One can also predict that individuals who operate from ego-based emotions would more readily subscribe to the morality of justice system, whereas individuals who operate from other-focused emotions would more readily value the morality of caring system. Both cultural and gender variations influence self-conception and morality construction issues.

Affective and Cognitive Congruence

According to Lazarus (1991), emotion, cognition, and motivation are three intertwined constructs. He argues that the following principles all hold true under certain conditions: emotions shape thought and action, actions shape thought and emotion, thoughts shape emotion and action, and the environment shapes thought, emotion, and action (Lazarus, 1991, p. 460). Casting these four principles in identity negotiation terms, our primary emotions that are associated with self-conception (such as anxiety/fear, guilt/shame, pride/dignity) can shape or drive our cognitive attribution process and behavioral actions. Disclosing certain aspects of our self or attaining another person's perspective, can change our thinking and feeling about the strangers. In addition, the way we cognitively appraise our sense of self-identification and other's sense of self-identification can change our affective reactions and behavioral tendencies. Finally, the cultural and situational environments frame emotion, thought, and action.

The overall key then to affect and cognition is the perceived congruence between the two systems. According to Lazarus (1991), "whereas *integration* is tantamount to mental health, disconnection among the constructs of the mind is tantamount to psychopathology, dysfunction, and distress. The three constructs of mind—cognition, motivation, and emotion—should generally be compatible, ideally in harmony; the mind as a system must also be in reasonable touch with environmental conditions; and actions should flow from this harmonious, coordinated system" (pp. 460-461). It is critical to point out here that individualists in Western cultures tend to perceive emotion, cognition, and motivation as located in the mind system, whereas collectivists in Eastern cultures tend to perceive the three constructs as stemming primarily from the heart system. There are more words and vocabularies that deal with the relationship between self-conception and cognition in the individualistic, Western cultures. There are, in contrast, more vocabularies and metaphors that deal with self-conception and emotional harmony issues in the collectivistic, Eastern cultures (Harre, 1986; Holland & Quinn, 1987; Markus & Kitayama, 1991; Ochs, 1988). Overall, however, congruence between affect and cognition facilitates individual/environment adaptation, and incongruence or disconnection promotes maladaptation.

Beyond being sensitive to the culturally grounded driving mechanisms of affect or cognition, one has to be affectively mindful in developing affective/cognitive congruence with symbolic interactions. Thus, the feelings about one's self-identifications have to be eventually brought into close alignment with cognitive orientation, and one's cognitive appraisals of self/other identifications have to be eventually converged with one's affective level. If one's affective sense about self-identifications goes counterintuitively against one's cognitive appraisal, then one has to learn to either change one's emotional reactions, change one's cognitive appraisal process, change one's behavioral actions, or change one's relational environment. In addition, one's emotional reactions to other's self-views and actions provide affective feedback into the cognitive labeling process. How we label our self-identification in a stranger encounter episode and how we label the stranger's self-identification, in turn, provide circular feedback to our emotional coping domain. Appropriate empathy, which arises out of the root emotion of compassion, can be regulated by cognitive mindfulness. Too much empathy leads to emotional contagion or burnout; too little empathy leads to the display of noncaring attitudes. The complementary balance of cognitive and affective congruence can be best observed through the resourceful regulation of empathy, which acts as both a cognitive and an affective construct.

In short, in developing a sound working relationship, one can learn to revise one's emotions, cognitive beliefs, and actions until they are congruent. Congruence conveys a sense of authenticity of self-coherence. Authenticity of self-presentation, however, takes on individual and cultural variations. In addition, one can learn to be congruent with others, and congruent with the particular relationship and situation (Fisher & Brown, 1988). Congruence with others means attuning one's emotions, cognitions, and actions with the other's emotions, cognitions, and actions (Scheff, 1990). This mutual attunement relies heavily on expressive and responsive communication. Finally, developing congruence to match the particular relationship and situation requires reflective relationship assessments, responsive expectation clarifications, appropriate empathy, and attention to the situational and contextual cues that surround identity expression.

Thus, to be affectively resourceful, we need to balance and counterbalance our self-conception emotions, monitor our culturally grounded reactive emotions, regulate ego-focused and other-focused emotions, and learn to develop affective-cognitive congruence that is sensitive to the parameter of the culture. Culture is both a state of the mind and a habit of the heart. Culture carries symbolic meanings and significance for an individual's sense of self-system. To be an affectively resourceful communicator, we have to learn to cross both cognitive and affective boundaries when appropriate. We also have to learn to adapt to existing boundaries and rules when appropriate. Overall, to work toward attaining affective-cognitive congruence, we need to continuously check our deep-leveled emotions and cognitions until they are congruent with our larger cultural frame of reference and with our basic sense of moral convictions and symbolic actions.

Behavioral Resourcefulness

Behavioral resourcefulness refers to the ability to attune to strangers' identities and needs, and the effective action tendencies to coordinate and affirm identities with strangers. Three behavioral resources are identified: managing self-esteem, monitoring mutual self-presentation behaviors, and displaying behavioral adaptation and flexibility.

Self-Esteem

Self-esteem is viewed as occupying a pivotal role in effective identity negotiation. Self-esteem or self-worth is grounded in the evaluational criteria of the "ideal persons" in their ideal positive performance in the sociocultural webs of the system. As Harre (1984) observes, "for me, a person is not a natural object, but a cultural artifact. A person is a being who has learned a theory, in terms of which his or her experience is ordered. . . . There are two primary realities in human life: the array of persons and the network of their symbiotic interactions" (p. 20). Learning the culturally endorsed values of behaviors, learning the cultural theories of what it means to maintain a positive versus a negative view of the self, serves as a good starting point for effective self-esteem management. As Markus and Kitayama (1991) comment:

> For those with independent selves, feeling good about oneself typically requires fulfilling the tasks associated with being an independent self, that is, being unique, expressing one's inner attributes, and asserting oneself. . . .

> Maintaining self-esteem requires separating oneself from others and seeing oneself as different from and better than others. . . . The motive to maintain a positive view of the self may assume a somewhat different form, however, for those with interdependent selves. Feeling good about one's interdependent self may not be achieved through enhancement of the value attached to one's internal attributes and the attendant self-serving bias. Instead, positive feelings of the self derive from fulfilling the tasks associated with being interdependent with relevant others: belonging, fitting in, occupying one's proper place, engaging in appropriate action, promoting others' goals, and maintaining harmony. (p. 242)

The locus of self-esteem stemming from independent construal of self emphasizes individual-oriented communicative motivations; the locus of self-esteem generating from interdependent construal of self emphasizes socially oriented communicative motivations. From the independent construal of self perspective, managing self-esteem means respecting and recognizing the stranger's unique personal attributes, competencies, and/or accomplishments. From the interdependent construal of self perspective, managing self-esteem means recognizing the importance of collective membership esteem, family background reputation, workgroup loyalty and commitment, and/or collective membership standing.

Managing personal and collective self-esteem is also closely related to the notion of managing interactive facework in a communication episode. From the independent construal of self perspective, facework is oriented toward personal self-esteem management. From the interdependent construal of self perspective, facework is emphasized on the collective self-esteem level. Although the concept of face or the claimed sense of self-respect is a universal construct, how we manage facework in a situation and how we negotiate the claimed sense of self-respect or self-esteem differs from one culture to the next (Ting-Toomey, 1988).

Situated face dialectics include the considerations and the weightings of maintaining a claimed sense of self-dignity or regulating a claimed sense of self-humility in interaction. Other face dialectics include the display of identity respect or irreverence in an interactive situation, and the considerations of imposition or nonimposition in an interactive episode. The three face dialectics of dignity-humility, respect-deference, and imposition-nonimposition govern situated facework interactions (Lebra, 1976; Penman, in press; Ting-Toomey, in press b). Thus, to be effective in facework negotiation, one needs to learn to manage the culturally grounded level of facework issues, the implicit social norms of facework interaction, and the appropriate rule boundaries of facework negotiation. In addition, one also needs to learn to balance or juggle the delicate dialectics of respect-deference on one hand and autonomy-connection intimacy on the other.

Managing self-esteem in the independent self construal system means respecting the personal accomplishments or unique contributions of the relational partner; managing self-esteem in the interdependent self construal system means respecting social face and acknowledging collective group work effort in the interaction. Finally, managing self-esteem in the independent self-construal system means respecting personal space and privacy need in the relational partner; managing self-esteem in interdependent construal of self system means respecting ingroup/outgroup boundaries, and the importance of practicing patience in crossing such intergroup boundaries.

Mutual Self-Presentation Behaviors

Individuals can use both protective self-presentation behaviors and assertive self-presentation behaviors to preserve and articulate their sense of self-esteem (Tedeschi & Norman, 1985). Protective/defensive self-presentation behaviors refer to a range of behaviors, from behaviors that aim to maintain the existing level of self-esteem to behaviors that actively restore the negatively spoiled personal or social identity in a communication episode. Assertive/diffusive self-presentation behaviors refer to a range of behaviors, from behaviors that affirm (or enhance) one's particular identities or attributes in the eyes of another to behaviors that diffuse (or deprecate) one's particular identities or attributes in order to take the attention away from the ego-focused self to the connected-focused other. Both sets of self-esteem maintenance behaviors can be traced back to the root dialectical interplay of existential identity security-vulnerability.

Persons who follow an independent construal of self orientation are more likely to use individualistic, self-focused identity presentation behaviors, and persons who use an interdependent construal of self orientation are more likely to use mutual-focused identity management behaviors. In addition, persons in individualistic, low-context cultures are more likely to use direct defensive and assertive identity presentation strategies, and persons in collectivistic, high-context cultures, in contrast, are more likely to use indirect and diffusive identity management strategies. Persons in individualistic cultures are more likely to use identity-autonomy preserving strategies, whereas persons in collectivistic cultures are more likely to use identity-connection enhancement strategies. Finally, persons in individualistic cultures are more likely to use assertive behaviors to protect individual self-esteem on the personal identity level, whereas persons in collectivistic cultures are more likely to use diffusive behaviors to protect collective self-esteem on the social face level (Ting-Toomey, 1988).

Protective/defensive identity interactive strategies can include the use of accounts (excuses and justifications), disclaimers, self-handicapping, apologies, restitution, prosocial behavior, mediated interaction, refracted interaction, anticipatory interaction, and ritualistic facework behavior. Assertive/diffusive identity interactive strategies can include the use of entitlements, enhancements, ingratiation, intimidation, exemplification, self-promotion, supplication, and conspicuous generosity (Lebra, 1976; Tedeschi & Norman, 1985). To become a behaviorally resourceful communicator, one can learn to accumulate a diverse set of behavioral repertoires—to protect mutual self-esteem and to verify/enhance one's self-views and other's self-views. In addition, one can learn to become more effective in managing mutual self-presentation process by attending to specific facework issues.

Based on the *positivity bias* principle, many researchers (Pelham & Swann, 1989; Robinson & Smith-Lovin, 1992; Swann, 1986; Swann et al., 1989) have tested the competing hypotheses between self-verification and self-enhancement of one's self-esteem. It seems that both interactive self-enhancement and self-verification relevant feedback play critical roles in different identity negotiation stages. Although positive self- enhancement feedback may be critical at the early stage of relationship development, relevant self-verification feedback may help to change one's differing aspects of self-conception. An individual's self-conception is sufficiently differentiated enough that both positive and negative attributes exist in the same system.

The key theme in mutual self-presentation behaviors rests on the importance of developing a wide range of verbal and nonverbal repertoires to deal with the diverse identity needs of different persons in different situations. The active monitoring of the mutual self-esteem protection need and the mutual identity self-enhancement need promotes effective identity coordination and attunement.

Behavioral Adaptation and Flexibility

Behavioral adaptation and flexibility refers to the importance of both behavioral responsiveness to strangers and behavioral openness to learn from the strangers or relational partners. Beyond the acquisition of the knowledge of communicative rules in the sociocultural system, one has to learn to acquire the critical cognitive and affective vocabularies that are related to everyday self-conception expressions and projections. Whether one culture endorses the rule of "disclosing" one's feelings or "wrapping" one's feelings intact, a resourceful communicator can learn to be observant, be accepting, be adaptive, and be flexible in his or her relational dialectics.

According to Baxter's (1988) research, three basic dialectics exist in any interpersonal relationship: novelty-predictability, openness-closedness, and autonomy-connection. The novelty-predictability and openness-closedness dialectics involve self-identity regeneration and self-identity expression; the autonomy-connection dialectic revolves around self/other identity space and intimacy issues. All three relational dialectics reflect the underlying negotiation of the basic identity vulnerability and identity differentiation issues. Whereas too much predictability in a relationship leads to "emotional deadening," too little predictability can lead to relational insecurity. Likewise, too much information openness leads to information overload and too little information openness leads to relational misunderstanding and perceptual inaccuracy. Finally, as too much connection leads to conjoint identity combustion, so too little connection leads to emotional alienation and loneliness.

Baxter (1988) suggests that three general dialectical strategy types are available to us in attempting to manage these interpersonal relationship dialectics: selection, temporal/spatial separation (cyclic alternation and segmentation), and integration (integrative moderation, integrative disqualification, and integrative reframing). *Selection* refers to the ability to use appropriate verbal and nonverbal relational strategies to regulate the importance of one dialectical pole over another dialectical pole. *Temporal/spatial separation* involves the ability to use verbal and nonverbal strategies to respond to each polarity of a given contradiction at different relational points. *Integrative reframing* refers to the resourceful use of verbal and nonverbal strategies to respond to the dialectical poles either by creatively moderating the notion of opposing dialectical tendencies, by being strategically ambiguous, and/or by employing transcendental meta-messages in overriding the relational dialectics.

Thus, how one creatively manages these dialectics with one's relational partner and how one meta-communicates about the underlying issues that revolve around these interpersonal dialectics are critical to the maintenance and the developmental pacing of the relationship

(Ting-Toomey, 1989b). The three basic interpersonal dialectics exist in all cultures, but the way one manages these dialectics and the meanings attached to them can differ from one culture to the next. Thus, for example, while members of individualistic cultures may tend to expend more energy in managing the dialectical poles of novelty, openness, or autonomy, members of collectivistic cultures may tend to invest more time and patience in managing the dialectical poles of predictability, closedness, or connection.

To be effective in the relational identity negotiation process, one needs to display verbal and nonverbal flexibility and sensitivity to the cultural, structural, family socialization, and relational nuances that exist within and external to the relationship. Relational problems and intercultural misunderstandings often occur because of the miscasting and mismanagement of the interpersonal dialectical sets. These dialectical sets are, for the most part, influenced by sociocultural and relational ideologies. These ideological/expectational frames, however, are often lodged in the implicit, relational messages rather than in the explicit, verbal messages. Thus, a flexible communication style is likely to lead to increased perceptual accuracy and relational empathy. Explicit meta-communication may also help to clarify identity vulnerability and identity anxiety issues that underlie these personal relationship dialectics.

To conclude, a resourceful communicator has to learn to act appropriately, effectively, and flexibly in multiple relational situations. In the context of the present identity negotiation perspective, appropriate identity negotiation means knowing the when, where, how, and with whom one should express one's sense of self-views and, at the same time, monitoring the implicit or explicit sense of self-views expressed by others. Effective behavioral identity negotiation also entails the attainment of mutual, interactive goals that may include instrumental, expressive, and, most important, identity protective and relational meaningfulness goals. Finally, a resourceful communicator learns to act creatively. One knows when to follow rules and when to transcend rules. One knows when to pursue certain interactive goals and when to modify such goals. One also realizes that moving beyond cultural and social scripts, interactants can co-create their relational standards that transcend the trappings of cultural and societal ideologies. A flexible, resourceful communicator can learn to empower oneself and stranger to change and diversify one's sense of self-conception and the stranger's self-conception. This leads to the final point of this section: the issue of ethics in communicative resourcefulness.

ETHICAL RESOURCEFULNESS

Although ethical resourcefulness is not displayed as part of the identity negotiation model in Figure 4.1, it is viewed as the underlying root source to all the three resourcefulness domains. To briefly explain, while ethical relativism emphasizes the importance of making moral judgments relative to the gender/cultural context, ethical universalism emphasizes the importance of universal moral principles in guiding all human behaviors. It is critical to acknowledge here that the identity negotiation perspective affirms the importance of cultural norms and values in shaping the ethical/moral system. However, it also recognizes that certain fundamental, universal principles guide all human behavior in all cultures. Such universal principles start with the basic concept of peace.

As Kale (1991) notes, the concept of peace applies not only to "relations between cultures and countries but also to the right of all people to live at peace with themselves and their surroundings. As such, it is unethical to communicate with people in a way that does violence to their concept of themselves or to the dignity and worth of their human spirit" (p. 424). An ethically resourceful communicator will learn to recognize which moral issues should be appropriately framed within the cultural context and which moral issues should take on the universal, human level of concern. Both the "morality of justice" and the "morality of caring" should be given equal weight in assessing a moral dilemma situation. Ultimately, an ethical, resourceful communicator will use the full capacities of her or his cognitive, affective, and behavioral resources to engage in multilateral, open-ended inquiry and dialogue—and to deal wisely with the partial and impartial truths, and with the relational and situational contingencies of the moral dilemma problem.

PROCESS AND OUTCOMES

Cognitive, affective, and behavioral resourcefulness contribute to effective identity negotiation and outcome attainment processes. The identity negotiation model presented in Figure 4.1 shows only person A's orientation (from left to right) toward effective identity negotiation process—readers should use their imaginative resources to add person B's orientation to the identity negotiation process (from right to left on the model). Thus, the complete imaginary model should involve both interactants negotiating the multiple facets of their identity and also negotiating dialectical interactions implicitly and explicitly in the Effective Identity Negotiation Process oval (see Figure 4.1).

The identity negotiation perspective recognizes the importance of both the process and outcomes of effective identity negotiation. Interactive identity confirmation, interactive identity coordination, and interactive identity attunement serve as both process and outcome dimensions.

Interactive identity confirmation requires the knowledge base and the abilities of cognitive, affective, and behavioral resourcefulness to affirm the sense of positive self-views and validate the sense of positive self-views in other. This affirmation process requires self-conception knowledge and other identity-salient knowledge on both the episodic level and on the global self-identification level. Appropriate and effective interactive identity confirmation across time should lead to strengthened identity security and identity comprehensibility. The identity security, in turn, should lead to a more positive-appraisal approach to strangers. Finally, a positive-appraisal approach to strangers would help to enrich one's self-conception in both scope and depth.

Both scope and depth of self-conception generate new motivational energy to interaction with strangers. Interactive confirmation, in and of itself, can be both self/other affirming and self/other accepting. In addition, interactive identity confirmation can signal interest and willingness between interactants to develop "intact social bonds." For Scheff (1990), the need for the "maintenance of social bonds" serves as the most important driving force for human interaction. He explains:

> Secure social bonds are the force that holds a society together . . . this force involves a balance between closeness and distance. . . . Optimal differentiation defines an intact social bond, a bond which balances the needs of the individual and the needs of the group. It involves being able to maintain ties with others who are different from self. . . . Optimal differentiation involves closeness since it requires knowledge of the other's point of view. . . . An intact social bond does not imply agreement but knowledge of both agreement and disagreement. (p. 4)

Intact social bonds fulfill the identity security-change need, and the inclusion-differentiation need. They also provide a sense of community webs in which identity can be centered, anchored, and rested.

The second dimension, *interactive identity coordination*, requires the self and stranger to coordinate their lines of meaning and action in order to engage in communicative synchrony. Interactive identity coordination includes the negotiation of personal meaning systems for self-identification, social/gender meaning systems for self-identification, and ethnic/ethical meaning systems for self-identification. These meaning systems are embedded in the cognitive and affective states of the person, and they are also embedded in the social structures and the social expectational frames of the larger culture. With communicative resourcefulness, interactants can learn to co-create or re-create their own relational scripts and cultures by being responsive to the feelings and the moods of their partners, and by not being rigidly trapped in their mental or affective reactive boundaries. Identity transformation can lead to the diversification and the extension of intact social bonds and can also ultimately lead to identity change and growth. Interpersonal attraction, trust, and identity security factors can serve to move the development of intact social bonds to intact personal relationships.

Finally, to be effective in identity negotiation, we must work to develop identity attunement with strangers in repeated interaction episodes across time. Attunement refers to the "joint attention to thoughts, feelings, intentions, and motives between individuals and also between groups" (Scheff, 1990, p. 199). In addition, attunement consists of not only "joint knowledge of meanings evoked during contact, but long-ranged considerations involving intentions and character. The same kind of attunement between groups is referred to as social solidarity" (p. 201). *Interactive identity attunement*, as cast in the identity negotiation perspective, refers to a coherent sense of understanding of self/other identity salience issue, a knowledgeable sense of culturally grounded self-esteem process, and an affective connectedness sense to strangers —especially as both move dialectically closer together or further away from each other.

In sum, interactive confirmation, interactive coordination, and interactive identity attunement are viewed as process and outcome dimensions. They serve as the pivotal feedback loops to existential security-vulnerability self-system and the sense of identity meaningfulness structure. Although identity security and change process can be resourcefully managed by effective identity confirmation and coordination, the sense of identity meaningfulness is attained through resourceful identity attunement. The self-other connection and group-to-group connection rest, ultimately, on effective identity negotiation process.

CONCLUSION

This chapter contains a newly developed perspective on communication competence, namely, the identity negotiation perspective. In a nutshell, the identity negotiation perspective emphasizes the importance of managing the identity security-vulnerability dialectic and the inclusion-differentiation need dialectic. However, the optimal degree of balance satisfying the existential security-vulnerability dialectic and satisfying the inclusion-differentiation need depends heavily on culturally grounded interactive motivations. Culturally grounded motivations influence how these dialectics can be interpreted and framed. These interpretations, in turn, influence how one manages these dialectics. Communicative resourcefulness is viewed as a facilitating factor in effective identity negotiation. More specifically, three resourcefulness domains have been identified: cognitive, affective, and behavioral resourcefulness. In addition, ethical resourcefulness undergirds all three domains. These resources should help an individual to work toward identity affirmation, identity alignment, and identity attunement.

Drawing from the assumptions and rationale for identity negotiation presented in this chapter, some basic theoretical propositions derived from the identity negotiation model can be summarized:

Proposition 1: The more secure we are in self-identification, the more open we are to stranger interactions.

Proposition 2: The more vulnerable we are in self-identification, the more anxiety we experience in stranger interactions.

Proposition 3: The higher our security need, the more vulnerable we feel in encountering strangers.

Proposition 4: The higher our inclusion need, the more value we place on relational/ingroup membership boundaries.

Proposition 5: The higher our differentiation need, the more distance we place between self and other, and/or ingroup and outgroup relationships.

Proposition 6: The more effective we are in managing the security-vulnerability dialectic, the more resourceful we are in identity negotiation with others.

Proposition 7: The more effective we are in managing the inclusion-differentiation need, the more resourceful we are in identity negotiation with others.

Proposition 8: The more secure we are in self-identification, the stronger our sense of identity coherence.

Proposition 9: The more secure we are in self-identification, the higher our global self-esteem.

Proposition 10: The higher our personal self-esteem, the more resourceful we are in approaching strangers.

Proposition 11: The higher our membership esteem, the more resourceful we are in approaching strangers.

Proposition 12: The more motivated we are in approaching strangers, the more likely we seek out communication resources to deal with strangers.

Proposition 13: The greater our cognitive resourcefulness, the more effective we are in identity negotiation.

Proposition 14: The greater our affective resourcefulness, the more effective we are in identity negotiation.

Proposition 15: The greater our behavioral resourcefulness, the more effective we are in identity negotiation.

Proposition 16: The more diverse our communication resources, the more effective in interactive identity confirmation.

Proposition 17: The more diverse our communication resources, the more effective in interactive identity coordination.

Proposition 18: The more diverse our communication resources, the more effective in interactive identity attunement.

Proposition 19: The more diverse our communication resources, the more flexible we are in co-creating interactive goals and relational contexts.

Proposition 20: The more diverse our communication resources, the more effective we are in developing mutual identity meanings and comprehensibility.

Boundary conditions: (a) Cultural, social, and personal socialization variations influence effective identity negotiation process; (b) social structural and contextual factors influence the latitude (or the degree of freedom/power) of effective identity regulation process; (c) individuals operate within optimal levels (with reasonable minimum-maximum threshold levels) of security-vulnerability dialectic and inclusion-differentiation dialectic; (d) group membership identities are much more salient in unfamiliar, novel situations, and personal identities are much more salient in familiar, intimate situations; and (e) the core identity negotiation process applies to both intercultural and intracultural encounters. More specifically, the identity negotiation theory can be applied to social and personal relationship development, intercultural adaptation, and intercultural training context.

To conclude, this chapter attempts to recast intercultural communication competence from an identity negotiation perspective. It is argued that in stranger interaction and beyond, both knowledge and the ability to apply communication resources creatively and flexibly help to promote effective identity negotiation. Cognitive, affective, and behavioral interactive resources have been identified to facilitate effective identity negotiation process. Finally, interactive identity confirmation, interactive identity coordination, and interactive identity attunement are viewed as critical tripartite processes and outcomes of effective stranger interaction.

It is assumed that communication holds the key to effective identity negotiation. However, the specific ways of communicating and the specific hows of communicating would differ from one culture to the next. A resourceful communicator, nevertheless, should learn both cultural-general knowledge concerning effective identity negotiation and, at the same time, cultural-specific knowledge in enacting, evoking, and maintaining the basic human bonds in different contexts in different cultures. A resourceful communicator learns to honor and respect both self-conception diversity and other-conception diversity, and, concurrently, learns to weave-in common everyday experiences on the universal, human responsive level.

5

Identity Management Theory

Communication Competence in Intercultural Episodes and Relationships

WILLIAM R. CUPACH • *Illinois State University*

T. TODD IMAHORI • *San Francisco State University*

The notion of communication competence continues to enjoy significant attention by scholars of intercultural interaction (for reviews see Collier, 1989; Hammer, 1989; Kim, 1991). As the field has grown to adolescence over the last 15 years, concomitant "growing pains" have been exhibited as well. Critics maintain that the conceptual literature is fragmented and generally lacking in theoretical direction.

Some of the more recent approaches to intercultural competence are shifting the emphasis from cross-cultural adaptation (e.g., Ruben, 1976, 1977; Ruben & Kealey, 1979) to effective and appropriate interaction in specific intercultural relationships. These more relationally oriented approaches typically adapt conceptualizations of competence found in the interpersonal communication literature (e.g., Collier & Thomas, 1988; Imahori & Lanigan, 1989). Indeed, Spitzberg (1989) has argued that "progress in the study of *intercultural* communication competence is going to derive mainly from the development of sound *interpersonal* communication competence theories that can be applied to the intercultural setting" (p. 261).

Our goal in the present chapter is to advance a particular emerging theory of interpersonal communication that we believe is generalizable to intercultural contexts, and can provide insight regarding competence in intercultural interactions and relationships. Tentatively, we have labeled our approach the *Identity Management Theory* (*IMT*). IMT represents the confluence of several distinct but related lines of scholarship. Our thinking has its intellectual roots in symbolic interactionism in general, and the writings of Erving Goffman (1967) on self-presentation and facework in particular. Among intercultural communication scholars, our work resonates with and draws from the conceptualizations of Collier (1989) and Ting-Toomey (1988), though our slant is different in some important ways.

We begin by outlining the chief assumptions and constructs attendant on identity management, and its interactional instantiation, facework. Then, we explore ramifications of IMT for conceptualizing intercultural communication competence, both episodically and relationally.

IDENTITY MANAGEMENT IN INTERPERSONAL (INTERCULTURAL) COMMUNICATION

Intrinsic to the process of communication is the development of personhood and relationship. Individuals develop an identity as a consequence of interacting with others. At the same time, ongoing interaction drives the development of a relationship, and relationships profoundly affect the definition of each partner's identity. Indeed, "the communication process is largely a negotiation process whereby persons reciprocally define their relationships and themselves" (Millar & Rogers, 1976, p. 88). Thus, the emergent relationship exhibits a dialectic association with the identities of the individual relational participants. Wood (1982) explains:

> To carve an identity within a particular relationship is to become a substantially different self than the one existing prior to the relationship. As a relationship becomes more intimate and a partner more significant, an individual's self-definition increasingly takes into account the understandings of the evolving relational culture. (p. 77)

The very construction of a relationship is a function of the extent to which individual identities merge and become interconnected (Schlenker, 1984).

Identity is defined here as self-conception—one's theory of oneself. Individual identity gives one a sense of one's own ontological status and serves as an interpretive frame for experience. It also serves as a source of personal motivations and expectations for social behavior (Hecht, Collier, & Ribeau, 1992).

Identity is complex, abstract, and amorphous. Given that there are different domains of self-conception, there are several corresponding facets or aspects to an identity. These domain-specific aspects of one's total identity are also referred to as identities; it is in this sense that persons are seen as possessing "multiple identities." For our discussion, it is useful to consider two primary interdependent facets of identity. First, Collier and Thomas (1988) define *cultural identity* "as identification with and perceived acceptance into a group that has shared systems of symbols and meanings as well as norms/rules for conduct" (p. 113). Broadly construed, culture can refer to numerous different types of social groups, including ethnic, racial, social-economic, occupational, and gender. Thus, a person actually possesses numerous interconnected cultural identities.[1]

Second, as interpersonal relationships evolve and develop, relational partners formulate a *relational identity*. This is tantamount to Wood's (1982) notion of relational culture, that is, "a privately transacted system of understandings" that coordinates meanings and actions of relationship participants (p. 76). In a sense, each developing relationship forms a unique miniculture. For every relationship one forms, one acquires a distinct relational identity that interacts with other aspects of one's identity, and contributes to the total individual identity.

Although different aspects of an individual's total identity can be distinguished, these domains are not orthogonal. The various aspects of identity are enmeshed and exert influence on one another. Thus, an individual's *total identity* is made up of the various facets, as well as their nonsummative interactions with one another. The resultant gestalt represents a person's holistic self-image.

Extending Collier and Thomas's (1988; Collier, 1989) discussion of cultural identity, it can be argued that the various aspects of identity vary along three interdependent dimensions: scope, salience, and intensity.[2] *Scope* refers to the number of persons who potentially share an identity. Thus, relational identity is always smaller in scope than cultural identity. *Salience* refers to the relative importance of a particular aspect of identity (e.g., cultural identity) in a specific situation, relative to the other aspects of one's total identity. *Intensity* refers to the strength with which an aspect of identity is communicated (Collier, 1989, p. 296). Variations in the scope, salience, and intensity of aspects of one's identity are influenced by the contextual parameters of interaction, including the nature of the relationship between interactants. This is reflected in our view of the distinction between intercultural and interpersonal communication.

INTERPERSONAL VS. INTERCULTURAL COMMUNICATION/RELATIONSHIPS

The episodic salience of particular aspects of interlocutors' identities is central to distinguishing intercultural communication and interpersonal communication. Intercultural communication is characterized by situations in which interlocutors possess salient but separate cultural identities, whereas intracultural communication occurs when salient cultural identities of interlocutors are shared and supported. Interpersonal communication, however, is characterized by the development of a relational identity, that is, a negotiated enmeshment of individual identities or maintenance and support of an established relational identity. Intercultural communication, therefore, is different from interpersonal communication with respect to which aspects of identities are salient to the interlocutors. However, the process of communication through which individuals' identities are developed, formed, maintained, threatened, and finally enmeshed is the same for both types of interactions.

Other intercultural scholars share the view that intercultural and interpersonal communication manifest the same processes. The stranger's paradigm by Gudykunst and Kim (1984) assumes that interpersonal communication and intercultural communication share the same dynamics except that the nature of interpersonal knowledge is highly cultural in intercultural interactions and highly personal in interpersonal interactions. Similarly, Gudykunst and Ting-Toomey (1988) and Collier and Thomas (1988) refer to the degree of "culturalness" and "personalness" in distinguishing intercultural interactions from interpersonal interactions. In general, intercultural and interpersonal communication can be distinguished in terms of the salience of cultural identity (Collier & Thomas, 1988).

Because of the situational nature of identity salience, more than one type of interaction can occur within a particular encounter or a particular relationship. Moreover, because of the complexity of an individual's total identity, more than one aspect of identity may be salient and negotiated in a given episode. "Communication can therefore be more or less interpersonal and simultaneously more or less intercultural" (Collier & Thomas, 1988, p. 101). Similarly, relationships can become more or less interpersonal and simultaneously more or less intercultural. If two individuals with separate cultural identities are able to form a relationship with an enmeshed relational identity, their relationship can be considered interpersonal to the extent that their relational identity becomes more salient and their separate cultural identities recede into the background. However, because their individual cultural identities cannot be entirely lost and can become salient in different situations (e.g., an interculturally married couple visiting their relatives), their relationship can become intercultural as well as interpersonal.

FACEWORK AS IDENTITY MANAGEMENT

Because it is complex, partially internal, and ever-evolving, one's complete identity is never directly observed in its totality. Aspects of a person's identity are revealed and recognized in communication through the presentation of *face*. Following Tracy's (1990) conceptualization, face "references the socially situated identities people claim or attribute to others" (p. 210). Thus, various elements of interlocutors' identities are tacitly offered, ascribed, and inferred through interaction in particular social contexts through the presentation and negotiation of face.

The maintenance of face is a natural and inevitable *condition* of human interaction (Goffman, 1967). As Brown and Levinson (1978) state:

> In general, people cooperate (and assume each other's cooperation) in maintaining face in interaction, such cooperation being based on the mutual vulnerability of face. That is, normally everyone's face depends on everyone else's being maintained, and since people can be expected to defend their faces if threatened, and in defending their own to threaten others' faces, it is in general in every participant's best interest to maintain each other's face, that is, to act in ways that assure the other participants that agent is heedful of the assumptions concerning face. (p. 66)

Brown and Levinson (1978, 1987) propose that there are two fundamental types of face: positive and negative. *Positive face* is most closely related to Goffman's original conceptualization, and refers to an individual's desire to be appreciated and approved of by important others. *Negative face* pertains to the desire to be autonomous and free from the imposition of others. Lim and Bowers (1991) argue that there may be two types of positive face: the want to be included and the want to have one's abilities respected. They label these *fellowship face* and *competence face*, respectively. They use the term *autonomy face* to refer to Brown and Levinson's notion of negative face.

Face threats represent challenges to a person's acclaimed and desired image in a particular interaction. One can threaten one's own face by performing awkwardly, losing poise, exhibiting a lack of tact, or violating a social or relational rule. One can threaten another's face by embarrassing, offending, criticizing, or constraining the other. Naturally, threat to one's own face can involve acts that simultaneously threaten another's face.

Face threats are counteracted by facework—communication behaviors that address the identity claims of self and other in interaction.

Preventive facework is designed to avoid or minimize potentially face-threatening acts before they occur and thereby defend one's own face and protect the face of others (Goffman, 1967). Disclaimers (Hewitt & Stokes, 1975) and forms of politeness (Brown & Levinson, 1987) are employed to mitigate the face-threatening implications of behavior. Corrective facework is designed to repair a transgression that has diminished face. Acts such as apologies and accounts (Cupach & Metts, 1990; Schlenker, 1980) are often used for this purpose. Different types of face are addressed by different forms of facework. *Solidarity* addresses fellowship face, *approbation* addresses competence face, and *tact* addresses autonomy face (Lim & Bowers, 1991).

Successful management of face involves paradoxical challenges. First, inherent in facework is a dialectical tension between satisfying one's own face wants and the face wants of one's interlocutor. For example, to the extent one respects the autonomy face of another, one is potentially threatening his or her own autonomy (Scollon & Scollon, 1981). Offering an apology generally supports the face of another at the expense of one's own face. Second, supporting one aspect of another's face may simultaneously entail a threat to a different aspect of face. Giving a compliment, for instance, may be seen as anointing the competence face of a fellow interactant, but it may also be taken by that interactant as a threat to his or her autonomy face. Third, an individual's own face wants can be in conflict with one another. The simultaneous desire for fellowship *and* autonomy represents a classic dialectical tension observed in interpersonal relationships (Baxter, 1988, 1990; Goldsmith, 1990).

Identity management is a culturally universal communication function, thus the desire to maintain face in interaction is presumed to be cross-culturally universal (Brown & Levinson, 1987; Holtgraves & Yang, 1990; Ting-Toomey, 1988; Tracy, 1990). Nevertheless, there are several ways in which the interpretation and management of facework varies across cultural groups: (a) the relative value placed on various aspects of face; (b) the behaviors construed to threaten face; and (c) the behaviors that are preferred to minimize or rectify face threats (Collier, 1989; Edelmann, 1990; Matsumoto, 1988; Scollon & Scollon, 1981). Ting-Toomey (1988), for example, suggests that members of individualistic, low-context cultures exhibit a greater degree of self-face maintenance and employ more autonomy-preserving strategies compared to members of collectivistic, high-context cultures.

We also believe that there are individual (personality) differences in orientation to face (Strzyzewski, 1987). The fact that writers typically refer to aspects of face concern as needs or wants is telling. Specifically, we hypothesize that individuals differ (in comparable contexts) with respect to the degree they desire autonomy, acceptance, or respect. Similarly, we suggest that persons differ in their ability to address the face concerns of others (Hale, 1986; Leichty & Applegate, 1991). Thus, some individuals are more sensitive to the expressed face needs of others in various situations and are better able to fulfill those needs than other people. Such persons may be seen as having higher levels of trait communication competence.

FACEWORK AND COMPETENCE

Following IMT, *interpersonal communication competence should include the ability of an individual to successfully negotiate mutually acceptable identities in interaction.* As Weinstein (1969) has indicated, "Skill at establishing and maintaining desired identities, both for one's self and for others, is pivotal in being interpersonally competent" (p. 757). Since identity management is endemic to all social interactions, facework is an important social skill. Virtually all social behaviors are modified by considerations of face. Hence, as Goffman (1967) explains, "Variation in social skill pertains more to the efficacy of facework than to the frequency of its application" (p. 13). The ability to effectively maintain face may be considered a reflection of one's interpersonal competence (Wiemann, 1977). This ability is demonstrated in particular episodes of interaction. In the following section, we consider this aspect of interpersonal competence in the context of intercultural encounters.

FACE MANAGEMENT IN INTERCULTURAL EPISODES

The assumption that effective face management is an element of interpersonal competence applies equally well to both intracultural and intercultural interactions. In intracultural interactions, cultural identities of the interlocutors may be salient but the identities are shared. In intracultural interactions where the interlocutors also share cultural norms for politeness, they are likely to be aware of what is appropriate and face supporting and what is inappropriate and face threatening. In addition, intracultural interactions are relatively free from complications in facework regarding the cultural identities of interlocutors. Because cultural identities are shared, supporting the other's face also supports one's own face. To tacitly communicate that "I value you because you are a Japanese like me" is to also confirm the notion that "I value being a Japanese." Thus, the dilemma of choosing to support one's own face or the other's face does not exist with respect to cultural identity in intracultural interactions, even though in other aspects of identity such a paradox may need to be resolved through complex face management and identity negotiation. Furthermore, their shared cultural identities allow the interlocutors to actively manage only each other's fellowship and competence faces in the domain of cultural identity; their autonomy face wants regarding their cultural identity generally is not problematic.

However, in intercultural interactions, where cultural identities of the interlocutors are also salient but different, face management becomes more complex. First, because the cultural norms for politeness are different (Ting-Toomey, 1988), lack of cultural knowledge can impair the ability to show appropriate face support. Moreover, in intercultural interactions, one of the interlocutors may intentionally try to show face support using his or her cultural politeness norms, but such behavior can be perceived as face threatening to the other interlocutor. For example, complimenting a Japanese person in front of other Japanese on the ability to speak English fluently can be face threatening.

In intercultural interactions where interlocutors lack knowledge about the other's culture, people often rely on *stereotypes* in managing the other's face. However, stereotyping, whether it is positive or negative in nature, threatens the other's face.

People of minority status often experience *negative stereotyping*. Both Afro-Americans (Hecht, Ribeau, & Alberts, 1989) and Mexican-Americans (Hecht, Ribeau, & Sedano, 1990) expressed that one of the most salient issues in communicating with Euro-Americans is that of being negatively stereotyped. Whether Euro-Americans directly speak about these stereotypes or indirectly reflect their stereotypes (e.g., talking about music and sports to Afro-Americans), these ethnic minority groups find negative stereotyping offensive. Other minority groups such as the disabled (Braithwaite, 1991a, 1991b) and the deaf (Jankowski, 1991) routinely must deal with inappropriate questions (e.g., "How did you get into that wheelchair?" Braithwaite, 1991a, p. 266) and stereotypes (e.g., people with physical disabilities are helpless). Although negative stereotyping is apparently incompetent facework, unfortunately it seems to occur frequently in intercultural interactions.

Even if the intercultural interlocutors have good intentions in complimenting the other's cultural identity (i.e., *positive stereotyping*), any stereotyping can potentially threaten the other's negative face. What stereotyping does is to *categorize* the other's identity. Hecht, Collier, and Ribeau (1992) refer to dialectic tension between subjective, private identities that are *internally defined*, and objective, public identities that are *externally imposed*. Stereotyping often is based on this externally imposed identity, which may not coincide with one's internally defined identity. Thus, in attempting to compliment the other's cultural identity, one pressures the other to avow the externally imposed identity rather than giving the freedom to express the internally defined identity. For example, when someone makes compliments about Japan or the Japanese culture to a Japanese, the Japanese feels "stereotyped" as a "Japanese." Thus, there is a fine line between confirming another's identity, and *freezing* it.

The paradox between supporting one's own face or the other's face clearly becomes an issue regarding interlocutors' separate cultural identities in intercultural interactions. This tension becomes more difficult to resolve to the extent that their cultural identities are more different and independent, and to the degree that their respective cultures have different symbols, norms, rules, and the like. In order to confirm the interaction partner's cultural identity through face support, one may need to threaten one's own face and consequently disconfirm one's own cultural identity. For example, consider a work team consisting of Japanese and U.S. Americans. If the work team failed to perform to its standard because of one Japanese team member, the Japanese politeness norm calls for an apology from other group members for not helping the failing team member. If the U.S. American team members are aware of this Japanese politeness norm, then they face a dilemma. From the U.S. American politeness norm, apologizing is face threatening, and it is inconceivable to apologize when one is not actually responsible. Thus, to confirm one's own cultural identity, U.S. American team members may not apologize. This lack of apology, however, communicates the desire to maintain autonomy face in Japan, and thus communicates a lack of collectivistic effort of teamwork and consequently threatens the Japanese fellowship face.

When cultural identities are separate but differences are not as great, then this particular paradox may become less of an issue. For example, a work team consisting of Chinese and Japanese may not face the same paradox as the work team consisting of U.S. Americans and Japanese because the Chinese and Japanese politeness norms in the particular episode may call for similar protocols.

The paradox of choosing to support the other's positive or negative face wants is always an issue as long as the two intercultural interactants have different and independent (separate) cultural identities. This paradox may be observed in three manifestations of dialectic tension between the aspects of face. First, there is a dialectic tension between fellowship face and autonomy face. When one of the intercultural interlocutors attempts to support fellowship face, there is a risk of threatening the other's autonomy face to have a separate and different cultural identity. The statement unskilled intercultural communicators often use, "We are both humans and we aren't really different," clearly ignores the other's autonomy face, and disconfirms the other's cultural identity. An overemphasis on fellowship face without deference to the other's autonomy face needs results in forced assimilation (Scollon & Scollon, 1981). However, although more tacitly communicated, support of fellowship face can become a competent act when the intercultural interlocutors begin to establish some degree of shared identity.

The second type of dialectic tension exists between competence face and autonomy face. One of the intercultural interactants may try to support the other's competence face either by saying positive things about the other's culture (as in ingratiation) or by asking questions about the other's culture, to allow the other to demonstrate knowledge about his or her own culture. Such an act certainly confirms the other's cultural identity. However, the other's autonomy face is threatened in the sense that the other's identity is "locked into" the cultural identity, and the other is allowed relatively little freedom to bring other aspects of his or her total identity into the interactions and the relationship. In other words, by focusing the nature of interactions on the other's cultural identity by either asking questions about or ingratiating the other's culture, the interlocutor has narrowly defined the interaction to be largely intercultural. If the other's intention is also to focus the discourse on cultural issues, this is not a particularly incompetent act. Indeed, an initial intercultural interaction is often characterized by an exchange of questions and answers regarding each other's culture, and at least in the narrow parameter of initial interaction or small talk, such an exchange can be considered episodically competent. However, when the other's intention is to steer away from discourse on cultural issues and "move on" to other issues (i.e., cultural identity may be less salient), then, emphasizing the other's cultural identity becomes a hindrance to the relational movement toward more interpersonal interactions. Indeed, Braithwaite's (1991a) study on physically disabled people showed that they sometimes prefer to delay disclosure about their disabilities, and instead try to first "establish themselves as a 'person first,' rather than being seen as a 'disabled person' " (p. 265).

The third dialectic tension exists between autonomy face and either fellowship or competence face. In this situation, one of the interactants tries to support the other's need to maintain independent cultural identity. This act can be competent in the situation in which two intercultural interactants do not wish to develop a relationship and there is no necessity to merge their cultural identities. However, if the two interlocutors are to somehow merge their separate cultural identities, supporting the other's autonomy face can threaten the other's fellowship or competence face because *overall*, supporting the other's autonomy face is to confirm the other's separate cultural identity (and one's own separate cultural identity). As a consequence, the differences between interactants are made salient in the relationship. Heightened saliency of cultural differences may threaten the other's fellowship face because it may suggest that cultural differences are going to make it difficult for the two interlocutors to be "fellows." The other's competence face may also be threatened because it may suggest the other's inability to accommodate or adjust to the cultural differences.

In summary, competent intercultural communication requires the ability to engage in appropriate facework during interaction. Successful facework entails managing the inevitable paradoxical challenges that occur in every episode of interaction. It is noteworthy, however, that some dialectical tensions may be effectively managed at a relational level, across multiple episodes (Baxter, 1990). For example, addressing autonomy face may be emphasized during one encounter while addressing fellowship face may be emphasized in another encounter. Indeed, we believe that careful "balancing" of dialectical tensions among various aspects of face wants is critical to the development of a successful intercultural *relationship*. In our following discussion, we briefly describe some ramifications of competent intercultural communication for developing competent intercultural relationships.

COMPETENCE AND RELATIONAL DEVELOPMENT

In explaining competence regarding the development of intercultural relationships, we find it useful to conceptualize the relational processes in three phases. These phases are highly interdependent, and have sequential and cyclical order. Intercultural interlocutors may go through these phases at varying pace. Some interlocutors are unable or unwilling to go beyond a certain phase; others may go through these phases rapidly. Intercultural communication competence affects the interlocutors' ability to move on to subsequent relationship phases.

The First Phase: Trial

The first phase represents early developmental processes of intercultural relationships exhibited in initial interactions. When intercultural strangers meet, their cultural identities are salient but different. Because competent intercultural communication can be defined as intercultural interaction that validates, supports, and confirms cultural identities, mutual confirmation of separate cultural identities is critically important in this phase. According to Collier (1989), mutual confirmation of cultural identities may be observed in two ways. First, researchers can focus on impressions of interactions. "Respondents can be asked to identify the cultural identities adopted in particular encounters and when cultural differences are evident, to agree upon competent behavior for both the cultural identities being adopted" (p. 297). Second, "the ascribed and avowed identities can be compared as they are evident in the discursive text and the more the cultural difference in identities *and* the higher the match between avowal and ascription, the higher the intercultural competence" (p. 297).

Although we believe that intercultural competence is revealed in these two ways, particularly in later phases of relationships, the first phase entails some additional complexities. First, intercultural interactants often lack knowledge about each other's cultural norms, rules, symbols, and so on. This hampers the abilities of intercultural interactants "to agree upon competent behavior for both the cultural identities being adopted" (Collier, 1989, p. 297). Second, in an attempt to support the other's cultural identity, one may refer to inaccurate information, such as stereotypes about the other's culture, which the other finds offensive. Again the dialectic tension between confirming versus freezing the other's identity is salient.

Because of the different cultural rules regarding politeness and different symbolic norms, intercultural interlocutors often do violate rules of the other's culture and threaten each other's face. Rule violation (with attendant sanctioning) is perhaps the most common method of obtaining rule knowledge. However, such apparently incompetent acts can help the interlocutors identify critical face wants that must not be threatened, and those that need to be supported if the relationship is to develop. Paradoxically, by being incompetent, one can learn to become competent. Moreover, intercultural interactants can discover the aspects of their identities that they mutually share through such interactions of trial-and-error. It can be assumed that the more distinct the interlocutors' cultural identities are, the more likely they need to find shared aspects of identities outside of their cultural identities.

Even when one of the intercultural interactants (with separate cultural identities) is able to speak the language, accommodate the communication styles, and follow the politeness rules of the other's culture, the initial interaction between such seemingly *intracultural* interlocutors must also go through the trial-and-error negotiation. For example, one interlocutor must discover the willingness of the other interlocutor to adjust to the first's own cultural norms for symbols, rules for politeness, and the like. One must also assess the degree of threat to the other's autonomy face due to requiring the other to make such adjustments.

Another way to view this trial-and-error process is to consider identity as a frame of reference (Hecht et al., 1992). One's identity is used to interpret one's environment, the other's identity, and so on. Thus, when intercultural interlocutors have salient but different cultural identities, they do not share a common frame of reference to be able to understand each other's cultural identity. This may result in low awareness of cultural differences in early phases of intercultural relationships (Gudykunst, Gao, Sudweeks, Ting-Toomey, & Nishida, 1991), or cultural differences may be viewed as factors hindering the relationship (Sudweeks, Gudykunst, Ting-Toomey, & Nishida, 1990). The interlocutors must discover an area of identity that provides them a common frame of reference, such as similarity in attitudes or interests.

There is an obvious corollary to the competence/incompetence paradox we have identified: For one to be competent in this first phase of intercultural interaction, one must be able to deal with incompetence. Throughout the trial-and-error process, one must be tolerant of one's own as well as the other's incompetence as both partners engage in the balancing act between the various dialectic tensions. One must be able to tolerate and risk the possibility of accidentally threatening the other's face, as well as the other inadvertently threatening one's own face. Tolerance for short-term incompetence, paradoxically, may be necessary for longer-term relational competence (Spitzberg, in press).

Many interactants, in fact, tend to fear rule violations and subsequent face threat, that is, they are discouraged by the paradoxical challenges endemic to intercultural interactions. Thus, an intercultural interlocutor may decide to engage in only one type of facework. Scollon and Scollon (1981) caution that excessive attention to fellowship face can result in an increasingly closed relational system, leading to negative relational outcomes. We believe, however, that exclusive attention to autonomy face also stifles relational development. The need to attend to both autonomy and fellowship is a constant dialectical challenge. Alternatively, interlocutors may avoid the intercultural interactions entirely, rendering them incompetent actors. Competent intercultural interlocutors, however, are able to use this first phase as a way to build a relationship further and move on to the second phase.

The Second Phase: Enmeshment

In the second phase, intercultural communication competence develops as the relationship between intercultural interactants grows. Intercultural communication competence, like cultural identity, is fluid and emergent (Collier, 1989). Thus, successful intercultural relationships involve increasing *enmeshment* of the identities of the individuals who each bring their own cultural identity to the intercultural encounter. Intercultural communication competence in the second phase requires that intercultural partners begin to develop a mutually acceptable and convergent relational identity, in spite of the fact that their cultural identities are still divergent. This view reflects the assumption that intercultural communication competence is necessarily judged in the context of a *relationship* between culturally heterogeneous interactants (Imahori & Lanigan, 1989). Communicators comprise a relational system in which interdependence and mutual influence are exhibited (Spitzberg & Cupach, 1989; Wiemann & Kelly, 1981). Thus, as Collier and Thomas (1988) contend, intercultural communication competence also involves "the demonstrated ability to negotiate mutual meanings, rules, and positive outcomes" (p. 108).

This fluid and emergent conceptualization of competence suggests that some specific outcomes begin to appear in competent intercultural relationships during the second phase. First, effective negotiation is reflected in increasing symbolic interdependence. Stephen (1986) and colleagues have elaborated a symbolic exchange theory of interaction, in which symbolic interdependence represents bonds growing out of an increased shared view of reality between interactants. Drawing from symbolic interactionism, Stephen (1986) argues that as individuals interact over time, they develop shared tacit assumptions and meanings regarding the nature of reality. This emergent shared meaning is referred to as *relationship worldview*. As Stephen (1986) indicates, "the unanticipated outcome of ongoing communication is a mutual restructuring of the individual interpretive frameworks that actors apply to the world" (p. 192). Similarly, Duck (1991) conceptualizes relationship development as "symbolic union" whereby individuals create and *share* a dyadic universe of meaning. It is not merely the objective similarity of meanings ascribed by two individuals that is important; rather, as Duck maintains, it is the *recognition* of shared meaning that is significant.

The symbolic interdependence construct applies to intercultural encounters as well as interpersonal ones. We predict that symbolic interdependence is positively associated with other interpersonal outcomes, such as relational satisfaction and stability. This is consistent with the position of Imahori and Lanigan (1989) that competent intercultural interaction should eventually lead to positive relational outcomes. Positive relational outcomes such as achieving a common goal (Hecht et al., 1989) or feeling relational solidarity (Hecht et al., 1990) are perceived as salient to interethnic communicators.

Another positive outcome of intercultural communication competence in the second phase is rule convergence, that is, the establishment and coordination of different rules and norms that will in turn determine the appropriateness of actions in the intercultural/interpersonal relationship. Rules are prescriptive guidelines for behavior in particular interaction contexts (Shimanoff, 1980). As Collier and Thomas (1988, p. 109) contend, "Actions that conform to mutually shared rules are more predictable" and more identity confirming. Developing mutually shared rules attending to face wants in relationships is critical to intercultural communication competence.

In the second phase, the emergence of symbolic interdependence and rule convergence is based on the trial-and-error process in the first phase, which has allowed competent intercultural interlocutors to identify mutually shared aspects of identities, and learn to mutually support those shared identity aspects. Competent intercultural interlocutors are able to steer away from the areas of identity that can be potentially face threatening and make salient the areas where they can support each other's face. In doing so, they have actually accomplished rule convergence regarding how they can appropriately support each other's face and appropriately avoid face-threatening acts.

Symbolic convergence is evidenced in the second phase when interactants share certain symbolic norms that they can use to talk about the areas of commonality (e.g., two foreign scholars discussing a theory). Terms of endearment, personal idioms unique to the relationship, and symbols of relationship identity also should emerge as manifestations of the developing relationship (Baxter, 1987; Bell & Healey, 1992).

Finding or establishing common aspects of identity signals the emergence of relational identity. However, at this second stage, relational identity is not yet entirely developed, because the separate cultural identities are just swept under the carpet and not yet incorporated into the emerging relational identity. In other words, the emerging relational identity is narrow in the sense that enmeshment of the individual identities is still relatively limited. Many intercultural interlocutors elect not to develop their relationship beyond this point. For example, in the studies of North American-Japanese relationships, moderately intimate same-sex intercultural relationships (Sudweeks et al., 1990) and opposite-sex friends (Gudykunst et al., 1991) indicated few cultural similarities, but reported some attitudinal, interest, and background similarities. As long as intercultural partners can interact within the parameters of their emerging relational identity (e.g., colleague, superior-subordinate, teacher-student, neighbors, friends), they can avoid more complex face wants. Such intercultural relationships may be considered competent from the standpoint that certain desired goals are achieved in these relationships. However, more intimate and interdependent relationships can be established if intercultural interlocutors can move on to the third phase. This is where intercultural relationships realize the potential to evolve into interpersonal relationships (i.e., they become more personal than cultural).

The Third Phase: Renegotiation

The third phase represents the emergence of enmeshed relational identity, and thus the emergence of a truly integrated relationship. Intercultural competence in the third phase is characterized by a nearly full integration of individual identities reflected in symbolic interdependence and rule convergence. Competent intercultural interlocutors use their narrowly defined but emerging relational identity from the second phase as the basis for renegotiating their separate cultural identities. Although the separate cultural identities may have been circumvented in early phases of their relationship, now the intercultural interlocutors are able to address their distinct cultural identities and potentially merge the two or cultivate greater sharedness in the cultural aspect of their respective identities. At minimum, the different cultural identities are evaluated positively (Gudykunst et al., 1991; Sudweeks et al., 1990).

Renegotiation of separate cultural identities begins in part as a result of the breakdown of the relational system that has increasingly become closed (Scollon & Scollon, 1981). The escalating attention to fellowship face can become dysfunctional if autonomy face needs are neglected. Consequently, there is increasing pressure to show deference to each other's autonomy face. This renegotiation of separate cultural identities is possible because the interlocutors have established some degree of symbolic interdependence and rule convergence. Because they now substantially share a framework for interpreting reality, their respective cultural identities are probably perceived as less distant and separate than perceived in early phases of their relationship. They may engage in symbolic acts such as mixing their respective native languages, or creating entirely new words to refer to certain concepts they share. As a result of such symbolic interdependence, they see their separate cultural identities becoming somewhat integrated or at least approaching each other.

Similarly, rule convergence has allowed the interactants to develop idiosyncratic rules such that their face wants for individual identity can be supported by confirming their emergent relational identity. For example, an interculturally married couple may develop a set of rules stating it is important for them to satisfy each other's fellowship face and competence face as spouses (i.e., being a good husband and a good wife) while keeping their cultural identities in the background. However, the same couple may also have a rule specifying that one must show appropriate politeness acts according to the partner's cultural norms when they visit the partner's relatives. One must support the partner's cultural identity fully in front of the partner's relatives. Although this latter rule could be interpreted as threatening the autonomy face of the partner who has to accommodate to the different cultural norms, the relational identity of being a good couple now supersedes and such accommodating behaviors are seen as supporting the fellowship face of each other.

The intercultural interlocutors experience various dialectic tensions again in this phase. One must manage dialectics in supporting one's own face as opposed to the other's face, and autonomy face as opposed to fellowship or competence face. However, these dialectic tensions are more easily managed because the increasingly enmeshed relational identity is mutually shared. Supporting the other's face supports the mutually shared relational identity, and in turn, one's own face is supported. Mutual face support becomes increasingly interdependent as relational identity is more salient. Even if one tries to support the other's autonomy face, it will not be a threat to the relational identity because the partners have identified independent areas of their respective identities that do not threaten the core of their shared relational identity. In short, the intercultural partners have become interpersonal partners, and dialectic tensions will now revolve more often around relational rather than cultural identity.

Although the highly enmeshed identities are achieved in the third phase, it is important to note that the individual identities cannot be totally isomorphic. Competent facework continuously must balance the needs for autonomy face and fellowship face. Successful relationships are not *solely* characterized by solidarity (i.e., mutual support of fellowship face). Instead, a competent relationship emphasizes fellowship face when it is appropriate for the partners to be connected and autonomy face when it is crucial for the partners to be independent. Similarly, intercultural relationships depend on the balance in the dialectic tension between autonomy face and fellowship face. This balance must be maintained in their cultural identities as well as in other areas of their total identities where some amount of convergence is achieved but some divergence also remains.

It is important to stress that the phases discussed here are highly interdependent and cyclical. Intercultural interlocutors are equipped to bond an interpersonal relationship in later phases because of their acts in the earlier phases. Some intercultural interlocutors may go through the three phases for each salient aspect of identity, and may repeat the phases cyclically over time. Indeed, the more two individuals interact and become interdependent, the more complex their relationship becomes and, therefore, the more aspects of identity will have to be negotiated and renegotiated.

CONCLUSION

We have sketched only briefly the outlines of an emerging theory of interpersonal relationships—identity management theory. This theory offers a useful and unique vantage point for understanding communication competence in intercultural interactions. First, the proposed theory explains interpersonal relationships more generally, and intercultural interaction is considered a special case of interpersonal communication. Thus, by applying concepts of identity and facework to intercultural episodes and relationships, we simultaneously inform about interpersonal communication competence in general as well as intercultural competence. Second, since the theory focuses on interaction and relationships, we think it is especially well suited to understand *intercultural* processes. Previous applications of the concept of face have been directed largely at drawing cross-cultural comparisons (e.g., Holtgraves & Yang, 1990, 1992; Ting-Toomey, 1988; Trubisky, Ting-Toomey, & Lin, 1991). Third, IMT articulates the connection between identity and facework. These concepts, relevant to both intercultural and interpersonal communication, have only been loosely connected in previous writing.

Finally, IMT offers considerable heuristic potential for research. We contend that many of the concepts are observable and the hypothesized empirical relations indicated by the theory are subject to falsification. Competent identity management via facework can be studied at both an episodic level and a relational level. Dimensions of identity such as salience can be measured by both self-report and the examination of discursive text from observed intercultural episodes. A comparison of ascribed and avowed identities within intercultural encounters is informative with respect to intercultural communication competence (Collier & Thomas, 1988). In addition, more direct self-report measures of perceived identity confirmation and face support can be developed and linked to other relevant episodic and relational outcomes (e.g., satisfaction).

A particularly important research priority is to document the *manner* in which symbolic convergence is accomplished over time in a relationship. One approach is to have members of developing intercultural relationships keep semi-structured diaries (Duck, Rutt, Hurst, & Strejc, 1991). The content of such diaries could be mined to discern how an emerging relational identity is manifested in everyday interactions. To fully understand the processual (developmental) nature of intercultural communication competence, longitudinal observation of intercultural relationships, following the three phases presented here, is warranted.

In this chapter, we have utilized examples of intercultural relationships primarily related to *national* cultural identities. Nevertheless, we believe that IMT is applicable to other types of cultural identities (e.g., ethnic, sexual preference, gender, disability). Whatever types of cultural identities may be salient in intercultural interactions, communicators must grapple with the dialectic tensions we have outlined here. Comparisons of face management across these relationship types would be informative. In addition, we recommend that the factors uniquely relevant to particular cultural identities (e.g., the power disparity experienced by ethnic minorities) be explored. These factors may influence the interpretation and management of face, as well as the process of symbolic convergence. Scholarship focusing on ethnic identities should offer some fruitful connections (Hecht et al., 1992).

Our description of IMT at this point is admittedly oversimplified and underspecified. The interrelationships among symbolic interdependence, rule convergence, facework, identity negotiation, and competence are complex. Serious effort needs to be devoted to stating more precisely the relationships among constructs, and to developing valid operational definitions. But we believe the heuristic and explanatory potential of IMT argues well for the effort. Our hope is that further elaboration of IMT, along with appropriate empirical substantiation, will illuminate processes fundamental to both intercultural and interpersonal interaction. In the end, we believe this route will offer useful insights about competent communicators and successful relationships.

NOTES

1. We see cultural identity as encompassing the notion of *social identity*. Tajfel and Turner (1979), for example, describe social identity as "aspects of an individual's self-image that derive from the social categories to which he perceives himself as belonging" (p. 40). They refer to membership in certain social-economic groups, occupational groups, gender classification, and so forth.

2. There are other useful dimensions of identity to consider (Hecht et al., 1992). However, the dimension that seems to have received the greatest amount of attention in the literature thus far is *salience*. Conceptually, we speculate that this dimension is one of the most potent.

6

Culture-Based Interactive Constraints in Explaining Intercultural Strategic Competence

MIN-SUN KIM • *University of Hawaii, Manoa*

Intercultural communication competence has emerged as one of the major concerns among intercultural communication scholars. The tradition of study of intercultural communication competence has provided a promising foundation built on practical need, ranging from sojourner adaptation to intercultural training (see reviews by Brislin, 1981; Gudykunst & Hammer, 1984; Ruben, 1989). Although many researchers conceptualize intercultural communication competence as either appropriateness (the ability to demonstrate a knowledge of the socially appropriate communicative behavior) or effectiveness (the degree to which personal or relationship goals are achieved; see Abe & Wiseman, 1983; Collier, 1989; Imahori & Lanigan, 1989; Martin & Hammer, 1989), the exact nature of intercultural communication competence is not well established.

Recently, there has been a growing consensus that global impressions of intercultural competence are strongly and positively associated with evaluations of strategy choices (Gudykunst & Ting-Toomey, 1988; Yule & Tarone, 1990). At the heart of the concept of culture is the notion that people from different cultures develop distinctive interaction styles and preferred communication strategies. Expectations about conversational style and preference for a particular set of verbal strategies may contribute to global assessments of strategic competence. This chapter attempts to investigate cultural variability in perceptions of communication competence from the perspective of conversational strategy choices by viewing strategic competence as one aspect of competence.

Researchers from communication, psychology, linguistics, and other related fields have focused on differences in strategy choices across

AUTHOR'S NOTE: *The author gratefully acknowledges constructive comments and suggestions from Drs. Steven Wilson, Mary Bresnahan, Gerald Miller, David Johnson, John Hunter (all at Michigan State University), and Narayan Raja on earlier drafts of this paper.*

cultures as one aspect of competence in the pursuit of conversational goals such as compliance gaining (Neuliep & Hazleton, 1985), work-related requests (Hirokawa & Miyahara, 1986), information seeking in initial interaction (Alexander, Cronen, Kang, Tsou, & Banks, 1986), self-disclosure (Barnlund, 1975; Nakanishi, 1986), conflict resolution (Ting-Toomey, 1987, 1988), management of compliments (Barnlund & Araki, 1985; Daikuhara, 1986), and the general use of verbal tactics, such as the degree of directness (Okabe, 1987; Tannen, 1981), apologies and thanks (Coulmas, 1981), and requesting (Blum-Kulka, House, & Kasper, 1989).

Much of the accumulated research testifies that intercultural communication competence can be characterized as a general impression of communication quality, with particular reference to the nature of strategy choices. However, most of the research is descriptive in nature, with some notable exceptions (Gudykunst & Ting-Toomey, 1988; Ting-Toomey, 1989a). Typically, such investigations have attempted to describe various communicative strategies or classes of tactics that people might use across cultures in the pursuit of some interaction goals. Although this research provides an important and rich descriptive base, two fundamental problems stand out: understanding and prediction of strategy choices.

First, why are certain types of verbal strategies preferred by a cultural group? Why would an average Korean prefer to choose "hint," and an average American "request," as a favor-asking strategy? A few researchers attempt to explore the origins of preferred communicative strategies by relying on norms, rules, and conventions. For instance, some researchers in communication and sociology have generated a corpus of rules (Collier, 1988; Cronen, Chen, & Pearce, 1988; Wiseman, 1980). Norms and rules, being specific to particular social situations, have a severely limited explanatory role in comparative research, since the findings and bits of information on the choice of strategies frequently appear as isolated entities without connection to other situations. The appeal to certain norms and rules, therefore, runs the risk of not being applicable to other situations. Jacobs (1985) argues that a conventional rule-based logic cannot (a) capture the ways in which actors infer beyond the information given to achieve coherence, or (b) organize communication functionally.

The second problem in most intercultural studies in strategic communication styles relates to the *predictability* of communicative strategy choices. Expressing interaction patterns declaratively restricts their predictability in other situations. One can imagine such scenarios as "What to say when a policeman pulls you over for speeding in Saudi Arabia," or "How to refuse a request from a best friend in Japan." Knowledge to handle such situations would be readily available if the interaction situations described were the ones frequently encountered by an individual. However, not all situations occur in standardized packages (i.e., scriptlike), and, of course, one cannot describe every possible strategy choice so as to account for every possible interaction goal across cultures.

A major purpose of intercultural communication competence research is to improve communication and understanding between members of different cultural groups. Thus, understanding others' intentions and predicting others' strategy choices should be the critical endeavors in intercultural strategic competence. This chapter posits the existence of culturally induced global constraints that are essential to this endeavor.

Specifically, this chapter examines how global impressions of intercultural communication competence are associated with the preference for interactive constraints. In positing culture-based interactive constraints governing the general impression of intercultural strategic communicative competence, two ideas are being proposed. The first is that culture in the area of communication is best seen not as complexes of behavior patterns (e.g., customs, habits, and norms) but rather as a set of governing mechanisms (e.g., goals, plans, instructions, and "programs") of communication behavior. Perhaps a way to understand this position is by an analogy with electronic computers: As we program computers to do what they do, our culture to a great extent *governs* us to do what we do and to be what we are. Hall and Hall (1985), for instance, likened culture to an enormous, subtle, extraordinarily complex computer: It programs the actions and responses of every person, and these programs must be mastered by anyone wishing to make the system work. Although people are not automatons programmed by culture, human beings are dependent on such cultural programs for ordering their behavior.

A second focus on intercultural competence concerns the way cultural information is organized on the individual level. Consistent with the "governing mechanism" view of culture, D'Andrade (1981, 1989) posits that the pool of cultural information constrains individuals' information processing systems, and their styles of reasoning. More specifically, von Cranach, Machler, and Steiner (1985), in their theory of goal-directed action, point out that "manifest behavior is governed by (partly) conscious cognitions that in turn are (partly) of a social origin, so that society (partly) creates and controls the individual's action by controlling his or her cognitions" (p. 22). Geertz (1973) argues that undirected by culture patterns, peoples' behavior would be virtually ungovernable, a mere chaos of pointless acts. Of course, not all interaction styles are culture-based—we all have a great number of idiosyncratic noncultural programs. But with respect to the predominant patterns of social interactions, it is mostly through culture that human groups organize, direct, and pattern their behavior. This chapter intends to extend our knowledge about what kinds of general interactive constraints shape people's beliefs in communication competence, and how interactive constraints are anchored in the wider cultural milieu.

The remaining sections are organized as follows: First, the nature of goal-oriented behavior is outlined. Interactive constraints and other goal-related concepts (e.g., tactics, strategies, and primary interaction goals) are defined, and the two interactive constraints—face support and clarity—are introduced as main factors in communication competence. Next, the origins of the two interactive constraints are explored at a cultural level. Then, the constructs of individualism and collectivism, as major pan-cultural, etic themes, are linked to the interactive constraints. Several predictions or propositions are formulated regarding differential assessments and choice of various verbal tactics (in terms of face concern and clarity). Finally, directions are outlined for testing the propositions, and for future development and refinement.

GOAL-BASED NATURE OF STRATEGIC COMPETENCE

In considering structures for understanding social behavior and strategic competence, a number of cognitive and social theorists (e.g., Miller, Galanter, & Pribram, 1960; Schank & Abelson, 1977; Wilensky, 1983) have argued that social interaction and the perceptions of competence can be analyzed in terms of people's goals, and the plans and strategies necessary to achieve those goals. Over the years, numerous terms related to goals have been used as the ends governing actions: motive (McClelland, 1985), values (Rokeach, 1973), and end-beliefs (Read & Miller, 1989). Goals are end states people desire to attain or maintain (Read & Miller, 1989).

Much of the knowledge about communication goals (or objectives of a conversation) has been formulated in terms of their degree of abstractness (Kellermann, 1989; Wilson & Putnam, 1990). The knowledge of interaction goals is cast at three principal levels of abstraction that are hierarchically organized from specific and concrete to general, abstract, and global elements: (a) tactical or strategic goals, (b) primary communication goals (outcome of a conversation), and (c) global constraints.

At the most specific, basic level, Kellermann (1989) posits that tactical goals are concerned with desires for specific behavioral action (e.g., desiring to ask a question). These goals pertain to short periods of time, such as a single turn or adjacency pair in a conversation. The idea of strategy and tactics has been postulated in describing relatively concrete communicative actions (Berger, 1987; von Cranach, Kalbermatten, Indermuhle, & Gugler, 1982). Generally, *strategies* are viewed as action sequences that are used to attain goals, and *tactics* as specific behavioral actions that persons manifest in their goal-directed interactions with others (Berger, Karol, & Jordan, 1989; Street & Cappella, 1985). Asking a question, breaking eye contact with someone, and turning away from someone are all examples of tactics.

The next level of goals consists of the numerous outcomes or primary goals that may be desired from an entire interaction (Kellermann, 1989). An overall strategy and specific tactics for carrying out that strategy are implemented only if one selects a functional outcome desired from interaction. Recently, interest has emerged in identifying and classifying a variety of situation-specific interaction outcomes or goals, such as gaining compliance, seeking information, de-escalating relationships, correcting others, and testing affinity (Argyle, Furnham, & Graham, 1981; Kellermann & Kim, 1991; McCann & Higgins, 1988; Rubin, Perse, Barbato, 1988; Schank & Childers, 1984). The situation-specific interaction goals are functional outcomes of a conversation, for which a wide range of different tactical goals can be used (Kellermann, 1989; Read & Miller, 1989). For instance, if one has the interaction goal of seeking information, there are a number of different tactics (i.e., hinting, asking, keeping eye contact with the partner) one can use.

At the most abstract, global level, several authors have argued for cross-situational goals that serve as criteria for making a choice among tactics in the pursuit of interaction goals. As people pursue primary communication goals such as gaining compliance, seeking information, or altering relationships, they generate messages within a variety of constraints. These higher-level goals or constraints have been named "meta-goals," "meta-plans" (Berger, 1987; Kellermann, 1989; Wilensky, 1981, 1983), "supergoals" (von Cranach et al., 1982), "life theme" (Schank & Abelson, 1977), "cross-situational goals" (Street & Cappella, 1985), "supermaxims" (Grice, 1975), "meta-strategies" (van Dijk & Kintsch, 1983), and "ritual-constraints" (Goffman, 1967). Although primary goals generate a sequence of tactics specific to the nature of the interaction, global constraints are usually responsible for generating the strategies and actions that guide an individual's conversational style in general (Kellermann, 1989; Wilensky, 1983).

Basic Assumptions

Some basic assumptions are made regarding goal-based strategic communication competence. Goal-oriented behavior requires evaluation of the success of each strategy attempted. Does it bring the desired goal nearer? This question reflects an important aspect of rationality, namely, the ability to weigh different means, and choose the one that best satisfies the desired goal. This chapter is based on the assumption that all competent adult members of a society possess certain rational capacities, in particular, consistent modes of reasoning from ends to means that will achieve those ends (Brown & Levinson, 1978). For example, if I want to find my nephew's phone number in Detroit, it would surely be irrational to call directory information in California. Although universal rationality remains an assumption, it enables us to understand human interactions in many different settings across diverse cultures.

This rationality does not imply that strategy choices are always processed consciously. Most of the time, one may not be consciously aware of these goals or strategy choices (Street & Cappella, 1985). However, when interaction mistakes occur, or actors have a particularly clear interaction goal in mind (e.g., making a good impression in a job interview), the strategies may very well emerge into awareness (Brown & Levinson, 1978; Street & Cappella, 1985).

Interactive Constraints

To account for cross-cultural similarities and differences in the choice of conversational strategies affecting perceptions of strategic competence, it is necessary to have available a limited set of shared interactive constraints (or conversational concerns). A culture-based interactive constraint is a collection of shared background knowledge that influences the overall choice of strategies across primary interaction goals. It is assumed that there are a limited number of universal interactive constraints that function as main factors in assessing communication competence.

Researchers from communication, artificial intelligence, psychology, linguistics, and other related fields have suggested two major dimensions that may serve as global constraints in conversational and planning situations: clarity and face support (e.g., Brown & Levinson, 1978; Grice, 1975). *Clarity* in conversational behavior is conceptualized as a concern about achieving a primary goal in the most explicit and the shortest way possible; *face support* is conceptualized as a concern about achieving a primary goal without hurting the hearer's desired social image and feelings.

In the past, several authors have suggested similar interactive constraints that are motivating forces in communication: "be clear" and "be polite" (Lakoff, 1977); "concern for clarity" and "concern with support"

(Greene & Lindsey, 1989); and "efficiency" and "social appropriateness" (Kellermann & Kim, 1991). Grice (1975) also put forward the "maxim of manner" in the use of language (e.g., be clear, be brief, try to avoid obscurity). Brown and Levinson (1978) also posited such desires as the want to be efficient or indicate urgency, and the want to maintain hearer's face to some degree. These major overarching interactive constraints (face support and clarity) are anchored to cultural orientations.

ORIGINS OF CONVERSATIONAL CONSTRAINTS

Face Support as Relational Concern

As people pursue primary interaction goals, they generate messages within a variety of constraints. One major type of conversational constraint that may influence the perceptions of strategic competence involves face support (Argyle et al., 1981; Brown & Levinson, 1978; Chen, 1989; Kellermann & Kim, 1991). Face support has been investigated under such labels as "politeness" (Brown & Levinson, 1978; Lim, 1988), "face" (Goffman, 1967; Ho, 1976), "identity goals" (Wilson & Putnam, 1990), "impression management goal" (Street & Cappella, 1985), and "concern with support" (Greene & Lindsey, 1989).

Concern for the other's face relates to the speaker's perceived obligation to support a hearer's desire for approval-seeking or the positive self-image that the hearer claims (Brown & Levinson, 1978; Ting-Toomey, 1988). Research on politeness focuses on strategies for minimizing threats to other's face and reinforces the importance of the concern for the other's face and feelings in conversational behavior (Lakoff, 1977; Scollon & Scollon, 1981).

The basic motivation behind the preference for face-supporting behavior is the sociological principle of relational harmony. In general, people in interaction prefer conflict-free interactions in which their face will be maintained and cooperate (and assume each other's cooperation) in maintaining face (Goffman, 1967). Thus, the preference for face-supporting communicative tactics is consistent with the desire to create and sustain positive identities, evaluations, and face in the eyes of others. The degree of face wants that are appropriate may differ across cultures, but the general concern to be seen as supporting the other's face in communicative acts is presumed to be universal.

Clarity as Task-Orientation

Need for clarity is another major global constraint that may influence choice of conversational tactics and strategies and determine one's perceptions of strategic competence (Blum-Kulka, House, & Kasper, 1989). The concern for clarity in conversation is defined as the likelihood of an utterance making one's intention clear and explicit. The clarity concern controls the degree to which a strategy is explicitly and unambiguously communicating to a listener the content of the message.

Given the energy and time constraints of social actors, it is assumed that interlocutors seek to use direct and clear tactics and strategies that will minimize the amount of time and effort expended to reach a conversational goal (Berger, 1987). The function served by clarity is to express information as clearly and succinctly as possible (Lakoff, 1977). In sum, clarity in a conversational contribution means that the speaker will not be wasting the addressee's time (Lakoff, 1977). Movement toward increased clarity typically results in the choice of more pointed and direct tactical means.

The idea of clarity frequently has been talked about in the literature on conversation (Blum-Kulka, Danet, & Gherson, 1985; Leech, 1983). Brown and Levinson (1978) explicitly argue that the want to be clear (i.e., indicate urgency) can be considered to be part of rationality. For instance, Grice's (1975) "maxim of manner" can be seen as a guideline for clear communication. Leech (1983) also posits the Economy Principle ("Be quick and easy") as a valuable precept in conversation for reducing time and effort in encoding and decoding.

The notion of avoiding unnecessary steps or being clear is a move in the direction of ultimate "taskification" (a word coined by Wilensky, 1981), or task-orientation, which can be contrasted with face-orientation. Argyle et al. (1981) argue that formal speech is guided by the principle of direct communication. For instance, the main function of a legal document, a scientific paper, or a recipe is to be clear, precise, and unambiguous, which is geared toward task-orientation. Brown and Levinson (1978) argue that the majority of natural conversations do not proceed in such a brusque fashion at all, and that the pervasive motive for *not* adhering rigidly to such maxims is the desire to give some attention to face.

Although preference for clarity (e.g., fairly direct and pointed verbal tactics via imperatives) can frequently interfere with the desire to satisfy another's face wants, the two constraints need not be in conflict on every occasion. For example, in cases of great urgency, little concern for face support is necessary (Brown & Levinson, 1978). Similarly, face concern takes on more importance in highly ritualized ceremonies (e.g., weddings; Kellermann, 1989). Most interactions, however, occur in situations where there is some tension between the two constraints (Kellermann & Kim, 1991).

There are some clues that the two interactive constraints proposed might apply across different cultures, even though cultures may differ in the relative importance attached to clarity and face support. Some existing empirical evidence testifies that face-saving interaction, which is partly a conscious suspension of clarity of communication, may be a cross-culturally transferable concern (Brown & Levinson, 1978; Holtgraves & Yang, 1990). Drawing on material from their own fieldwork in India and Mexico, and on data from England, Wales, and America, Brown and Levinson (1978) claim that the basic constraints (i.e., face wants and need for clarity) on effective interaction appear to be essentially the same across cultures and languages. Specifically, they say, any rational and competent agent will take into consideration the relative importance of the want to be efficient or direct and the want to maintain the hearer's face to whatever degree. Several authors (Blum-Kulka et al., 1985; Lakoff, 1977; Tracy, 1990) also argue for the potential universality of conversational constraints in interaction: certain adherence to directness concerns is as essential for the successful achievement of interactional balance as is maintaining face.

Although the two interactive constraints are probably based on universal principles, the manifestation of the role of each constraint might differ systematically across cultures, because of differing social norms operative in different societies. For example, Brown and Levinson (1978) allow for the possibility of clarity concerns being part of the considerations subject to cross-cultural variation: Cultures may differ in the degree to which wants other than face needs (such as the need for efficiency, directness, or for the expression of power) are allowed to supersede face needs. If there is a norm of sincerity and directness in talk, for example, sincere disapproval is less of a face-threatening act than it would be in societies not having such a legitimization of non-face wants. For instance, speakers of Hebrew attach a high value to sincerity in speech. In her ethnographic study of the ethos of directness in Israeli society, Katriel (1986) shows that the notion of *dugri*, direct straight talk, is positively associated with concepts such as *sincerity* (truthful expression), *naturalness* (simplicity, spontaneity), *solidarity*, and *anti-style*, thus legitimizing a conscious suspension of face concerns over clarity or directness of communication. This leads to a communicatively competent style that, in Israeli culture, is perceived as honest and forthright, but that, in other cultures in which face-maintaining considerations play a more central role in interaction, is seen as inconsiderate and rude. A host of studies give evidence of systematic ethnic/national differences (Blum-Kulka et al., 1989; Carrell & Konneker, 1981; Gumperz, 1982; Scollon & Scollon, 1981; Tannen, 1981) in the valuing and use of politeness and, more broadly, in the importance attached to a set of face wants and, presumably, to the need for clarity.

To summarize, the two interactive constraints (clarity and face support) may serve as pressures that shape and give rise to the nature of strategic competence. Cultural values are one major determinant of the importance of these interactive constraints in any given situation. That is, the degree to which each interactive constraint is elaborated or emphasized may vary from culture to culture. Although people are not automatons programmed by the culture, cultural values regarding the preferred modes of conduct guide the salience of conversational constraints.

The assumption that cultural values, as a control mechanism, affect the salience of each constraint requires one to extract pan-cultural or etic themes that are important to the patterning of conversational behavior. Out of various dimensions of culture, the individualism-collectivism constructs address relational orientations of human groups, thus potentially affecting the operation of overarching conversational constraints and global impressions of strategic competence.

In the following section, it is proposed that the origins of interactive constraints are the value contents that may serve either individualistic or collectivistic values. Specifically, the constructs of individualism and collectivism are analyzed and linked to the importance of each conversational constraint in the production of competent conversational behavior across cultures. Briefly put, it is postulated that the inclination toward the clarity constraint is deeply rooted in the individualistic orientation, while the inclination toward a preference for the face concern is similarly rooted in the collectivistic orientation.

INDIVIDUALISM AND COLLECTIVISM: THEIR RELATION TO INTERACTIVE CONSTRAINTS

The concept of individualism-collectivism has been described by Triandis et al. (1986) as perhaps the most important dimension of cultural differences in social behavior across the world. Numerous cross-cultural studies (Hofstede, 1979; Hofstede & Bond, 1984; Hui, 1984; Hui & Triandis, 1986) have provided empirical evidence supporting the usefulness of the individualism-collectivism dimension as a way of categorizing cultures. Hofstede (1980), for instance, has identified individualism-collectivism as one of the four major dimensions in his factor analytic study of work values in 40 countries. Hui (1984) and Hui and Triandis (1986), after surveying cross-cultural anthropologists and psychologists from all parts of the world, conclude that the dimension of individualism-collectivism can be used as a powerful theoretical construct to explain the relational differences and similarities between cultures.

Triandis, Bontempo, Villareal, Asai, and Lucca (1988a) posit that collectivist cultures emphasize people, whereas individualistic cultures emphasize task. Specifically, Triandis et al. (1988a) have defined collectivism as having a great emphasis on (a) the views, needs, and goals of the ingroup rather than of oneself, (b) great readiness to cooperate with ingroup members, and (c) intense emotional attachment to the ingroup. Individualism is reflected in (a) self-reliance, (b) low concern for ingroups, and (c) distance from ingroups. In other words, individualism is defined as the tendency to be more concerned about one's behavior for one's own needs, interests, and goals, whereas collectivism refers to the tendency to be more concerned about the consequences of one's behavior for ingroup members, and to be more willing to sacrifice personal interests for the attainment of collective interests and harmony (Leung, 1987; Triandis et al., 1986).

Individualism and collectivism have been recognized under various pseudonyms as addressing relational aspects of cultural groups. Miller (1984) distinguishes between *individualistic* (stressing autonomy, self-aggrandizement, and the sense of personal inviolability apart from society) and *sociocentric* (holding the person to be fundamentally related to others, stressing empathy and the readiness to adjust one's behavior to the situation or group) concepts of the person. Hsu (1981) differentiates between *individual-centered life* (the emphasis is on the predilections of the individual) and *situation-centered life* (the emphasis is on an individual's appropriate place and behavior in situation-centered life). Yang (1981) has articulated a similar position: *social orientation* (a tendency for people to act in accordance with external expectations or social norms) versus *individual orientation* (focus on internal wishes or personal interest). Parsons, Shils, and Olds (1951) similarly distinguish between *self-orientation* (the permissibility of one's pursuing any interests private to oneself) and *collectivity-orientation* (one's obligation to pursue the common interests of the collectivity). Similar distinctions have been proposed to study individual differences: *allocentric* versus *idiocentric* orientation (Triandis, Leung, Villareal, & Clark, 1985) and *social orientation* versus *goal orientation* (Frese, Stewart, & Hannover, 1987).

Recently, Schwartz and Bilsky (1987, 1990), in their theory of the universal types of values, confirmed the idea that the distinction between values serving the individual's own interests or those of the collectivity is universally meaningful. Using data from Australia,

Finland, Hong Kong, Spain, and the United States, individual task-achievement and self-direction values were found to serve individualistic interests; prosocial tendencies were found to serve collective interests. This consensus about the usefulness of the individualism and collectivism constructs across cultures reinforces their validity for the current theoretical framework. That is, the differences in priorities across cultures reflect real differences in emphasis on individual versus collective interest.

Concern for face support is postulated to be closely connected with collectivistic traits, and concern for clarity with individualistic traits. The following section explores the significance of these cultural orientations in influencing the salience of interactive constraints.

Concern for Face Support as Collectivist Ethos

The degree of collectivist orientation in a particular society systematically affects the importance of face concern in guiding the perceptions of strategically competent conversational behavior. Collectivism is often associated with a strong emphasis on interpersonal harmony (at least within the ingroup[1]) and preferences for affiliation, succorance, and nurturance (Hui & Villareal, 1989; Yum, 1988), interpersonal concern (Hui, 1984), protecting one's face (Chinese Culture Connection, 1987), maintaining good face-to-face relationships (Argyle, Bond, Lizuka, & Contarello, 1986), and the *we* identity rather than the *I* identity (Ting- Toomey, 1988). When one's personal identity is rooted collectively in the soil of interdependent relations with others, one tends to be very concerned about others' feelings. It is difficult for people from a collectivistic culture to overlook negative interpersonal consequences of their actions, and this is at the root of the collectivistic value orientation.

Deep-rooted in the emphasis on social relationships is the theme of face. In the collectivistic Chinese society (and in other East Asian societies, such as Korea and Japan), the individual is not inner-directed but controlled by a need for not losing face. Face—a literal translation of the Chinese *lien* and *mien-tsy*—is lost when the individual, either through his or her action or that of people closely related, fails to meet essential requirements placed on the individual by virtue of the social position he or she occupies (Ho, 1976). Ting-Toomey (1987) points out: "Members in the collectivistic cultures live the 'face concept' twenty-four hours a day. They breathe it, they honor it, they despise it, they can't do without it" (p.12). In fact, some Korean phrases strongly manifest the importance of face in relation to social grace: When someone can not fulfill an obligation, the person will typically say to a third party, "I have no face to see him/her" (*bol-myeon-mok-up-da*). In addition, one Korean proverb states: "Better to die rather than to live in dishonor/disgrace," which is an interesting contrast to the American "Give me liberty or give me death." Thus, the notion of face has both psychological and emotional components that manifest themselves through behavioral interaction patterns. For collective cultures in which saving face is a critical matter, the style of face-supporting behavior, rather than efficient and direct goal orientation, may be effective and may produce desirable consequences in the long run.[2]

The contrast between cultural emphasis on different conversational norms concerning face support (at least toward ingroup members in the case of collectivistic cultures), as against clarity, has been recognized by various authors. One of Grice's maxims for cooperative conversation is manner, which suggests that speakers should avoid ambiguity and obscurity of expression (Grice, 1975). Several writers have written that although this direct communication is a norm in North America, an individualistic society, Grice's principle would not be accepted as a norm in cultures with a different value orientation (Yum, 1988). Okabe (1987), for instance, has shown that in Japan, the traditional rule of communication that proscribes demanding, rejecting, asserting oneself, or criticizing the listener straightforwardly, is a more dominant principle than Grice's maxim of manner.

These ideas, as applied to conversational behavior, would mean that collectivists have, as a general cross-encounter goal, the desire to avoid loss of face and to be accepted by ingroup members, which strengthens their preference for face-saving means of achieving primary goals. For relatively highly collectivist cultures, in which saving face is a critical matter, relationally sensitive behavioral style, rather than being direct and clear, may be effective, and may be considered to be strategically competent. Given the same situational contingencies, the propriety of one's tactics will become a more important consideration in judging one's strategic competence as the culture moves toward a more collectivist orientation. Therefore:

Proposition 1: Members of more collectivistic cultures attribute higher importance to face support in the pursuit of primary goals.

Given that the strategies presented are sufficiently differentiated in terms of face support, some classes of speech acts and tactics[3] (i.e., warn, criticize, disapprove) for achieving primary goals may be perceived as a greater threat to the other's face in a more collectivist culture, and thus will not be judged acceptable or strategically competent. The more collectivist a culture, the more the classes of acts that are perceived as threatening to basic face wants by members of that culture. Therefore:

> *Proposition 2:* Members of more collectivistic cultures have a higher threshold for acceptable levels of face support.

Assessment of strategy acceptability should affect one's strategy choices. Many of the interaction goals pose a certain amount of conflict between face and clarity concerns. For instance, when one's goal is to ask a favor, the most face-saving ways to accomplish this goal (e.g., hinting) are also least likely to be direct in leading to the outcome. When interaction goals pose conflict between the face and clarity concerns, the constraint deemed to be less important is left unfulfilled (Descott & Latombe, 1985), which can be seen as one aspect of strategic competence. Given that people typically focus on the more important constraint (Kellermann, 1989; Waldinger, 1977):

> *Proposition 3:* Members of more collectivistic cultures select a greater number of strategies that involve maximizing the face support constraint.

Concern for Clarity as Individualist Ethos

The concern for clarity, as a general guideline in the choice of conversational action, seems to serve the major individualistic concern of self-interest. The desire for maximum directness or clarity is at the heart of such individualist traits as meeting personal needs (Wheeler, Reis, & Bond, 1989), task orientation (Triandis et al., 1988a), maximizing the satisfaction of individual interests (Kluckhohn & Strodtbeck, 1961), and subordination of others' goals to one's own (Triandis et al., 1986). Strategic competence in individualistic societies is thus geared toward the achievement of personal goals, and is often dominated by the instrumental function of maximizing the outcome for individuals (e.g., coming directly to the point). Yum (1988) elaborates on the outcome orientation of individualistic culture (i.e., North America) and its communication patterns:

> The main function of communication is to actualize autonomy and self-fulfillment[;] the outcome of the communication is more important than the process. With short-term, discontinuous relationships, communication is perceived to be an action which is terminated after a certain duration and then replaced by a new communication. Tangible outcomes in terms of

> friends gained, opponents defeated, and self-fulfillment achieved become the primary function of communication. (p. 381)

A major aspect of an outcome orientation is related to practical principles that govern and guide how communication is to be employed to achieve goals. One's conception of desirable consequences is arrived at through a practical empiricism (Stewart, 1972; Yum, 1988). Consequently, outcome orientation, as a value serving individualistic communication goals, gives significance to getting things done (Stewart, 1972) with least expense of effort and time. Generally speaking, outcome emphasis coincides with individuals striving toward directness and clarity in communication.

An important consequence of the individualistic value orientation is the preference for clear and direct communication behavior in judgments of strategic competence. This preference for clarity is reflected in the reaction to violations of clarity rules such as "Why don't you get to the point, dammit," or "Why can't he say what he means?" (Lakoff, 1977). Gudykunst and Ting-Toomey (1988) have made a similar claim that communication in the United States (an individualistic culture) affords little room for the cultivation of ambiguity. The predominant forms of communication in individualistic cultures call for clear and direct communication, exemplified by such expressions as "Don't beat around the bush," and "Get to the point." Direct imperatives increase the communicated urgency, and are intended to reduce the time and energy expended in attaining a conversational outcome. For instance, the more direct a given request strategy type, the shorter the inferential path to the requestive interpretation (i.e., illocutionarily transparent; Blum-Kulka et al., 1989). Therefore, an individualistic orientation systematically increases the importance of directness concerns in guiding tactical choices and in perceptions of strategic competence. The general tone of social interaction is concerned with being as pointed, direct, clear, unambiguous, and concise as possible in the choice of verbal tactics. Consequently:

> *Proposition 4:* Members of more individualistic cultures attribute higher importance to clarity concern in the pursuit of primary goals.

Given that the strategies presented are sufficiently differentiated in terms of the level of clarity, certain tactics (speech acts) with low communicative urgency (i.e., hinting, implying) will be assessed as less direct, and thus less acceptable and less strategically competent, in a more individualist culture. Thus:

Proposition 5: Members of more individualistic cultures have a higher threshold for acceptable levels of clarity.

Assessment of the degree of incompatibility between the two constraints should affect one's strategy choices and one's perceptions of strategic competence. The degree of individualistic orientation will bias the constraint satisfaction move toward directness whenever interaction goals involve incompatibility between the two constraints. As a part of strategic competence, people typically focus on the more important constraint. Consequently:

Proposition 6: Members of more individualistic cultures select a greater number of strategies that involve maximizing the clarity constraint.

DISCUSSION

Theoretical Implications

This chapter has put forth some predictions regarding culture-based conversational behavior and perceptions of strategic competence, based on the integration of different lines of research in the areas of intercultural and interpersonal communication. In everyday social interaction, people have various social goals (i.e., gaining compliance, affinity-seeking, seeking favor, seeking information, revealing information). To achieve those goals, people must have strategic competence—the procedural knowledge necessary to reach their goals. The notion of *culture-based interactive constraints* guides the choice of communication strategies and the general assessment of communication competence.

This research is based on the assumption that the concern for clarity serves individualistic interests, and the concern for face support serves collectivist interests. The extent to which individual versus collective interests in social interactions are served by different interactive constraints has important consequences for the preference that people attach to interactive constraints, and their perceptions of strategic competence. Even if people have identical desired outcomes in an interaction (e.g., striking a business deal), their assessments about acceptability of strategies can still vary because of different pressures exercised by each constraint. Perceptions of strategic competence among people with individualistic value orientations are often dominated by the instrumental function of goal achievement with a preference for direct and efficient means. In contrast, the main function of communication in collective value orientations is to create or maintain social propriety. The different interest served by each interactive constraint will affect the priority attached to the constraints, the different modes or approaches to achieving social goals, and, ultimately, overall impressions of communicative competence.

The prediction above should not be interpreted as implying that in any situation members of a particular culture may totally disregard one constraint in favor of the other. As mentioned earlier, in any culture the urgency of a situation will increase the importance of clarity in goal achievement (Brown & Levinson, 1978). Similarly, in any culture, face support will take on more importance in highly ritualized ceremonies (i.e., weddings).

In sum, given the implicit, yet powerful, link between cultural values and the priorities attached to interactive constraints, investigation of this theoretical prediction among various cultural groups should be informative, and should provide insights into how cultural variability influences the pattern of tactical choices for fulfilling conversational goals, and assessments of strategic communicative competence.

Practical Implications

Conversing and communicating competently across cultures is becoming a major concern for many people. The current line of research has important practical implications for intercultural communication competence. Knowing the cultural way of communication entails more than a command of syntax and lexicon—it requires an understanding of cultural perceptions and of the usages regarding different types of communication tactics. According to Leech (1983), the transfer of the norms of one community to another community may well lead to pragmatic failure, and to the judgment that the speaker is in some way being impolite and uncooperative. Tannen (1981), for example, has remarked on the pragmatic failure caused by the fact that her indirectness in a second language (Greek) was different from that of her native-speaker hosts: While chatting, she mentioned that she associated Greece with grapes, and was surprised at not having seen any since she came to Greece. She also mentioned that Americans have a special way of fixing eggs, namely, scrambling them. These utterances, meant as polite conversational topics, were taken as hints by her hosts, and she was faced with scrambled eggs and grapes for breakfast from then on. Unfortunately, neither was one of her favorite dishes. This incident can be accounted for by the notion of pragmatic or strategic competence.

The competent use of language lies in knowing how to use words to get listeners to make the right inferences about what is meant (Gibbs, 1985). Simply knowing the meanings of individual words is not sufficient to ensure the proper accomplishments of conversational goals. People need to know additional information about the value attached by each other to interactive constraints. This pragmatic information constitutes the shared or mutual knowledge that allows interlocutors to achieve communication. Failure to produce successful strategies might be seen as reflecting a general knowledge deficit, or communicative incompetence. This factor probably accounts for much stereotypical intercultural misunderstanding; it represents perhaps the major limitation to the universal intelligibilities in the interaction between people from differing cultural assumptions.

Highly relevant in this context is the work of Gumperz (1982), which shows that cross-cultural differences in expectations of linguistic behavior can lead to breakdowns in intercultural communication. Examining interactions between British-English and Indian-English speakers in England, Gumperz (1978) found that differences in cues resulted in systematic miscommunication about whether a question was being asked or whether a person was being rude or polite, among others. This line of research shows that when speakers of different cultural backgrounds interact, the problems that develop in communication are often the direct result of misunderstanding each other's global goals or constraints in conversation.

Culturally based studies of different aspects of communicative competence have many implications for teachers, clinicians, and researchers who work in multicultural contexts. One of the most important implications of this study is that different cultures do not necessarily share the same assumptions concerning what constitutes appropriate choices of strategies (Gumperz, 1978). Some of the learner's speech act behavior results from overgeneralization, simplification, or reduction of sociopragmatic knowledge. To the extent that strategies are linked to interactants' assessments of constraints and to the extent that cultures differ in their assessment of these values, misunderstandings can occur. Given that global constraints contribute to consistent performances across varying contexts, and can influence the establishment of stable and/or preferred interaction exchanges, the idea of the different restraining force of various interactive constraints can provide a useful framework for explaining intercultural misunderstandings.

NOTES

1. One of the distinguishing characteristics of collectivists is that they delineate sharply between ingroup and outgroup. For example, Triandis et al. (1988a) note that in collectivist cultures people share and show harmony within ingroups, but that the total society may be characterized by much disharmony and nonsharing. Therefore, concern for proper social relationships among collectivists is not universalistic, but mainly applies to ingroup members.

2. However, the emphasis on proper social relationships and their maintenance is geared toward the ingroup rather than indicating any abstract concern for a general collective body. Therefore, appropriate human relationships under Confucianism are not universalistic, but apply to a particular ingroup member.

3. Following Brown & Levinson (1978): *Act* is what is intended to be done by a verbal or nonverbal communication. A *speech act* is what is intended to be done by a verbal communication.

III

RESEARCH PERSPECTIVES

7

Methodological Issues in the Study of Intercultural Communication Competence

MYRON W. LUSTIG • BRIAN H. SPITZBERG •
• *San Diego State University*

The study of communication competence is both an old and a new endeavor on the social scientific landscape. The recorded scholarly concern with excellence in interpersonal relations dates back at least to the ancient Greeks (Spitzberg & Cupach, 1984). Its more scientific origins begin in the 1920s with the early investigations of social intelligence as a factor of general intelligence (e.g., Thorndike, 1920). Later, interpersonal communication competence came to be conceptualized as a basic ability underlying such characteristics as social maturity and intellectual capacity (Bradway, 1937; Doll, 1935), healthy family functioning (Foote & Cottrell, 1955), and social relations in general (Bochner & Kelly, 1974; Weinstein, 1969). Its origins appear to have been rooted in medical models of defect (Wine, 1981) and ability models of deficiency (Baldwin, 1958), but its more recent manifestations can be found in action-oriented models of information processing (Welford, 1980) and generative skills (Trower, 1982, 1983, 1984). Currently, there is a conceptual morass of models and perspectives toward competence in human relations (Spitzberg, 1989; Spitzberg & Cupach, 1984; Wiemann & Bradac, 1985). It should come as little surprise, therefore, to discover a parallel fragmentation of methodologies and measurement approaches (Spitzberg, 1987, 1988; Spitzberg & Cupach, 1989). The various attempts to investigate interpersonal communication competence in intercultural and cross-cultural contexts have reflected this same trend.

Interpersonal competence can be defined as the quality with which interaction is, or can be, performed. The inherent subjectivity of competence becomes obvious when one chooses the referents for what constitutes quality in human interaction, as several metaphors have been used to define quality. For example, if competence is viewed as a synonym for *ability* (Foote & Cottrell, 1955), then a person does not have to manifest actual skilled performance, but only knowledge of or capacity for skilled performance (McCroskey, 1982). In contrast, if competence is viewed as synonymous with skill conceived as a repeatable goal-oriented sequence of actions (Argyle, 1981), then manifest behavior is the primary attribute that should be assessed. If competence is defined in terms of a *clarity* metaphor (or perspecuity, accuracy, understanding, coorientation, or uncertainty reduction; Powers & Lowry, 1984), then measurement generally will have to ascertain cognitive overlap between interlocutors. If competence is defined according to the communicative *effectiveness* (Parks, 1985), then either interactants' perceptions of goal-achievement or more objective task outcomes would need to be analyzed. Finally, if *appropriateness* is the primary conceptual metaphor (Hymes, 1972a), then the subjective impressions of social actors involved are likely to be the best candidates for assessment. The point is that one's underlying metaphors of communicative quality clearly should influence the selection of measurement schemas.

The selection of an underlying conceptual metaphor for communication competence is even more complicated when multiple cultures are the object of study. For example, the appropriateness metaphor may be much more subjectively salient to collectivist cultures than to individualistic cultures. The objectives of clarity and effectiveness may make more sense to low-context cultures than to high-context cultures. When it is realized that even these comparisons require gross overgeneralizations, the difficulties involved in selecting appropriate metaphors for measurement are formidable.

Most theorists seem to have accepted either implicitly or explicitly the importance of *appropriateness* and *effectiveness* in defining interpersonal competence. Appropriate interaction avoids the violation of extant valued rules or expectancies for a given context. Effective interaction functions to produce relatively valued outcomes or objectives.

Even when these criteria of appropriateness and effectiveness are not explicit in measures of competence, they are likely to be implicit. For example, if clarity is valued, then clear communication is part of an ideology of accuracy in which concise communication is assumed to be more appropriate and effective. If competence is equated with the manifestation of specific skills (e.g., disclosure, assertiveness), it is because these behaviors are presumed to lead to valued outcomes in a variety of social contexts. If subjects are responding, in a specific instance, to a series of items intended to assess their perceptions of the level of competence manifested by target individuals, they are likely to instantiate standards of evaluation based on their personal weighting of the competence criteria. Ultimately, therefore, competence is an evaluative judgment (Pavitt & Haight, 1985; Spitzberg & Cupach, 1984). If a given behavior can be competent in one context and incompetent in another, then competence cannot inhere in the behavior itself but is instead a function of social evaluation and context (Spitzberg, 1983).

If interpersonal competence is defined in terms of appropriateness and effectiveness, then it becomes incumbent upon researchers of intercultural communication to ascertain the salience of these criteria in the populations observed. Furthermore, given that some cultures may value one criterion more than another in any set of episode types, researchers may need to permit subjects to provide their own subjective weightings of these standards of competence.

All attempts to study intercultural communication competence will have to address certain *topoi* of decisions. These decisions concern *what* is assessed, *who* is assessed by *whom*, *when* competence is assessed, *where* competence is assessed, *why* competence is important to assess, and *with what effect* competence is assessed. Each of these topics will be discussed in the subsequent sections of this chapter. There is no choice in each of these decisions that is necessarily right or wrong. However, it is relatively easy to overlook the importance of these decisions, thereby jeopardizing methodological validity.

WHAT: THE CONTENT OF COMPETENCE RESEARCH

The question of what should be assessed has occupied a considerable proportion of research efforts. For example, Spitzberg and Cupach (1989) identified over 100 distinctly labeled constructs extracted from over 30 factor-analytic studies of interpersonal competence. However, the issue of what to assess runs much deeper than this. As Øyen (1990) has pointed out, comparisons across cultures are rarely without imperfections, largely because of the inherent difficulties in making such comparisons. Thus, careful attention to what should be assessed can usually reduce the likelihood that methodological imperfections will lead to distrust of the results. Deciding what to assess involves at least five issues: the level of abstraction, the equivalence of assessment procedures, the level of analysis, the type of comparison, and the content of the competence measures.

Level of Abstraction

The level of abstraction is concerned with whether to assess the competence of relatively microscopic interactional behaviors (e.g., eye gaze, question use, verbal-nonverbal synchrony), mezzoscopic behaviors (e.g., politeness rituals, assertiveness routines, speech acts), or macroscopic behaviors (e.g., patterns of self-disclosure, empathy level, conflict styles). These different levels reflect mapping rules in which the more molecular behaviors represent or are translated into meaningful patterns at the more molar levels (D'Andrade & Wish, 1985; Spitzberg, 1989; Wish, D'Andrade, & Goodnow, 1980). However, to date, such interconnections are relatively unexplored.

Assessment Equivalence

Some concepts are culture-specific. That is, a specific belief, value, attribute, or behavior may be used appropriately to refer to a particular culture, but there may be no comparable concept within other cultures of interest to the researcher. Such concepts are called *emic* (Hall, 1985; Pike, 1966), and the methods for assessing such emic concepts can only be used in and are only generalizable to the specific culture(s) within which the concept is relevant. Consequently, emic concepts are most useful for understanding single cultures and for developing procedures to observe and measure those cultures. For instance, the Greek concept of *philotimo* (Vassiliou & Vassiliou, 1973) and the social expectations about appropriate behaviors at a Japanese tea ceremony are examples of emic beliefs and behaviors.

Other concepts are more universally appropriate, as they deal with beliefs, values, attributes, or behaviors that are common to people across many varied cultures. Such concepts are called *etic* (Pike, 1966). Etic concepts are preferred if the research goals include either comparisons across cultures (cross-cultural) or comparisons among interactants who come from different cultures (intercultural). Only methods and procedures that are valid within the specific cultures of interest should be used to investigate etic concepts.

Ideally, of course, a standardized research protocol should be used for all experimental methods that are employed, such that the questionnaire items, social settings, experimental interventions, and observational procedures are all identical. Yet etic procedures, though desirable, are not common; rarer still are attempts to verify that the concepts and procedures actually employed are indeed etic. Because it is a difficult and laborious process to confirm that the research concepts and methods are etic, *pseudoetic* constructs or methods are frequently employed in published research. A pseudoetic concept or method is one in which an emic idea or procedure is developed in a specific culture—most often, in a Euroamerican culture—and is simply assumed to be etic and therefore universally generalizable to other cultures (Pepitone & Triandis, 1987; Triandis, 1972, 1983).

Many of the measurement issues that must be considered when conducting research on intercultural communication competence can be subsumed under the general rubric of assessment equivalence. Issues related to assessment equivalence address the kinds of problems that lead to incomparability among research samples because of differences in the interpretations of the stimulus materials used to gather information (Hui & Triandis, 1985).

Level of Analysis

The level of analysis is concerned with the units that are used for purposes of comparison. Research may compare individual, group (or relational context), or cultural levels, or any combination of these. For example, a group-level question might ask whether communication among friends is perceived as more competent than it is among strangers. An individuals-within-groups-by-culture question might ask if assertive subjects in organizational contexts are less competent negotiating in high-context cultures than they are when negotiating in low-context cultures. Each level of analysis will determine what statistical procedures are appropriate for conducting investigations and developing interpretations (Kenny, 1990; Kenny & La Voie, 1985). Table 7.1 provides a description and some examples of the types of research hypotheses that one might formulate given various combinations of individual-, group-, and cultural-level analyses. Table 7.1 also can be used as a heuristic device for helping to differentiate among these levels.

Type of Comparison

Decisions about the type of comparison focus on the unit of occurrence of the phenomenon being assessed (Lustig, 1991). Comparisons among particular attributes or behaviors might be made in four general ways. First, the *typicality* or mean amount of communication may differ across individuals, groups, or cultures. For instance, high-affiliative individuals may self-disclose more than low-affiliative individuals, friends may disclose more than acquaintances, and low-context cultures may value self-disclosure more than high-context cultures.

Second, the *variability* of certain forms of communication may differ across individuals, groups, or cultures. For instance, the variability in the disclosure patterns of Malaysians may be greater (more heterogeneous) than is the variability in the disclosure patterns of Thais. That is, though Thais and Malaysians may exhibit similar levels of self-disclosure

TABLE 7.1 Individual, Group, and Cultural Levels of Analysis

Analysis Type	*Examples (General & Specific)*
Individual (I)	Are I_1 individuals more likely to X than are I_2 individuals? High-affiliative individuals self-disclose more than low-affiliative individuals.
Group (G)	Are G_1 groups more likely to X than are G_2 groups? Friends self-disclose more than acquaintances.
Cultural (C)	Are C_1 cultures more likely to X than are C_2 cultures? Low-context cultures value self-disclosure more than high-context cultures.
I w/in G	Are I_1 individuals within G_1 groups more likely to X than I_1 individuals would typically X? Low-affiliative individuals within close friendships self-disclose more than low-affiliative individuals typically self-disclose.
I x G	Are I_1 individuals more likely to X in G_1 groups than in G_2 groups? High-affiliative individuals self-disclose more within close friendships than within acquaintanceships.
I w/in C	Are I_1 individuals within C_1 cultures more likely to X than I_1 individuals would typically X? High-affiliative individuals within low-context cultures self-disclose more than high-affiliative individuals typically self-disclose.
I x C	Are I_1 individuals more likely to X within C_1 cultures than within C_2 cultures? High-affiliative individuals self-disclose more within high-context cultures than within low-context cultures.
G w/in C	Are G_1 groups within C_1 cultures more likely to X than G_1 groups would typically X? Friends within low-context cultures disclose more than friends typically disclose.
I w/in G w/in C	Are I_1 individuals within G_1 groups and within C_1 cultures more likely to X than I_1 individuals would typically X? Low-affiliative individuals within close friendships who are from low-context cultures self-disclose more than low-affiliative individuals would typically self-disclose.
I w/in G x C	Are I_1 individuals within G_1 groups more likely to X within C_1 cultures than I_1 individuals within G_1 groups would typically X? High-affiliative individuals within close friendships are more likely to self-disclose within low-context cultures than high-affiliative individuals within close friendships typically self-disclose.
I x G w/in C	Are I_1 individuals more likely to X within G_1 groups that occur in C_1 cultures than I_1 individuals are likely to X within G_1 groups that occur within C_2 cultures? High-affiliative individuals are more likely to disclose within friendships that occur within low-context cultures than they are likely to disclose within friendships that occur within high-context cultures.
I x G x C	Are I_1 individuals in G_1 groups and C_1 cultures more likely to X than are I_1 individuals in G_1 groups and C_2 cultures? High-affiliative individuals who are close friends in low-context cultures are more likely to self-disclose than are high-affiliative individuals who are close friends in high-context cultures.

when interacting with acquaintances, the Thais may display a homogeneous pattern of disclosure such that most people self-disclose at a level that is similar to the cultural mean, whereas Malaysian individuals may behave with far more heterogeneity and variability, and therefore with less predictability, in their self-disclosing behaviors.

Third, the kinds of *associations* among variables may differ within individuals, groups, and cultures. Thus, communication competence and amount of self-disclosure may be positively correlated in a low-context culture such as the United States, negatively correlated in a high-context culture such as Japan, and uncorrelated in another culture.

Finally, the *pattern* or process of particular aspects of communication may differ at the individual, group, and cultural levels. For instance, the consequences of self-disclosure may typically evoke symmetrical or reciprocal self-disclosure among dyads from one culture and complementary or compensatory responses among dyads from a different culture. Alternatively, the relational trajectories in the development of friendships may vary as a function of other aspects of the culture, group, or individual psyches.

The four comparison types described above can be combined with the analysis levels depicted in Table 7.1 to provide a matrix of research issues. Although the examples in Table 7.1 refer to typicality issues, analogous examples could be identified for variability, associations, and processes.

Content Level

The final attribute of *what* is measured concerns behavioral content. Reviews of relevant literature (Chen, 1990; Dinges & Duffy, 1979; Imahori & Lanigan, 1989; Spitzberg & Cupach, 1984; Wiemann & Kelly, 1981) as well as empirical analyses (Abe & Wiseman, 1983; Collier, 1989; Cui, 1989; Gudykunst, Nishida, & Chua, 1987; Martin & Hammer, 1989; Olebe & Koester, 1989; Ruben & Kealey, 1979; Wiseman, Hammer, & Nishida, 1989) have attempted to identify the basic components of intercultural communication competence. Although various attempts have been made to integrate and synthesize the many constructs involved in intercultural relations (Fiske, 1991; Osgood, May, & Miron, 1975; Spitzberg, 1989), there still seems to be minimal consensus.

At the level of the individual, Spitzberg and Cupach (1984) and others (Imahori & Lanigan, 1989; Spitzberg, 1989; Spitzberg & Brunner, 1991) have argued that most constructs in the domain of interpersonal and intercultural communication competence can be integrated under the concepts of motivation, knowledge, and skills. That is, the more motivated, knowledgeable, and skilled a communicator is, the more competent the person is likely to be perceived as being. Motivation can include such constructs as values, anxiety, goals, and openness to experience. Knowledge involves such disparate constructs as self-monitoring, cognitive complexity, strategy repertoire, rule comprehension, familiarity, and language competence. Skills include all the various behavioral abilities such as disclosure, interaction management, expressiveness, language facility, and immediacy.

Other approaches might examine the *what* question by defining different types of competence according to the relational models predominant in the cultural milieu. For example, Fiske (1991) argued that all social relations, whether between individuals or nations, operate according to one of four basic relational structures: communal sharing, authority ranking, equality matching, and market pricing. These structures can be described in overly summary fashion by several characteristics. The motivation of parties is one of intimacy in communal sharing, power in authority ranking, equality in equality matching, and achievement in market pricing. Social identity is defined by group membership in communal sharing, as revered leader or loyal follower in authority ranking, as separate but co-equal peer in equality matching, and as occupation or economic role in market pricing. Although a gross oversimplification, such relational prototypes imply different criteria for assessing competence, depending on which structure is operating. For example, effectiveness is a more important criterion of competence in the authority ranking and market pricing models, appropriateness is more important to the communal sharing model, and reciprocity or homophily would be more important to the equality matching model.

The content of competence measures depends on the conceptual criteria selected as relevant, either by the researcher or the subjects of research. These criteria may then be analyzed in terms of their level of abstraction, the equivalence of assessment procedures, the level of analysis, the type of comparison, and the content of the competence measures. Inattention to such distinctions makes comparisons of competence findings across research traditions highly problematic.

WHO: THE LOCUS OF COMPETENCE EVALUATION

A complicating issue in the study of intercultural communication competence is one of determining whom to observe to obtain the information needed to make the desired comparisons. Extensive research suggests that actor, coactor, and uninvolved observers perceive the interactional world from widely divergent perspectives (Adams-Webber, 1985; Kuiper & Rogers, 1979; O'Connor & Day, 1989; Sandelands & Calder, 1984; Watson, 1982). Even well-acquainted couples appear to share only approximately 50% common perception of their behavior (Christensen, Sullaway, & King, 1983; Jacobson & Moore, 1981; Robinson & Price, 1980). It appears that self, other, and observer simply decode and use observed behavior differently (for reviews, see Spitzberg, 1987; Wilson & Stone, 1985). The question is less who is right, and more which perspective provides the most useful information.

Some populations may be in the best position to report on their own competence. When competence is conceived in terms of goal achievement, personal fulfillment, and self-actualization, the actor may be the only judge who can report on relevant psychological data. In contrast, when appropriateness, normality, and propriety of behavior are important, such impressions are most legitimately made by observers or recipients of the behavior being judged. Furthermore, some populations are studied *because* of their presumed lack of competence (e.g., children, recent immigrants, mentally disturbed), in which case self-perceptions are likely to be biased by virtue of the distorted information processing of the subjects.

The apparent solution to the problems of interpersonal disparity in competence impressions is to collect perceptual data from actor, coactor, and observer(s). Aside from the resource intensiveness and potential reactivity problems with using observers, there is still no calculus for combining such perceptions, or for determining the meaning of disparities when they are found.

Ultimately, the researcher should make an argument for the legitimacy of any given *perceptual locus*. This may be based upon the public availability of the behavioral or psychological data referenced in evaluating competence. Strictly private or psychological information (e.g., past experiences, affective states, goals) requires self-report methods. More public, discrete, and behavioral information permits ratings from many perceptual perspectives, as well as with more objective techniques (e.g., coding recorded behavior). A further qualification requires that evaluations of competence be provided by minimally socially competent persons. Inaccuracy of social perceptions is often a hallmark of incompetence itself, thereby constraining the validity of ratings made by incompetent interactants.

Research on intercultural communication competence requires the selection of subject samples from whom data are obtained. Ideally, such samples are selected so as to insure that they are similar to the larger population they represent, and therefore valid inferences about that larger population can be made. Researcher claims of representativeness, and research designs to assess results obtained from samples alleged to be comparable, require that two features be fulfilled. First, the samples must be selected such that each member of the population has an equal chance of being included (random selection). Second, the subjects so selected must be assigned randomly to the various levels of the experimental conditions on which observations are intended (random assignment). In practice, neither of these requirements can usually be fulfilled completely.

The selection of a truly random and therefore representative sample of subjects from a given population presumes some current and accurate list of all population members, along with the means to contact them. More commonly, constraints of time, budget, and subject availability require that convenience samples of accessible subjects must be used. Similarly, the random assignment of subjects to experimental conditions is often precluded by insurmountable constraints. When culture is the independent variable of interest, random assignment is, in effect, impossible. One's culture, like one's family, is a fixed rather than a random effect.

Problems caused by the absence of a randomized selection process can never be removed completely, though they can often be overcome to a degree sufficient for accomplishing the research objectives. The principal way to accommodate such samples is to provide sufficient details about both the experimental procedures that were used to obtain the subjects and the relevant details or characteristics of the subjects that were ultimately selected. Such information may allow others to recognize the limits of the postulated results and might suggest plausible rival hypotheses that could be posed as alternative interpretations (Lonner & Berry, 1986).

Problems caused by the absence of procedures to randomly assign subjects to experimental conditions can also be overcome to a limited degree. As suggested earlier, such problems are particularly noticeable when researchers wish to make comparisons involving people from two or more cultures. Because individuals can not be randomly assigned to culture-of-origin, biases of self-selection always exist in cross-cultural and intercultural comparisons. All individuals from a given culture bring with them a host of characteristics that exist in addition to but inseparable from their culture. Samples of subjects from two or more cultures may therefore differ from one another in an infinite number of ways, including their ages, educational levels, incomes, occupations, prior experiences, physical attributes, living arrangements, proximity to mountains, diet, degree of left-handedness, and a plethora of others.

Fortunately, many of the unwanted but plausible alternative explanations that exist because of the inability to use procedures that randomly select or assign subjects to experimental conditions can be mitigated or eliminated as a viable threat to the validity of the knowledge claims that one wishes to make. Such experimental controls, even when not obtained through the use of randomization procedures for subject selection, can often occur statistically in research designs that measure, and ultimately control or test for, the plausible alternatives of interest. Thus, for instance, if a researcher believes that some outcome of interest may be related to subjects' age or the strength with which a particular cultural value is held, those plausible alternatives can be measured directly and controlled statistically. Alternatively, it would be naive for a researcher to assume that all members of a culture will differ in specified but unmeasured ways from all members of another culture, and therefore the obtained differences among the cultures on some outcome variable are attributable to those unmeasured causal forces. A more detailed discussion of these and related issues of measurement and interpretation are discussed in the sections to follow.

WHEN: TIME IN COMPETENCE ASSESSMENT

The issue of time enters into the assessment of competence at three levels. First, competence can be conceptualized as an *episodic* or *dispositional* phenomenon. Episodic competence is manifest in a particular encounter, episode, context, or discrete sequence of activity. Competence, in this instance, requires measurement that is sensitive to the vicissitudes of the particular episode. The obvious advantage of episodic assessment is that it permits the evaluators the luxury of inferences that are closer in time to the actual behaviors and experiences being judged. Further, questions regarding cross-situational consistency virtually require episodic-level measurements to examine the extent of behavioral variability. However, these advantages may be outweighed by the drawback that results from episodic studies may not permit generalizations beyond the episodes actually observed, which may make their scientific value unknown.

Other views of competence are dispositional in nature. If competence is viewed as a cross-situational trait, then measures can collapse time and place to provide a summary indicator of a person's competence. Although traitlike conceptions and operationalizations of competence are quite common (Spitzberg & Cupach, 1989), traits in general have revealed rather questionable relationships to actual abilities and performances

(Andersen, 1987; Argyle & Little, 1972; Cupach & Spitzberg, 1983). Further, viewing competence as a trait runs into difficulties when the defining characteristic of competence is adaptation. If competence presumes adaptation, and adaptation requires change, then competence is unlikely to be revealed by cross-situational consistencies of behavior or even by behavioral tendencies.

A second time issue involves a related concern of *cross-sectional* versus *longitudinal* research design. If competence is indeed manifest in relational forms (Gottman, 1979; Imahori & Lanigan, 1989; Spitzberg & Hecht, 1984), then longitudinal research designs may be required to uncover the dynamics by which such competence evolves over time as relationships develop. For instance, studies of sojourner adjustment seem to require longitudinal designs to examine the ways in which individuals adapt over time to the constraints of a foreign setting. In contrast, if the research question concerns issues about how competently people respond to particular situations, or issues about the degree of competence of a group of people in a normative sense, then cross-sectional designs are more appropriate.

A third and related issue of time involves *short-term* versus *long-term* perspectives toward competence. Research indicates that people's perceptions and evaluations of their own and others' behavior change over time (Croxton, Eddy, & Morrow, 1984; Moore, Sherrod, Liu, & Underwood, 1979; Wyer & Bodenhausen, 1985). If asked to evaluate an episode just elapsed, a person is likely to present significantly different impressions than if asked about the same episode weeks later. For example, people's impressions of past encounters may become increasingly negative over time (Spitzberg, 1987), or conflict encounters that begin with initially unfavorable impressions may soften over time. Furthermore, behaviors and episodes often become reframed by later events. Initially awkward interactions may become the stuff of future bonding and a resource for humor and ritual. If assessed contemporaneously, research would reveal relatively incompetent encounters, which become redefined into the corpus of competent interaction by the actors over time.

A similar but more esoteric issue arises in assessing effectiveness in interpersonal relations. The concept of losing the battle in order to win the war may have parallels in competence. Thus, an actor may strategically play the fool in early encounters so as to boost the self-perceived competence and superiority of the coactor. Politeness phenomena may be perceived as competent in part because the coactor's status is elevated relative to that of the actor, and this short-term diminution of the actor's status may permit longer-term success in the relationship.

Unless the long-term view is taken, such chronemic features are lost in time-bound assessments.

WHERE: THE ROLE OF CONTEXT IN COMPETENCE RESEARCH

One of the most axiomatic claims of the competence literature is that competence is contextual. However, the corollaries implied by this assumption are not entirely understood. For example, some might claim that because what constitutes competence varies according to context, different concepts and measures of competence are required for each primary context. Such reasoning has led to measures of organizational competence, heterosocial competence, marital competence, assertion competence, intercultural competence, and so forth. This list further suggests problems with the assumption that competence is contextual: The concept of context is itself underspecified.

Another school of thought argues that if competence is contextual, research must "account for how interactants account" for context. Specifically, if contexts are viewed as intersections of physical setting, actor purposes, cultural milieu, and relational definition (Spitzberg & Brunner, 1991; Spitzberg & Cupach, 1984), then theory and research should be sensitive to these features. Ultimately, all interactants must cope with these contextual features if they are to engage in an episode of interaction successfully. Researchers can choose to manipulate some of these features, hold them constant, or assess how the actors perceptually construct these features. However, it is clear that these features significantly affect impressions of competence (Spitzberg & Brunner, 1991) and adaptation (Argyle, Furnham, & Graham, 1981; D'Andrade & Wish, 1985; Wish et al., 1980). The danger is in assuming that these contextual features are held constant when they are not. For example, combining representatives of multiple cultural backgrounds and assuming that they are equally different from a comparison group, or combining them to examine the factor structure of intercultural competence, merely washes out important contextual differences rather than operationalizing them.

WHY: THE RELEVANCE OF COMPETENCE RESEARCH

The *why* decision concerns an issue that surprisingly has gone virtually unexamined. The question is whether or not competence is a relevant evaluative concern in a culture. Although culture is a product of interpersonal interaction, there are conceivable instances in which the evaluation of competence may be relatively insignificant within a culture. If the interactional requirements of a culture or context are relatively restricted, then the variance of competence in that culture may be relatively small, and its assessment will likely reveal few insights. Alternatively, in a culture that views the surface behavior of persons as irrelevant to the worth or evaluation of the person, competence may take on substantially different meanings and values. Colson (1967) described an instance of a culture in which technical requirements of competence evolved over a period of time because of social and political change. It is not a long stretch to assume that cultural and social evolution alters standards of competence as well (Nicolson, 1956; Wine, 1981). Such changes may occasionally diminish or inflate the actual relevance and importance of the very concept of competence itself. To date, there seems to be virtually no available research on the relevance and cross-cultural importance of competence qua competence. Consequently, researchers need to address why competence is considered important to a given culture or cultures.

WITH WHAT EFFECT: ETHICAL ISSUES

Communication researchers who would investigate competence phenomena in other cultures are always faced with a difficult set of ethical choices. Primary among these is in locating oneself comfortably on a continuum that stretches between moral absolutism and moral relativism. Moral absolutism—a stance that asserts that a single prescriptive set of beliefs, values, norms, and behaviors are, or ought to be, universally held—is clearly untenable. Indeed, the research purposes themselves often are predicated on the assumption that there will likely be systematic differences among cultures in the cognitions, affective states, and behavioral indicants of communication competence. Alternatively, however, a stance asserting moral relativism, and therefore a tendency toward nonjudgmental acceptance of all possible beliefs and behaviors, creates problems in attempting to accommodate incommensurable worldviews.

The limits of cultural relativism are often confronted when some belief or behavior in another culture directly violates a fundamental ethical principle that is central to the researcher's personal code of moral integrity. Such a limit might be reached, for instance, when a researcher must contend with differences in the importance or sacredness of human life. Fortunately, though, problems of such an extreme magnitude are uncommon in research on intercultural communication competence. A more likely challenge to one's morally relativistic stance could occur because the customs and expectations within the cultures of interest might inordinately constrain the potential researcher solely on the basis of her or his gender, age, ethnicity, religion, or other personal attributes.

Another set of ethical issues that face researchers of intercultural communication competence involves decisions about the relationship of the researchers to the research subjects. All research has the potential to harm, either physically or emotionally, those from whom information is gathered. For instance, in the social-scientific equivalent of the Heisenberg principle, the mere act of inquiring about people's perceptions of their close interpersonal relationships may sometimes change those relationships in undesirable ways. Similarly, though deception in communication research is always an issue of concern (Littlejohn, 1991), it may become even more problematic when cultural boundaries are crossed. A related ethical issue is one of obtaining informed consent, as subjects may have little understanding of the premises and presumptions that guide the research endeavors.

A further set of ethical issues that face intercultural communication researchers involves decisions about the relationship of the researchers to host-culture colleagues and collaborators. By their very participation, some of these collaborators may be placing themselves at risk. Alternatively, the collaborators may provide access to particular cultures with little recognition or reward for their efforts, and often with little or no input into the goals and objectives that guide the research efforts.

CONCLUDING REMARKS

We have attempted to touch on a variety of methodological issues that researchers must confront when they attempt to study intercultural communication competence. Following an initial analysis of definitional concerns about how intercultural communication competence is conceptualized, our focus has been on the *topoi* of decisions concerning what, who, when, where, why, and with what effect intercultural communication competence is assessed. Though the problems and obstacles in conducting research on intercultural communication competence are formidable, the potential rewards of such research are also enormously gratifying.

8

Competence as Cultural Pragmatics

Reflections on Some Soviet and American Encounters

DONAL CARBAUGH • *University of Massachusetts, Amherst*

Several years ago I had occasion to discuss dimensions of communicative conduct with a multicultural group, including people from Portugal, England, Korea, the United States, and the Soviet Union. During the discussion, I found this group was particularly interested in the increasing "privatization" of American public life, as when personal matters such as sexual practices, marital problems, family life, relationships with relatives and neighbors, and so on became themes and warrants for public discussions. We explored together what Richard Sennett called in the title of his book *The Fall of Public Man*, and the associated rise of "the intimate society." The description of American society as such seemed to strike a chord of accuracy to many in this group, at least as a general characterization of some prominent American scenes, but it also was no less perplexing and puzzling to them, especially to those whose public conduct, elsewhere, ran sharply counter to this apparent, recent American trend.

After our discussion, I returned to my office to find a Soviet member of the above group waiting for me.[1] I invited him in, and we continued discussion of public and private communication, cultural configurations of each, and the various ways these are invoked in social interaction. Following his lead, we spent a good deal of time characterizing the Soviet expressive system, and its clear distinction between public and private life. Then, it seems, it was my turn. I was challenged to justify and defend all of this "parade of personalness" in American public life. Before I could describe what I took to be some features of this trend, he gestured to pictures of my wife and children rather hidden behind some books and papers and said: "Why make your family pictures available?

You devaluate your family and experiences and memories by doing this." As I began mumbling something about family ties, kin, individualism, and American culture, my Soviet interlocutor, apparently unsatisfied with my explanation, asserted another, closer to his home: "We don't discuss [or display] our personal experiences whatever they are [in public], love, sex, relations with God. We cannot express these in words. You make it shallow if you speak it in public." His pronoun, *you*, in this last sentence (note the switch from the earlier *we*), upon reflection, served ambiguously as a description of life among his Russian contemporaries, and as an accusation of life so lived among Americans, including my own display of intimacies in public.

This rather routine episode introduces a kind of intercultural contact that is central to this essay, the everyday contact among people who use different culturally shaped systems of communication. Exploring this kind of everyday contact between people from different speech communities is important. As many readers can attest, moments such as these are occurring with greater regularity and among more of us. Such moments span a variety of settings from organizational to educational to legal, and require a kind of practical competence, an ability to at least reflect upon our own cultural ways, and be able to identify and perhaps even momentarily shift cultural frames of reference within ongoing, everyday social interactions. Creating this general kind of intercultural competence requires another more particular knowledge. We need a better understanding of specific, culturally based patterns of communication. For example, we know very little about Soviet patterns of communication, surprisingly little about middle American patterns of communication, and even less about the dynamics involved when one contacts the other. Our empirical literature on specific sociocultural fields of communication competence, and the resulting dynamics in intercultural contacts—with regard both to Soviet-American interactions—is extremely lacking. And further, if we turn to some of the prominent studies we do have of communicative competence, as important as they are, we find little assistance, for they tend to generalize on the bases of abstractions, rather than to particularize on the bases of sociocultural patterns. How has this come to be?

TWO VIEWS OF GENERAL COMPETENCIES, AND ONE GENERAL VIEW WITH PARTICULAR INTERESTS

One view of competence is indebted to the work of Noam Chomsky (1965). Chomsky's starting points are the limited grammatical properties of any one language and the human ability to create unlimited, grammatically correct sentences within a language. Competence, from this standpoint, means that one has mastered an abstract rule system (with one's biologically given language organ), which enables the production and interpretation of an infinite number of sentences, including some that have not been previously produced. It means further that the standard speaker has acquired the ability to discriminate between sentences that are grammatically correct or sensible, and others that are incorrect or nonsensible. On these bases, the competent production of linguistic sequences and sentences requires transformations of more underlying, deeper structures. Competence, as a *grammatical universal*, is grounded in a universal linguistic and biological apparatus, with specific and actual speech situations, interactional dynamics, and sociocultural fields being wholly elided.

In response to Chomsky's views, Habermas (1970a, 1970b, 1976) suggests alternate starting points. Rather than beginning with universal grammatical properties of language and human creativity, Habermas begins with universal validity claims for the existence of speech action, and the attendant universal domains or dimensions of the world that these claims foreground. Claims about reality, self, and society are presupposed for the existence of, and addressed in the expression of, any speech action. Dimensions of communicative action that are predicated on such claims are its comprehensibility, appropriateness, truthfulness, and sincerity. Realization of such claims in dialogue, and adjudicating counterclaims through means of the dimensions, provides for "idealized features of speech situations in general" (1970b, p. 367), or the "ideal speech situation." Communicative competence, then, means "the mastery of the [abstract] means of construction necessary for the establishment of an ideal speech situation" (1970b, p. 372), something we do not typically realize but can only anticipate. Competence becomes a *universal pragmatics* that hovers over actual speech situations, an ideal standard or abstract system of rationality that is presumed by the ideal speaker, and through which communicative actions are somehow produced, with systematic distortions recognized and critiqued (cf., Huspek, 1991).

Some of the parallels between Chomsky's and Habermas's theories of competence are notable. Each posits a universal standard from which communication is viewed, these being abstractions of a linguistic (grammatical) and universal (pragmatic) type; each locates the site of explanation outside of social interaction, within either an innate language organ (Chomsky) or a species-wide system of claims and dimensions (Habermas); each suggests a view of competence that is situated in a presumably abstract, aseptic, out-of-this-world environment; each relegates actual, situated, concrete communicative action into a contaminated order of errors (Chomsky, 1965), or a corrupted order of distortions (Habermas, 1970b); and each ignores (Chomsky) or gives minimal attention to (Habermas) the meaningfulness of communication to those who create it, the various means by which those people actually conduct and evaluate their communicative lives, and the cultural bases guiding communicative action such as the intercultural encounter that began this essay.

As a response especially to Chomsky, Dell Hymes (1979) proposed yet a third set of starting points for the study of communicative competence. Hymes suggested starting with grammatical knowledge (as does Chomsky) and tacit societal knowledge of communication conduct (similar to Habermas's dimensions of intelligibility and appropriateness), but moreover focusing on ability for use of specific communication patterns in actual scenes of ongoing social interaction. Rather than view competence in the abstract, Hymes takes concrete communicative action in its sociocultural context to be the basic datum of concern, the rendering of it from the vantage point of those who produce it, to be—at least in part—a basic theoretical concern. Hymes (1979) elaborates four "sectors of competence" that operationalize competence in concrete scenes of communication: "(1) whether (and to what degree) something is formally *possible*; (2) whether (and to what degree) something is *feasible* in virtue of the means of communication available; (3) whether (and to what degree) something is *appropriate* (adequate, happy, successful) in relation to a context in which it is used and evaluated; and (4) whether (and to what degree) something is in fact done, actually *performed*, and what its doing entails" (p. 281; italics in original). Each sector can be applied at the level of an individual in a context (e.g., whether possible, feasible), at the level of a specific interaction or interactional routine (e.g., what it makes possible, feasible), or at the level of a communication system. Hymes (1972) proposed an analytic vocabulary that is designed to produce such studies, what he calls "ethnographies of communication," and several such studies have been produced (Bauman & Sherzer, 1989; Carbaugh, 1990a; Gumperz & Hymes, 1972; Philipsen & Carbaugh, 1986). Foregrounded in such studies are *concrete social interactions*, in which "the systemically possible, the feasible, and the appropriate are linked to produce and interpret actually occurring cultural behavior" (Hymes, 1979, p. 286).

Returning for a moment to the example of the Soviet student in my office, I can briefly sketch how each view of competence might operate. First, by viewing this speech situation from the vantage point of grammatical universals, one could explore the general cognitive knowledge necessary to perform transformations of an abstract rule system into linguistic structures and sentences. Attention would be drawn to the ideal, innately derived grammatical competence exhibited by each individual speaker, with each sentence being further evidence of this human ability. Speakers, the Soviet male and myself, would be treated alike, as evidence of innate grammatical abilities. Viewing the speech situation from the vantage point of universal pragmatics would yield a sense in which the presupposed validity claims of our world norms differ with various dimensions of communication, especially those of comprehensibility and appropriateness providing possible sources of confusion as well as possible remedies for possible misunderstandings. What one has, then, with Habermas, are universal *topoi* for the identification of presuppositional slips, and the suggestion of abstract dimensions along which trouble might be diagnosed in some *possible* world, but no general elaborated conceptual system through which to discover the *actual* patterns of communicative action in context. What norms animate communicative action here?

Viewing our opening exchange as socially produced, culturally shaped communicative conduct, as Hymes suggests, yields a view of competence based less on universal grammatical knowledge, or species-wide ability, as crucial to our understanding as these are, and more on the communicative "means and meanings"—as Hymes puts it—of people in, and of, a place. Is it feasible and appropriate, even possible from the standpoint of Soviet life, to produce public communication about personal matters? If not, what other communicative patterns are in its place? What public means of communication are available? What meanings are associated with these? And likewise, what means and meanings are associated with an American pattern of public-personalness? By probing actual communication patterns that are used within social contexts, and treating them as of cultural systems, we uncover, or render, not just human grammatical abilities, or species-wide universal capacities, but sociocultural assessments, the communicative means and meanings that people use in their actual, natural environments—a grounding of competence in what I will call *cultural pragmatics*.

TWO INTERCULTURAL EPISODES AND THE SHIFTING GROUNDS OF COMPETENCE

Several definitions of communication competence revolve around the central criteria of effectiveness and appropriateness, or the relationship between communicative practices and the practical and moral context(s) they implicate (Spitzberg & Cupach, 1989; Wiemann & Backlund, 1980). However, what constitutes effectiveness and appropriateness is a complex matter, including not only the doing of proper things properly but also, as any thief knows, the doing of improper things properly, and further, as any Burundi—among others—knows, there are times and occasions when one ought to exhibit incompetence to artfully communicate to others the competence of being incompetent (Albert, 1972). With each such situated assessment, competence gets configured culturally, through local symbols, symbolic forms, and their meanings. One of the main objectives of ethnography of communication research is to describe and interpret these cultural configurations of competence, to identify the various features and dimensions of competent communicative performance as it gets done in local symbolizing contexts (Briggs, 1988). Ethnographic studies explore competence in performance by beginning typically with the creation of communicative texts in contexts, searching the nature and use of verbal means and meanings in social life, and exploring, for example, how the use of specific verbal genres or symbolic forms accomplishes various cultural meanings within these ongoing events and scenes.

Starting with this conceptual orientation, let me briefly explore two further episodes of Soviets and Americans interacting in an effort to track shifts between these two cultural configurations of competence. After this exploration, I will discuss the investigative procedure, erected on Hymesian foundations, that is used to analyze these episodes. The empirical demonstration and methodological discussion show how one can theorize about competence on the basis of actual intercultural encounters. In turn, I hope it suggests ways to interrogate one's own practices while in such encounters. This attention to theorizing on the basis of actual interactional practices, to the methodological concerns in such study, and the continuing commitment to exploring locally distinctive patterns of communication in contexts, as well as a critical examination of their use, makes this an exercise in the cultural pragmatics of competence.[2]

Soviet-American Episode 1: Public Speech

The 1991 Miss Universe contest, hosted by the popular American media figure Dick Clark, was shown on American television in the summer of 1991. The field of contestants had been narrowed to the final three, Miss Netherlands, Miss Mexico, and Miss USSR. As is typical in such events, the final stage of judging involved an evaluation of how each contestant responded to the "same" question, while the others were secluded in a soundproof booth. The question this year as posed by Clark was: "What are the main problems confronting your country and what should be done about them?" Both Miss Netherlands and Miss Mexico responded without pause by describing some prominent problems in their countries, and sketched some general solutions to them. Miss USSR, however, was left literally speechless. Feigning the question as inaudible, she asked that it be repeated. Upon hearing it again, she replied with a brief utterance and what appeared to be extreme embarrassment, "They're all over now" (giggle).

Most American viewers whom I interviewed about this exchange interpreted her reply, or lack of a reply, in individual terms, as an unfortunate slip in her poise or personality. After all, one should be able to speak in public—with talk about problems being the hallmark of many prominent American scenes (Carbaugh, 1988, pp. 127-142). If one is asked to produce such talk, and does not, several inferences may be forthcoming. Perhaps, as some American viewers suggested, the Soviet woman simply lost her composure and couldn't gather her thoughts in order to be responsive; or perhaps she was being disingenuous, or maybe was being silenced by some hidden force (such as the government).

Soviet responses, however, suggest deeper forces at work in this public communication event. From the vantage point of a Soviet expressive order, when one is in public, and especially in the presence of outsiders, there is a strong moral (and in the recent past, governmental) imperative that one ought not speak about problems; one should espouse the virtues that are the bases of social life. Further, these should be predicated to a collective agent, and presented as exercised patterns of behavior, "such as occur in the Motherland"—as Soviets have put it (Smith, 1976, p. 21). So, to ask Miss USSR about "the main problems confronting [her] country and what should be done about them," was to create an agonizing public exigence for Miss USSR.

Miss USSR could have addressed the question or not. If she talked about the problems, she would perhaps exude competence to the pageant judges (and American, Western audiences) and enhance her standing with them, but she also would risk accusations of incompetence, perhaps even betrayal, by those in her motherland. If she did not speak about problems, she would fail to address the question, thus lose standing within the pageant, but she would uphold the expressive system of her homeland. Each of these two possible and feasible public speeches, with the inherent counterforces of patriot and pageant, was clearly suboptimal for at least some crucial part of her audience. Against these dynamics, her eventual utterance appears rather artful, for she indeed addressed the topic, if hesitantly, and did so in order to dismiss it, "They're [the problems] all over now." In an utterance, she ably straddled two cultural audiences. But such verbal artistry apparently failed to impress the pageant judges, since Miss USSR, on the basis of this interview, was ranked third of the final three contestants.

Cultural characters, such as Miss USSR and Dick Clark, find their interactional footing with distinctive and cultural frames of reference, including at times different assessments of what is proper (and improper) for public speaking. The question posed by Dick Clark, then, is not really the "same" one at all for these contestants, for it holds fundamentally different meanings in their cultural communication systems. Apparently its form resonated with two countries' representatives (Netherlands and Mexico), who ably addressed the objective facts of the matter, but the third (USSR), whose natural discursive desires foregrounded the moral and ideal, was left without a place, or in the last place. And thus different standards of appropriateness, of competence, are invoked within a multicultural event, with the one being used as the standard of final judgment.

Soviet-American Episode 2: Sex Talk

In February of 1987, the popular American television program *Donahue* broadcast five hours of programming from the Soviet Union. Each show involved Soviet citizens in conversations with at least one American, Phil Donahue, the American host and moderator of the program. During the first two minutes of the second show, Donahue initiated a discussion about, as he put it, "sex." He asked:

DONAHUE: Did you use a contraceptive when you practiced [audience laughter] sex at age 18?
SOVIET MALE: Yes.
DONAHUE: Did you take care of this matter yourself or did the girl insist that you do it?
SOVIET MALE: Yeah, I knew about it before.
Before that I knew quite a bit.
[Pan to audience laughter, smiles]
I knew how, when, what, etc. I was well prepared.
DONAHUE: Are most Soviet boys conscientious, like you, in protecting the girl from pregnancy?
SOVIET MALE: Basically, yes. Why don't you ask the others?
[Pan to audience smiles]

On viewing this segment in my office, a female Russian viewer concluded: "They are talking about two completely different things." She asked of me, "When you say 'use a contraceptive' what do you think of? Health issues, right?" I agreed. She went on to discuss the American preoccupation with physiology and rationality, eventually saying Americans are "puritan," "unlike many Europeans," in that they "keep emotions to themselves." She went on, "They [Americans] talk about sex but they talk about sex, as like, well, it's very, very mechanical. 'This goes here, that goes there.' [laughing] I mean, in biology [class], when you talk like reproductive system, I just laugh at the way they do it. Well, 'this goes here and the temperature is (.)' It's like, yep, then the computer turns on." In fact, she added laughingly, "He doesn't 'come,' or have an orgasm, no, he ejaculates!"

Our Soviet viewer draws attention to two different cultural vocabularies that are invoked to talk about and listen to a topic of discussion. An American produces terms such as "sex," "use a contraceptive," "practiced sex"; locates responsibility for contraceptive use on an individual boy or girl; and discusses protection . . . from pregnancy. From the standpoint of our Soviet viewers, this all sounds rather odd and funny. Why is this topic even being discussed here in public, and done with terms of physiology (e.g., pregnancy), a tone of scientific rationality (e.g., sex can cause pregnancy/disease; contraceptives can prevent the same), or technical mechanisms (e.g., who brought the condom, and who was responsible for putting it on)?

The implication the Russian viewer invites the American to draw is that another vocabulary grounds Soviet utterances and interpretations about sex. First, she pointed out that talk on this topic, although feasible, is not really appropriate for public contexts. The topic is inappropriate to Soviets for at least two reasons: It brings private, intimate matters into a public place; and it suggests problems rather than virtues. However, if the topic is addressed (preferably in more intimate, private contexts), its primary terminological base would not include sex and contraception, but rather feelings, passion, and marriage. As she put it, sex brings up "a propriety issue." In so many words, she described how the topic, as discussed by Americans, is mechanical and without human sensuousness and passions. As such, it lacks what Russians call *dusa* (soul), and is heard as rather funny, even inhuman, for it—sex—is something animals can do. This is hardly, so Russians believe, the way to structure the topic for discussion (Wierzbicka, 1989). If discussed, it should include the proper emotional, passionate tone, and the interconnectedness of humans within a properly affected domain (e.g., marriage). But discussing this topic, even in these terms, in this relational domain, would also constitute a breach from the standpoint of the Soviet expressive order. For such topics, those that are deeply intimate and passionate, should be reserved for private rather than public, especially those being televised for outsiders. Needless to say, from this Soviet vantage point, Donahue's comments exuded not competence, but were bewildering and laughable, as indicated in the transcript above (Carbaugh, in press).

CULTURAL PRAGMATICS AND HEARING DIFFERENCE

The episodes described above involve particular, situated communication events in which at least two standards of competence, two culturally configured systems of symbolic action, are being creatively used. For Soviets, public contexts support sayings of individually and collectively exercised patterns, which are distinguished from others more intimate and private. For Americans, one senses a prominent freedom to say whatever one wants whether in public or not. With regard to public discourse, especially with outsiders, when a topic is introduced, Soviet speech motivates not just individual experiences but positive themes of shared virtues, the valued and connected fabric of the collective life. For Americans, after topics are introduced, they are often problematized, precipitating individual disclosures with great amounts of talk given to identifying and publicizing the flaws—rather than the virtues—of society. Considering the topic of sex, Soviets find such matters more appropriate to private rather than public discussion, and if discussed, prefer that it be done in terms of distinctively human passion, sensuousness, and within the proper relational domain of marriage, rather than in rational, analytic, biological terms, or within an individual domain (e.g., focusing on experiences of *one* who had sex or was responsible for contraceptive use).

The study of such intercultural episodes and the social patterning of them hopefully demonstrates some ingredients in an ethnographic view of communication competence. What is demonstrated is the utility of exploring what is possible, feasible, appropriate, and indeed performed as communication in contexts. Discovering in such routine intercultural scenes the cultural colorings of interactions, and being able to hear each as shaped by local systems of symbols, symbolic forms, and their meanings, is a main objective of ethnographic study. Through such study, it is hoped a better understanding will be created of the different cultural ways of speaking that are used on such occasions. This suggests a view of competence focusing on actual communication in contexts and explores its shapes as possibly cultural. It examines not only the means of communication that are used but also others that are feasible, possible, and appropriate, as well as the meanings implicated. This view also invites particular attitudes regarding intercultural competence. Brought to such encounters would be a willingness to learn and an eventual ability to hear, when relevant, different communicative acts and events with each being culturally situated in its own system, of its own form, with its own symbolic meanings. Such a hearing loads locally produced communicative means and sequences with their own communal *motives* and meanings. Note the dramatically different motives that are culturally compelling actors to so act and, in turn, the dramatically different ends toward which each is directed. In short, the concept of competence, especially when applied to intercultural encounters, requires attention to the means and meanings of communication, with a hefty part of the meaning being the actors' motives, and the interactional goals being sought.

Why would one fail to address a "simple" question, or balk at factual discussion of sex? One response would sketch the communal motives involved, that is, the felt need for doing such symbolic action in the first place and the end-in-view while the cultural *person* so speaks. Alternate communal motives run across each episode discussed above (one set for Soviets and another for middle Americans). Each can be summarized with its own cultural imperatives, formulated here as a Soviet motivational exigence (rather than a middle American one): Express soul (rather than disclose self). What is being presumed as a motive and targeted as a goal with each Soviet action is that one speaks in the proper spirit (as much as analytic reason), about virtues and morality (as much as problems and facts), with a connected and collective voice (as well as a personal and individual one). Culturally distinct motives and goals are being implicated in communicative actions with each presumed to exude some sector of competence. Hearing actions as possibly so colored, is to attempt to grasp from whence one and an other speaks. In this sense, hearing competence in communication involves knowing the actual means and their meanings that are available and used for symbolic expression, as well as the larger scene in which social action is done, including the culturally coded exigence(s) compelling actors to do what they do, to seek what they may, whether expressing soul, or disclosing self.

A Russian informant, bicultural and bilingual in Russian and American English, uttered the following words on hearing the second episode above: "They think they're talking about the same thing but they're not." Given the interpretations above, one is better equipped to hear what she meant, that is, to hear each as competent contributions, with each being formulated in response to different concerns and directed to different ends. The American is seeking factual disclosures of personal experiences in a serious and rational tone, while the Russian speaks morality with an eye to shared virtues and the properly personal, passionate, and transcendent tone that accompanies them. In short, the self-disclosive style of individual yet factual experiences meets the soulful expressive style of a socially exercised morality. Although the intercultural actors share a stage, it is as if together they are performing in different plays, with each artistic move of the one being read into the script of the other.

Each communication system (each cultural play) is being summarized here with special reference to the different beliefs about both the cultural person so communicated, and the communication such a person produces. With each such system of belief, however, the other can look or sound absolutely confusing or confused, if not downright wrong. From the standpoint of the Russian soul, the sounds of self ring of problems and are morally vacuous, overly analytical or rational, too intensely individual. From the standpoint of self, soul can sound moralistic, unreasonably passionate, fact-skirting, too transcendent. Each respective motive for acting, or end-in-view for action, can escape the other. Thus, culturally compelling motives for social action, the ends one has targeted, as well as the available means and their meanings guide competent communication, and need to be understood if we are to grasp some of the crosscurrents in such intercultural encounters (Scruton, 1979).

Yet, how does one unravel such a complex morass of cultural features in conversations? How does one identify in such encounters the various motives, means, and meanings of communication that construct these cultural configurations of competence? Note that the description of each episode above begins with *a focus on the principal activity getting done, and a framing of that activity as a culturally distinctive practice*, whether speaking in public, or talking about sex. So, for specific communicative actions, such as being rather unresponsive to a question and laughing during contraceptive conversation, a hearing is suggested beyond an individual's activity, or any one cultural standard—that is, as a slip of composure or taciturnity, all from an American frame of reference—and as something intercultural, as a single line caught within two cultural plays, a signaling that suggests shifts in the cultural grounds of discussion. Is this moment an interactional site of intercultural confusion? If so, in what cultural systems are these acts and events thus transpiring? What different cultural frames, what motives, means, and their meanings, if any, might be grounding the action? Within what distinctive systems of symbols, symbolic forms, and their meanings are these actions coherent, effective, and/or appropriate (Carbaugh, 1991)?

The framing and probes above suggest ways to elaborate these communicative actions as instances of cultural pragmatics. But how is this done? By generating data enabling one to describe and interpret the expressive orders distinctive to each cultural system. In this case, that involved describing several different symbols implicated in the intercultural communication, including the different cultural forms for such action, the different norms used to structure the interaction, and the dimensions of meanings relevant to each pattern (Carbaugh, 1990b). The analyses involve sustained attention to locally distinctive *systems of symbols, symbolic forms, and their meanings*. As examples, the interpretation suggests several areas of exploration. First, one must examine the *symbols used in the structuring of content*, including (a) contrastive forms of action and premises of meaning for the "same" symbolic frame, such as speaking in public; (b) contrastive symbols and their meanings, such as problems versus virtues, "self" versus "soul"; and (c) the domains of meanings associated with these, such as factual versus moral, or individual versus institutional (marital). Second, one views *symbolic forms* for communication, which consist of (a) particular sequences, such as topic initiation/shared virtues, or topic initiation/problems/responses; (b) different tones of discussion, such as serious and analytic versus passionate and playful; and (c) conversational rules or norms, such as what ought to be said, in which contexts, in what way, to whom, and so on. Third, *general dimensions of meanings* associated with these symbols and forms are analyzed, including what each cultural *persona* presumes as motives and goals for communication (i.e., express soul or disclose self), and the attendant beliefs about communication itself, whether activating morally transcendent expressions or personal disclosures. Dimensions of meanings also run within systems, such as Russian distinctions between public-private contexts of expression, outsider-insider audiences, taciturn-voluble levels of expressiveness, and the proper intensity of feeling attached to each, shallow to deep.

Hearing intercultural episodes as involving different cultural frames for action, different ways of structuring both content and interaction, different systems of symbols, their motives and meanings, is to hear different beliefs about persons and talk that are being coded into the pragmatics of intercultural conversations (Carbaugh, in press). Such is one ethnographic approach to communication competence in intercultural encounters.

This view of competence focuses attention on situated actions and sectors of action, as well as the communal motives, means, and meanings associated with each. Methodologically, an interpretive framework has grounded this view, an investigative procedure in which specific actions find their natural place within their cultural system of symbols, expressive forms, and their meanings. As a practical matter, the above suggests that one be willing to hear situated intercultural actions as involving perhaps cultural matters, and thus be better able to explore from whence other, and self, speaks.

Why, then, did the Soviet male tell me that displaying my family pictures in my office was a way of "devaluating" my private life? From a Soviet position, such display improperly brought private matters (such as sex and societal problems) into a public context, my office being a place, he presupposed, for conducting public affairs. The Soviet frame of publicness did not fit the symbolic content, private family matters, and even rendered such matters inappropriate in this context, since public communication is heard to be, relative to private, rather shallow in feeling. What should have been in its place? Perhaps in public, especially in educational contexts, symbolic images such as diplomas, certificates, professional pictures, or the like, which supported my role within the educational institution, would have sufficed. Not of course that one can or even should conform to cultural other's expectations, but to interact efficaciously with other, it helps to be able to reflect upon and react better to the shifting of cultural grounds in such interactions, so to move from naive evaluations from the vantage point of one, to a sense—if limited—that an Other has indeed spoken. In this case, from a Soviet's vantage point, my personal life had inappropriately spilled into a public context, and had been rendered rather shallow as a result. From mine, the display of an individual and personal world, dear to me, had been made a problem. And thus goes at least some Soviet and American encounters, where the corporate feeling of the individual and collective, built differently in public than in private, confronts the cross-contextual, individual, and personal view of the one.

As one is engaged in intercultural episodes such as these, it is helpful to attempt to hear not just an interaction gone haywire or—as many Americans so often infer—an unusual individual, but to sense the event as an encounter, as an instantiation of a deeper difference, a difference not just between individuals but between two cultural systems in action, two different ways for structuring communication competently. The more general orientation used above and some relevant studies are discussed in detail elsewhere (Carbaugh, 1990a; Carbaugh & Hastings, 1992), with the present essay displaying some of the possibilities in the approach. As in ethnographic approaches to communication generally, sustained attention is given to local systems of communication in order to discover what actual standards of competence ground such practices. What must be heard—what cultural frames and structuring norms are presumed to be operating—for this communicative action to be done in this way? By unraveling some of the strands in the cultural cloth, one seeks to describe, then begins to render the cultural bases of competence that ground such communicative practices. The theoretical framework discussed and referred to above suggests probes and a conceptual vocabulary for such analyses. How do different configurations of communicative competence get woven into particular episodes of social interaction? By exploring such episodes, the ethnographer is equipped better to move reactions to intercultural encounters from naive understandings of both, or unreflective evaluations of one by the other, or utter puzzlement about the other, to the unveiling of each as an other. As a result, ones whose ways were once thought confusing are now, at least from some point of view, more comprehensible, even appropriate (if no more agreeable). In turn, one is better able to critically reflect on one's own cultural ways that were not previously as scrutable (if now less agreeable).

On another level, and similarly, this exercise in cultural pragmatics is also an exercise in general theory, a view that foregrounds the shifting cultural bases of competence within intercultural encounters. As such, an effort has been made to demonstrate an ethnographic orientation that is general, which can apply to any cultural case, to any culturally configured system of communicative competence. One needs a general way of inquiring, a systematic way of asking in order to unravel the cultural particulars of concern, especially if two sets of particulars animate a single communicative occasion. This general approach involves searching such occasions for the cultural frames that ground the communicative action, the various structuring norms of content and for comportment that are guiding the face-to-face interaction, and the loci of motives and goals, among other features of cultural identities, that are coding the interaction as a cultural performance. Investigating this way, then, may begin to reveal the particular systems of competence that operate, such as Soviet and American patterns of cultural pragmatics, and also help lay a general path for conduct and critical inquiry—that is, a cultural pragmatics of communication competence.

NOTES

1. Given the rapid political changes in the new Commonwealth of Independent States, it is important to clarify why I use the term *Soviet*. I use the term as a way to identify

interactive patterns because my informants so identified these patterns. Each instance of the pattern was identified and used by people from more than one republic and some instances of the particular patterns were jointly produced by participants from various republics. Where the patterns appear distinctively Russian, I refer to them as such. Following conventional usage, I refer to popular communication patterns in the United States of America as American, as a way of designating the geographic and national place where such patterns are most pronounced (see Varenne, 1986). For each American pattern discussed, instances have been produced across genders, races, classes, geographic regions, and various ethnic groups.

2. The episodes were collected as part of an ongoing study of Soviet and American interactional styles (Carbaugh, in press). Data were generated over a two-year period and include five hours of videotapes from the *Donahue in Russia* series (televised in February of 1987), transcripts of all of these shows, co-observations of segments in this series between myself and Soviet co-investigators, audio recordings of these co-observations, interviews with Soviets in America and Americans who had spent considerable time in the Soviet Union, observations of Soviets and Americans interacting other than those televised, and of course literature on Soviet and American social life. I do not however claim to be an expert in Soviet languages, the Russian language, culture, or literature. My main objective is to hear in some intercultural encounters, features of two cultural systems at work. Toward this end, I sought the aid of others who are, or have been, participants in such patterns and encounters. Thus, the interpretations of the Soviet communication system were collaboratively produced with the invaluable assistance of Vicki Rubinshteyn, Laszlo Dienes, Diane Chornenkaya, Olga Beloded, and Joseph Lake. Even with such excellent help, I consider the brief descriptions and interpretations of Soviet patterns presented here to be more-or-less sketchy, suggestive, and incomplete. The discussion of middle-American patterns draws on more detailed, fine-grained study (e.g. Carbaugh, 1988). All data were analyzed using a particular model (i.e., Carbaugh, 1988, esp. pp. 177-184, 1990b, 1991; Carbaugh & Hastings, 1992) parts of which are discussed in the final section of this paper.

9

The Applicability of Interpersonal Communication Competence to the Intercultural Communication Context

VIRGINIA H. MILHOUSE • *University of Oklahoma*

The construct of *interpersonal competence (IPC)* has been the focus of a number of social and behavioral studies for several years. IPC has been associated with effective interactions in classrooms (Andersen, Norton, & Nussbaum, 1981; Milhouse, 1986), organizations (Argyris, 1965; Miller, 1972), health settings (Henderson & Byran, 1984; Kreps & Query, 1990), counseling (Corrigan, 1980), social encounters (Argyle & Kendon, 1967), and marital relationships (Olson, 1981).

In addition, a variety of interpersonal communication competence approaches have been investigated in both intercultural and cross-cultural contexts, including attitudinal (Abe & Wiseman, 1983; Gudykunst, Nishida, & Chua, 1987; Wiseman, Hammer, & Nishida, 1989), behavioral (Collier, 1989; Martin & Hammer, 1989; Olebe & Koester, 1989), and cognitive approaches (Collier, 1989; Collier, Ribeau, & Hecht, 1986; Collier & Thomas, 1988). However, reviews of those studies indicate that a consensus about a conceptualization of IPC competence in either intercultural or cross-cultural contexts has not yet been reached. Recently, Spitzberg (1989), Imahori and Lanigan (1989), Spitzberg and Hurt (1987), and Yingling (1986) have argued for a relational competence model that allows the integration of these research approaches to intercultural or cross-cultural contexts.

The purpose of this study is to investigate the applicability of the relational competence model from an intercultural communication context perspective. First, the relational competence model upon which

AUTHOR'S NOTE: *A small portion of this manuscript was partially supported by a research grant from the Office of Research Administration at the University of Oklahoma. The author thanks Gustav Friedrich, George Henderson, Robert Shull, Todd Mercer, and the reviewers who commented anonymously on the first version of this chapter.*

IPC research is based is explained. Second, the model is discussed from an integrative perspective, which allows past behavioral, attitudinal, and cognitive approaches to be examined holistically within the intercultural context (Imahori & Lanigan, 1989; Ruben, 1989; Spitzberg, 1989). Third, research measures that test the model's skills (behavioral), motivation (attitudinal), and knowledge (cognitive) components are described and then discussed in terms of their cross-cultural validity and reliability. This is followed by the test of three research hypotheses.

The relational competence model (Hammer, 1989; Spitzberg, 1989; Spitzberg & Hurt, 1987) views interpersonal competence as comprising the components of motivation (attitude), knowledge (cognitive), skills (behavioral), context, and outcomes. According to Spitzberg and Hurt (1987), "a person who is motivated to communicate, knowledgeable in communicating, skilled in communicating, and sensitive to the context is more likely to be viewed as competent and to achieve desired objectives (outcomes)" (p. 29). This model assumes that a substantial relationship exists between skills (molecular behaviors) and the molar evaluations or impressions of the competent use of the skilled behaviors. For instance, Spitzberg and Cupach (1984), in an extensive review of both experimental and descriptive studies, identify *molar impressions* of interpersonal competence as involving *interaction management* (topic initiation, encouragements, and turn-taking), *altercentrism* (self and other references that include supportiveness and approval indications), *expressiveness* (appropriate use of verbal and nonverbal behaviors such as expressing opinions and body posture), and *composure* (relaxation and confidence).

Coker and Burgoon (1987), Spitzberg and Hurt (1987), and Bochner and Kelly (1974) identified specific molecular behaviors (verbal and nonverbal) related to molar impressions of competence. Their investigations reveal that competent (appropriate and effective) use of (a) interaction management is evidenced by fewer vocalized pauses, good speech coordination, and topic follow-up; (b) altercentrism is communicated by greater other-references, good body orientation, and supportiveness; (c) expressiveness is provided through appropriate use of humor, nonmonotone voice, and greater use of vocal variety; and (d) composure is communicated by fewer speech blockages, greater response relevance, and less object manipulation or fidgeting.

The molar-molecular relationship as envisioned by the relational competence model is an empirical conceptualization of 4 single-level molar evaluations (interaction management, altercentrism, expressiveness, and composure) with 10 associative molecular behavioral items for each evaluation. As noted by Spitzberg and Hurt (1987), the single-level molar evaluations (and associative molecular behaviors) are (a) *interaction management* (topic initiation, questioning, topic follow-up, encouragements, interruptions, talk time, fluency, vocalized pauses, restatements, and response time); (b) *altercentrism* (supportiveness, seek clarification, self-references, other-references, approval indication, head nods, body lean, smiling, eye contact, and body orientation); (c) *expressiveness* (personal opinion expression, appropriate use of humor, monotone voice, vocal variety, brevity of speaking turns, gestures, appropriate facial expressions, smiling/laughing, body posture and orientation, and use of illustrators); and (d) *composure/relaxation/confidence* (response shortness, speech rate, speech blockages, vocal tension, response relevance, object manipulation, eye contact, extraneous movement, fidgeting, and postural rigidity).

Intercultural research implies that these interpersonal molar-molecular items may significantly influence impressions (self-rated, other-rated) of intercultural communication competence (Hammer, 1989; Martin & Hammer, 1989; Spitzberg, 1989). Although Hammer's (1989) research does not investigate the relationship between objective behaviors and behaviors that function as impressions of competence, it indicates that interpersonal communication competence research would be more theoretically applicable if the relationship between "the higher-order, abstract impressions [molar] and/or functions of competence and the more specific behaviors [molecular] that serve to functionally create these impressions are discovered and described more precisely" (p. 253). In other words, his research strongly implies a relationship among these functions and recommends research to examine such relationship. For instance, what are the specific molecular behaviors (e.g., eye contact, body orientation) that lead to impressions of respect (molar)? Ruben (1976) argues that the ability to express respect (e.g., a molar impression of competence) is important in effective interpersonal and intercultural communication relations. Ruben's research does not treat molecular behaviors and molar impressions of competence as interdependent factors.

Instead of investigating competence as either a behavioral, attitudinal, or cognitive approach, proponents (Imahori & Lanigan, 1989; Spitzberg, 1989; Spitzberg & Cupach, 1984) of the relational competence model argue for an interdependent relationship among these factors in intercultural contexts. Spitzberg (1989) theorizes that the relational competence model is invariant in its prediction of impressions of a person's self- and other-referenced competence whether the context is intra- or intercultural. In other words, the model's fundamental components do not change with different cultural contexts. According to

Spitzberg (1989), impressions of communication competence depend largely on perceived "motivation to communicate, knowledge of the communicative process and context, and skill in implementing motives and knowledge given the constraint of the context" (p. 250). Conceptually, Imahori and Lanigan (1989) argue that "the most ideal condition of ICC [intercultural communication] competence occurs when an individual possesses high degrees of intercultural knowledge, motivation and skills" (p. 272). These authors have developed an ICC competence model that is designed to transport IPC theory to a level of measurement in ICC contexts.

A prerequisite for comparing the relational competence model in intercultural contexts is the degree to which it obtains equivalence in conceptual or functional structure, construct operationalization, and item and scalars similarity across cultures (Berry, 1980; Brislin, Lonner, & Thorndike, 1973; Hui & Triandis, 1985). According to Hui and Triandis, conceptual equivalence is related to functional equivalence in that both pertain to similarity between the goals of two constructs or behaviors. That is, "a behavior of Culture A and a behavior in Culture B are functionally equivalent when they have similar precursors, consequences, and correlates" (p. 134). Regarding the issue of construct operationalization, Hui and Triandis establish two requirements, (a) operationalization is the transition from theory to measurement and (b) if a construct is operationalized in the same procedure in different cultures, the instrument thus derived is equivalent in construct operationalization across cultures. In an attempt to address these requirements, this research relies on Imahori and Lanigan's (1989) Relational Competence Model of ICC to demonstrate the transition of theory to an operational level of measurement, and on Spitzberg and Hurt's (1987) IPC measurements to examine the equivalency of the operationalized constructs in the intercultural context.

In demonstrating the transition of theory to a level of measurement, the relational competence model of ICC competence treats the issues of (a) operationalization of competence and relational outcome, (b) relationships among three components of competence, and (c) relationships among competence, relational outcome, and other variables. First, competence is operationalized by the variables of motivation, knowledge, and skills. These variables have been measured in both intra- and intercultural contexts, but not from a relational perspective. For example, *motivation* (e.g., social distance, positive regard, ethnocentrism, and open-mindedness) has been studied in several cross-cultural adaptational studies (Collier, 1989; Hammer, 1987; Hammer, Gudykunst, & Wiseman, 1978; Wiseman et al., 1989). *Knowledge*, which is concerned with understanding interaction rules, culture-general and culture-specific knowledge, and linguistic aspects, has also been investigated in a number of cross-cultural studies (Abe & Wiseman, 1983; Gudykunst & Hammer, 1984; Hammer, 1989). *Skills*, the third operational variable of competence, is generally agreed on as comprising behaviors such as interaction management, expressiveness, social relaxation, altercentrism, composure, coordination, and vocalics (Coker & Burgoon, 1987; Hammer, 1989; Ruben, 1976; Spitzberg, Brookshire, & Brunner, 1990; Spitzberg & Hecht, 1984).

These three components influence judgments about relational outcome that is operationalized in terms of intercultural effectiveness (Chen, 1989; Imahori & Lanigan, 1989; Nishida, 1985), communication effectiveness and appropriateness (Imahori & Lanigan, 1989; Olebe & Koester, 1989; Spitzberg, 1989; Spitzberg & Hurt, 1987), relational validation and goal achievement (Collier et al., 1986), avoidance of the violation of valued rules and expectations, and achievement of valued objectives (Spitzberg, 1989). Relational outcome, therefore, is a function of both parties involved in the interaction. Hammer (1989) states that "it is not the communication skill per se that contributes to the various adaptation and/or effectiveness outcomes. . . . Rather it is the individual interactants' judgments of self and other competence based upon the communication performances engaged in that influence the individuals' success in achieving cross-cultural adaptation" (p. 251). Others agree that relational outcome is viewed as an evaluative impression of communication competence; thus competence is a function of both appropriateness (i.e., adherence to valued rules) and effectiveness (i.e., achievement of goals) given a specific communication episode (Collier et al., 1986; Spitzberg, 1989).

Another issue of the relational competence model of ICC is the presupposition of a relationship among the three components of competence. Although these components have been studied mainly from either a behavioral (skills), attitudinal (motivation), or cognitive (knowledge) perspective, Imahori and Lanigan (1989) argue that ICC competence comprises all three factors. Their argument is supported by previous IPC research that suggests that an interdependent relationship exists among the three components. For example, Spitzberg and Cupach (1984) conceptualized these constructs as integral elements of a comprehensive model of interpersonal competence. A later study conducted by Spitzberg and Hurt (1987) concluded that interdependently and operationally the constructs accounted for a significant amount of the variance-covariance in their model; although skills accounted for the highest percentage of unique variance, it was followed by motivation and then knowledge.

The present research is concerned with whether interpersonal communication competence measures will obtain a similar degree of equivalence in meaning and operationalization at both the underlying and relational structural levels for each of the two cultural groups studied. A measure is equivalent in construct operationalization when the cultures being studied use it in the same way procedurally and assign like meaning to its properties such as item and numerical values (Berry, 1980; Hui & Triandis, 1985). Moreover, this research will attempt to demonstrate that the numerical values assigned at the entire scalars levels and for each individual item of the IPC instruments are equivalent in degree, intensity, or magnitude among the cultures under study.

To determine the measure's equivalence for each member of the two cultures being studied, this research uses a multistrategy method recommended by Hui and Triandis. This approach allows for the several types of equivalence in an experiment: (a) a factorial analytic strategy is used that is designed to examine functional/conceptual equivalence (e.g., the way the cultural members respond to the underlying factor structure of the CSRS measure); (b) a direct comparison strategy is used to examine both item equivalence and equivalence in construct operationalization (e.g., the way the respondents understand the relational structure and item meaning of the CSRS, and total MOT and KNO); and (c) a multistrategy approach or a regression method is used to determine whether or not the scales' properties are generalizable to an external criterion (e.g., whether the two different sets of scores obtained relate similarly to self and other judgments of intercultural communication quality). Before the results of these strategies are discussed, the conceptual/functional equivalence of the IPC measures is provided. This is followed by the three research hypotheses designed to test the measures' construct, item, and scalar equivalence.

CONCEPTUAL EQUIVALENCE OF THE ICC MEASURES

The conceptual foundation contributing to the development of the interpersonal competence measures is found in the works of Spitzberg and his colleagues (Dillard & Spitzberg, 1984; Spitzberg et al., 1990). After an extensive review of interpersonal communication competence literature, Spitzberg and Cupach (1984) concluded that competence was relational in nature. In other words, these authors integrated divergent perspectives regarding the behavioral, attitudinal, and cognitive nature of competence into a relational model of IPC competence. The model consists of five components of interpersonal competence: motivation, knowledge, skills, context, and outcomes. In addition to the model's relational nature, Spitzberg and Hecht (1984) argue that competence is also interactive in nature; that is, competence is viewed as an evaluative impression of both parties' successful exchange of the relational components during interpersonal interaction.

The five interpersonal competence measures used in this study are based on Spitzberg and his colleagues' research. The first measure is the *Conversational Skills Rating Scale (CSRS)*. This 30-item measure is designed to provide a relatively molecular-level assessment of perceived competence in specific, face-to-face episodes of interaction. The first 25 items of the scale are behavioral, and the last 5 items are general impression items. The episodes assessed can be recalled, imaginary, or immediately precedent to the rating. Furthermore, this measure can be adapted as 30-item Self-Rating (SRC) and Other-Rating (ORC) Competence Scales (Spitzberg & Cupach, 1984).

The CSRS was developed and refined over a series of studies. The original rationale was to provide a more behaviorally diagnostic measure. According to the authors, most extant self-report measures contain either highly molar items (e.g., "trustworthy," "cooperative") or a mix of inference levels. Therefore, they extracted the items for the original CSRS from extensive literature reviews, extant measures, and pilot studies (Spitzberg, 1987; Spitzberg & Hecht, 1984). Subsequent studies refined the scale's item content, scaling, and format.

Currently, the item content is reported to reflect four skill clusters: altercentrism (e.g., asking questions, distributing talk time, immediate body orientation), composure (e.g., nervous fidgeting, tense voice, postural rigidity), interaction management (e.g., turn-taking, interruptions, topic initiation), and expressiveness (e.g., vocal variety, opinion expression, use of humor). Subsequent research has been generally supportive of this factor structure, although some analyses suggest a fifth factor comprised exclusively of the vocalics items (Bennett, 1987; Chin & Ringer, 1986; Spitzberg et al., 1990). The items can be used as independent predictors, or they can be summed into either subscales or across all 25 of the CSRS behavior items to provide an overall measure of conversational skills. The five general impression items are typically summed to provide a validity criterion for the behavioral items and also a molar impression variable.

In development of the CSRS, Spitzberg and associates had to solve two major scaling problems. In any given behavior, respondents may be competent in one context and incompetent in another. Therefore, behavioral scales must include behaviors that normatively are multivalent (e.g., interruptions, though sometimes viewed as inappropriate, can be performed in a competent manner). Thus, the first problem was to devise scaling not based upon the simple occurrence of a behavior. The second problem was that behavior usages may be complex and curvilinear in relationship to competence. That is, a complete lack of eye contact is likely to be viewed as incompetence, but so too is a prolonged stare or gaze. The scaling of the CSRS was designed to permit the rating of both normatively positive and negative behaviors on the same measure as a continuum of competence. The continuum ranges from "inadequate," through "somewhat adequate," "adequate," "good," to "excellent." Recently, some normative prompting is provided in the item content (e.g., vocal confidence—neither tense nor nervous sounding). To date, the CSRS has revealed high internal reliability and strong validity coefficients with measures such as satisfaction (Cranley & Brunner, 1988; Curran, 1982); the Simulated Social Interaction Test (Dawson & Spitzberg, 1987); and self-rating of competence, motivation, knowledge, and general impression items (Cupach & Spitzberg, 1981; Spitzberg & Brunner, 1991; Spitzberg & Hurt, 1987).

The second IPC measure used in this study is the 10-item *Motivation (MOT)* measure that assesses a person's desire to interact in a particular conversational episode and a 10-item *Knowledge (KNO)* measure that reflects a person's perception of his or her own comprehension and awareness of what to do and say in a particular conversational episode (Spitzberg & Hecht, 1984). Both constructs were found by Spitzberg and Hecht to be significantly correlated with partner ratings of competence and self-reports of communication satisfaction. These constructs were conceptualized by Spitzberg and Cupach (1984) as integral components of the comprehensive model of interpersonal competence and to assess the validity of the CSRS measure. In Spitzberg and Hurt's (1987) study, both measures attained coefficient alpha reliability estimates of .83 and .74, respectively.

The third measure, the *Conversational Relational Outcome Scale (CROS)*—a revised version of Spitzberg & Canary's (1987) conversational appropriateness and effectiveness (CAE) scale—was designed to assess perceptions of a particular conversational episode in terms of its appropriateness and effectiveness. Appropriateness is referenced by items concerning the awkwardness or smoothness of behavior and specific remarks, the extent of embarrassment experienced, and general impressions of propriety. The initial version of the CAE was semantic differentially scaled, but the factor structure was unstable across samples (Spitzberg & Phelps, 1982). The next version was elaborated into a Likert-type format in the hope of providing more tangible referents and more factor stability (Spitzberg & Canary, 1985).

Effectiveness is assessed by items referring to success, control, and goal achievement in the conversation. The CAE items variably refer to the other person (e.g., "Some of the things he or she said were awkward"), to self (e.g., "I achieved everything I hoped to achieve in our conversation"), or to the conversation (e.g., "The conversation was unprofitable"). In general, given that propriety is more a social judgment and effectiveness idiosyncratic to one's private objectives, appropriateness items refer to the conversational partner while effectiveness items tend to refer to self.

The CROS's factor structure has consistently displayed a unidimensional structure for effectiveness, and two dimensions of appropriateness, labeled *specific appropriateness* and *general appropriateness* (Canary & Spitzberg, 1987). The specific factor reflects judgments of particular remarks or behaviors, whereas the general factor represents a judgment of the entire episode of interaction. Item wording and content was varied slightly depending on application. To date, the measures have displayed highly sensible validity coefficients with measures of conflict strategies, satisfaction, trust, intimacy, and mutuality of control (Canary & Spitzberg, 1987, 1989), self-rating of competence (Cupach & Spitzberg, 1981), rating of alter-competence (Spitzberg & Canary, 1985), and loneliness (Spitzberg & Canary, 1985).

Since Hypothesis 3 was concerned with impressions of overall communication quality as the external criterion for actor and coactor, the two CAE components were combined herein to obtain a total score. Henceforth, they are referred to as the CROS and used along with the SRC-ORC Scale as external measures of competence.

Using a holistic approach similar to the one employed by Spitzberg and his colleagues in the conceptualization and measurement development of the IPC scales, Imahori and Lanigan (1989) developed a holistic conceptualization of ICC competence. Included in their conceptualization are five testable theorems, which I draw on to help demonstrate the equivalence of IPC scales across cultures. The first of these theorems states: "Knowledge, Motivation and/or Skills dimensions of ICC Competence independently or interdependently influence the relational outcome, one's goal and/or experience" (p. 280). If in this research the skills, motivation, and knowledge of the U.S. and non-U.S. respondents influence their relational outcome, goals, and experiences, then the scales used to examine these constructs are interpreted similarly for these cultures. To test these scales in the intercultural communication context, the following hypotheses were stated:

Hypothesis 1: The internal structure of the CSRS measure is similar regardless of the participants' cultures.

Hypothesis 2: The CSRS, MOT, and KNO measures are similar in meaning and operationalization regardless of the participants' cultures and past intercultural experience.

Another theorem of Imahori and Lanigan's (1989) ICC model predicts a relationship among competence, relational outcome, and other variables. Here other variables are referenced by appropriateness (e.g., past experiences that impact the adherence to valued rules and expectancies) and effectiveness (e.g., the achievement of anticipated goals or objectives). Appropriateness and effectiveness are viewed as evaluative impressions of self- and other-rated communication quality and as external measures of competence (Spitzberg, 1989). In this research, communication quality depends on both self and other impressions (SRC-ORC) of appropriateness-effectiveness (CROS). To examine the relationship of the IPC measures to external criteria of competence, Hypothesis 3 posits:

Hypothesis 3: Items of the CSRS and total MOT and KNO relate similarly to external measures of self- and other-rated impressions of communication quality regardless of the participants' cultures.

METHODS

Respondents and Procedures

In order to examine the similarities and differences in the CSRS factorial structure among different cultures and to assess whether the IPC scales were equivalent across cultures regardless of past intercultural experience, two different samples of 150 respondents each (total $N = 300$) were used to collect the data for this study. Sample 1 was comprised of 75 U.S. military personnel (Euro-Americans, Afro-Americans, Hispanic-Americans) stationed at Ramstein AFB, Germany, and 75 German respondents living in adjacent communities. Sample 2 was comprised of 75 U.S. (Euro-Americans, Afro-Americans, Hispanic-Americans, and Asian-Americans) and 75 non-U.S. respondents (Chinese, Germans, Japanese, Africans, and Iranians). Both samples were comprised of persons regarded as qualified to comparatively evaluate conversationally appropriate and effective behaviors. This was important because the IPC Model assumes that the conversational behaviors of both parties contribute to the overall impression of competence.

The 75 U.S. military respondents were selected from graduate-level human relations courses offered at Ramstein AFB, Germany, by a major Midwestern university. The 75 U.S. respondents were enrolled in the same graduate-level courses offered at the university. As part of the course requirements, each participant was instructed to hold a 15-minute conversation with a person from a different culture. To ensure that the person selected possessed a background that made it possible for him or her to determine if his or her partner demonstrated interpersonally satisfying behaviors, three additional instructions were required: (a) the partner selected should have obtained at least an undergraduate education; (b) the partner selected must have had at least one of the following communication courses—interpersonal communication, interpersonal dynamics, applied interpersonal dynamics, group dynamics, or introduction to communication; and (c) both parties must have had some past intercultural experience. This third requirement was important for all participants because it allowed the researcher to determine if the IPC scales were equivalent regardless of past intercultural experience.

The participants were further requested to complete the questionnaire packet containing the five IPC measures immediately following their conversations to avoid problems with elapsed time between the events of conversational recall and assessment (Spitzberg & Cupach, 1990). Section 1 of the questionnaire packet asked the participants to provide information concerning the demographic variables of sex, ethnicity, age, education, and past intercultural experience (e.g., Have you ever had an intimate, working, or social relationship with someone from a distinctly different culture? If so, how long?). This section also provided space for the participants to indicate which of the five communication courses listed above they had as part of their educational program.

Analysis of demographic information revealed that 60% of the participants (both samples) had graduate-level education and 40% had an undergraduate education. Fifty-four percent of the German participants had two of the five communications courses listed above, while 21% had at least one of the communication courses. Almost all of the international participants (72) had at least two of the required communication courses, while only 3 had just one of the courses required.

As for past intercultural experience, 85.3% of the U.S. participants in Sample 1 reported having 5 years of experience, while only 14.7% had 4 years or less. Similarly, 78.7% of the German participants indicated 5 or more years of past intercultural experience and 21.3% reported having 4 years or less experience. Overall, Sample 2 participants reported having more past intercultural experience than Sample 1 participants. For instance, 97.3% of the U.S. participants had 6 to 10 years of past intercultural experience, while only 2.6% had less than 6 years of experience. Likewise, 92.0% of the international participants had 6 to 10 years experience, and 8.0% had less than 5 years of past intercultural experience. Sample 1 consisted of 45 U.S. males and 20 German males; 55 of the participants were U.S. females and 30 were German females. There were 43 U.S. males and 22 international males in Sample 2; 65 of the females were from the United States, and 20 of the females were international participants.

Statistical Design

Confirmatory factor analysis (Jöreskog & Sörbom, 1984) was used to determine if Spitzberg et al.'s (1990) CSRS factor structure was similarly present in the U.S. and non-U.S. samples. The model was assessed using χ^2/df and the goodness of fit index (GFI). Based on its original assessment, the model was considered a reasonable fit if: (a) the χ^2/df was 5 or below; (b) five components produced eigenvalues greater than unity; and (c) the factor structure represented the components—expressiveness, composure, altercentrism, interactional management, and vocalic features (Spitzberg et al., 1990). Thus, subsequent components principal analysis with orthogonal and oblique rotations was also used (Kim & Mueller, 1978).

To test the hypotheses, two Multivariate Analyses (MANOVA) were employed to assess the two independent variables and the three dependent variables in each sample. The independent variables were: (a) culture—total American respondents versus total German respondents; and (b) past intercultural experience—American × experience, German × experience, American × German × experience (Sample 1); American × experience, international × experience, American × international × experience (Sample 2). The three dependent variables were: (a) conversational skills, (b) motivation, and (c) knowledge. Further analysis of the six variables was conducted only if the multivariate statistics produced an F-ratio significant at the .05 level. Main effect interactions and simple interactions were tested using the group error term of the corresponding dependent variable. Means for the dependent variables by independent variables were compared using Newman-Kuels test (Winer, 1971).

Multiple regression analysis was used to test Hypothesis 3 treating self- and other-rated communication quality (SRC-ORC) as well as relational outcome (CROS) as the external criterion measures and the items of the CSRS and total MOT and KNO as predictor variables.

RESULTS

The confirmatory factor analysis for the U.S.-German sample yielded a χ^2 of 579 (125df, χ^2/df = 4.63) and a GFI of .70. Subsequent exploratory statistics produced five factors with eigenvalues greater than unity. The five factors that accounted for 53.2% of the common variance appear to represent expressiveness, composure, altercentrism, coordination, and vocalics. Similar results were obtained for the U.S.-non-U.S. sample: χ^2 = 581 (125df, χ^2/df = 4.65) and a GFI of .65. The five factors expressiveness, composure, altercentrism, coordination, and vocalics produced eigenvalues greater than 1 and explained more than 55.8% of the common variance for this sample. These results appear to confirm Spitzberg et al.'s (1990) factorial model: expressiveness, composure, altercentrism, interaction management, and vocalics accounting for 56.1% of the common variance. Extracted factor loadings, eigenvalues, and the amount of unique variance for both samples are presented in Table 9.1.

Using Cronbach's coefficient alpha, the reliabilities for all scales were .91 for CSRS, .73 for MOT, and .67 for KNO. Homogeneity of variance was employed with Cochran's *C* statistic (Winer, 1971). The homogeneity of variance hypothesis was accepted for all scales: CSRS (C[7/25] = .06, $p > .05$); MOT (C[7/10] = .04; $p > .05$); and KNO (C[7/10] = .04, $p < .05$).

To examine the equivalency in item meaning and operationalization of the relational competence scales across cultures, Bartlett's test of sphericity (7310.4, 300df, $p < .001$) indicated that multivariate analyses were warranted. The MANOVA procedure for the CSRS, MOT, and KNO scales yielded insignificant *F* approximation for the interaction between culture; for the American (Δ = .93, F[3/69] = 1.9, p = n.s.) and German (Δ = .94, F[3/69] = 1.4, p = n.s.) samples; and American (Δ = .94, F[3/69] = .9, p = n.s.) and international (Δ = .94, F[3/69] = 1.0, p = n.s.) samples. Similarly, multivariate tests were not significant for the two three-way interactions or two-way interactions for past intercultural experience. In addition, no significant main effects were found for culture and past intercultural experience. Cell frequencies, means, and standard deviations for each scale are presented in Table 9.2. Multivariate and univariate analyses of variance for the CSRS, MOT, and KNO scales are reported in Table 9.3. Power for the univariate test was .88 for a small effect size of .10 (Cohen, 1977).

Testing Hypothesis 3 required multiple regression analyses with all 25 behavioral items, the total CSRS, MOT, and KNO comprising the predictor set and the dyadic rating of communication quality for each

TABLE 9.1 Factor Analysis of Conversational Skills Rating Scale

	*Factors: U.S.—German**					*Factors: U.S.—Int'l***				
Item	1	2	3	4	5	1	2	3	4	5
Eye contact	*.60*	.13	.11	.28	−.21	*.55*	.01	.22	.31	.21
Topic initiation	*.40*	−.20	−.20	.28	.25	*.59*	.05	.15	.32	−.04
Topic maintenance	*.63*	−.06	−.29	.01	−.06	*.65*	−.11	−.22	.09	−.26
Speaking time	−.10	−.26	−.31	*.66*	−.05	.09	.30	−.36	*.67*	−.23
Interruption	.04	−.17	−.00	*.74*	−.28	−.28	.09	.12	*.69*	−.01
Speaking rate	−.14	−.30	.11	.03	*.60*	.26	−.05	−.27	−.14	*.72*
Speaking fluency	.02	−.22	.26	.29	*.55*	.12	−.10	−.35	−.14	*.74*
Vocal confidence	−.09	−.31	.20	−.06	*.63*	.18	.13	−.38	−.25	*.69*
Articulation	.25	−.39	.17	.00	*.66*	−.05	−.12	−.34	−.13	*.78*
Nervous twitches	.04	*.58*	.35	−.14	.03	.32	*.67*	−.36	.19	−.11
Posture	−.08	*.65*	.31	.34	−.24	.14	*.77*	−.12	.30	−.08
Fidgeting	.15	*.52*	.38	.18	.27	−.33	*.56*	−.22	.25	−.37
Questions	−.21	−.06	*.54*	.17	.17	.16	.38	*.64*	.03	−.08
Head nods	.13	.44	*.63*	.17	.18	.35	−.02	*.66*	.27	−.07
Body lean	.38	.23	*.43*	.11	.19	.42	.28	*.70*	.10	.11
Altercentric speech	−.29	.18	*.63*	.31	.03	.41	.24	*.71*	−.18	−.22
Egocentric speech	.09	.09	*.63*	−.27	.23	.16	.15	*.75*	−.33	.02
Encouragements	−.22	.07	*.63*	.16	.29	.15	.14	*.76*	−.31	.07
Humorous stories	*.67*	.10	−.30	−.32	.17	*.66*	−.24	.00	−.13	−.29
Vocal variety	*.63*	.13	.22	−.26	.32	*.66*	−.34	−.04	.28	−.04
Vocal volume	*.64*	−.25	−.04	−.27	.03	*.69*	−.25	−.02	.17	−.11
Opinion expression	*.66*	.00	−.14	−.31	−.24	*.66*	−.36	.04	.14	.26
Facial expression	*.72*	.26	−.04	.09	−.23	*.76*	−.21	.17	−.04	−.15
Gesture	*.62*	.39	−.18	−.15	−.27	*.72*	−.19	.16	−.23	.09
Smiling	*.65*	.36	−.16	−.00	−.32	*.79*	−.07	.21	−.11	.03

*Primary factor loadings are italicized.

*Factor**	*Eigenvalue*	*Pecentage of Variance*
1. Expressiveness	9.4	29.3
2. Composure	2.0	4.4
3. Altercentrism	1.7	8.4
4. Coordination	1.5	4.0
5. Vocalics	1.4	7.1

*Factor***	*Eigenvalue*	*Pecentage of Variance*
1. Expressiveness	12.0	33.0
2. Composure	1.7	4.3
3. Altercentrism	1.6	7.5
4. Coordination	1.3	4.7
5. Vocalics	1.0	6.3

TABLE 9.2 Cell Frequencies, Means, and Standard Deviations

		CSRS		MOT		KNO	
Cell	*f*	*x*	*SD*	*x*	*SD*	*x*	*SD*
Sample 1							
American experience	5	96.90	7.60	35.30	10.34	32.70	10.57
German experience	4	76.40	14.63	29.60	5.41	29.60	5.12
American-German experience	8	86.65	11.12	32.45	7.87	31.15	7.84
Culture*	52	107.21	9.24	37.13	8.06	36.21	7.87
Culture**	52	105.13	13.36	35.03	8.14	35.38	9.65
Sample 2							
American experience	10	109.91	11.75	36.83	8.57	35.50	8.92
German experience	9	82.08	11.01	32.83	7.19	32.83	5.79
American-international experience	18	95.99	11.31	34.33	7.83	31.31	7.92
Culture*	55	108.94	10.11	37.72	7.61	38.00	6.89
Culture**	55	108.21	10.24	36.72	7.48	36.67	8.45

*U.S. culture
**Non-U.S. culture

TABLE 9.3 Multivariate and Univariate Analyses of Variance for CSRS, MOT, and KNO

	MANOVA			ANOVA F's			
Source	*df*	Δ	*F*	*df*	*CSRS*	*MOT*	*KNO*
Sample 1							
American x Experience	3/69	.99	.99	1/74	1.16	1.17	1.08
German x Experience	3/69	.96	.95	1/74	1.54	1.12	1.81
American x German x Experience	3/69	.97	.87	1/74	2.79	1.07	1.21
Culture*	3/69	.93	1.88	1/74	2.40	1.99	1.41
Culture**	3/69	.94	1.42	1/74	2.63	1.83	1.61
Sample 2							
American x Experience	3/69	.95	1.52	1/74	1.94	1.43	1.18
International x Experience	3/69	.86	1.04	1/74	1.37	1.26	1.42
American x International x Experience	3/69	.97	.92	1/74	2.03	1.56	1.11
Culture*	3/69	.94	1.78	1/74	2.15	1.48	2.30
Culture**	3/69	.94	1.03	1/74	2.06	2.10	1.71

*U.S. culture
**Non-U.S. culture

sample as the criterion variable. In order to obtain the best 27-variable model possible (e.g., 25 items plus MOT and KNO), the maximum R^2 improvement technique was employed for all regression analysis. First, as a summed scale, the CSRS was significant at predicting impressions of competence for both the U.S.-German sample ($R^2 = .63$, $F[2,73] = 60.1$; $p < .001$) and the U.S.-international sample ($R^2 = .65$, $F[2,73] = 67.0$; $p < .001$). The strength of MOT to predict impressions of communication quality for both the U.S.-German and U.S.-international samples was also powerful: ($R^2 = .05$, $F[2,73] = 3.7$; $p < .05$), and ($R^2 = .11$, $F[2,73] = 4.3$; $p < .05$), respectively. Similar results were obtained for the predictor variable KNO on the U.S.-German sample ($R^2 = .09$, $F[2,73] = 3.5$; $p < .03$) and the U.S.-international sample ($R^2 = .16$, $F[2,73] = 6.8$; $p < .002$).

DISCUSSION

This study extended previous research by testing the equivalence of Spitzberg and his colleagues' (Spitzberg et al., 1990; Spitzberg & Hecht, 1984; Spitzberg & Hurt, 1987) relational competence model to the intercultural context. The model comprises three interpersonal communication competence components—skills (CSRS), motivation (MOT), and knowledge (KNO)—as well as relational outcome variables. These components were tested for the following types of equivalence: conceptual/functional (similarity in meaning across cultures), construct operationalization (similarity in use), and scalar equivalence.

The tests of equivalence of the model's scales produced some encouraging results for intercultural communication competence research. The replication of a similar factor structure for the CSRS for both the U.S.-German and U.S.-international samples offers support for the first hypothesis that posits a similar factor structure for the CSRS regardless of the respondents' culture. For both samples, the items loading on the CSRS scale were characteristic of Spitzberg et al.'s (1990) five-factor model: Factor 1 appeared to represent the expressiveness component comprising the items of homous stories, vocal variety, vocal volume, opinion expression, facial expression, gestures, and smiling behaviors. This factor was followed by composure, which is represented by the items nervous twitches, posture, and fidgeting. The third factor was altercentrism. Factor 4 was interaction management and Factor 5 emerged as the vocalic component. These factors explained more than 50% of the common variance in both samples.

Statistically, these findings appear to satisfy Hui and Triandis's requirements for conceptual cross-cultural equivalence. The results are encouraging for the CSRS use in intercultural research. However, it is important to point out that the respondents in this study identified some behaviors, namely, vocal variety and vocal volume, as expressiveness behaviors. These perceptions are inconsistent with the most recently reported model in which the behaviors are described as denoting vocal characteristics. These differences may be due to the scales' design and item relationship. Concerning the latter possibility, Sypher (1980) cautions that problems with item identification may mean that a scale is tapping semantic similarity rather than actual communication behavior. Concerning the structural domain of the CSRS items, Spitzberg et al. (1990) point out that vocal variety and vocal volume are closer in proximity to the expressiveness behaviors than they are to the vocalic behaviors. As such, the respondents "may [have] perceptually associated [the vocalic items] with expressiveness" (p. 148). I join those authors in suggesting future research that explores the CSRS with randomized item order.

In addition, further research is needed to distinguish between verbal vocalic behaviors and nonverbal vocalic behaviors. The CSRS scale consists of both types of behaviors but they are not clearly categorized. It is possible that subjects do not clearly differentiate between the two types of expressions when completing this type of assessment. In research reported by Martin and Hammer (1989), vocal characteristics were identified as nonverbal expressiveness behaviors used to create favorable impressions of intercultural communication.

The second hypothesis, which stated that the CSRS, MOT, and KNO scales would be equivalently operationalized across cultures, was also supported. When compared at the cultural and past intercultural experience levels, insignificant differences were obtained for the three scales. "When attempts are made to establish cross-cultural equivalence, significant difference between groups indicate non-equivalence" (Olebe & Koester, 1989, p. 343). Thus, the finding of no significant differences in the way the scales were used for both cultures in both samples offers some support for theoretical and conceptual claims that the relational competence scales are transferable to the intercultural context (Spitzberg, 1989). This finding is particularly interesting, since one sample consisted of American-international (non-European) respondents whose cultural communication patterns are considered to be quite different (Nishida, 1985) and the other consisted of American-German respondents whose cultural communication patterns are considered somewhat analogous (Stewart, 1972), and since nonequivalence is attributed to actual cultural differences (i.e., in knowledge, skills, and/or motivation to communicate) or a combination of cultural differences and dissimilar use of the scales (Olebe & Koester, 1989). However, the results are reported with some caution. First, the research instructions provided to the participants in this study required some prior past intercultural experience. This may have contributed to the respondents' overall impressions about intercultural communication competence. Past intercultural experience has been reported to improve levels of skills, knowledge, and motivation resulting in positive impressions about future intercultural encounters (Imahori & Lanigan, 1989).

It is also important to point out that the participants were required to have had some previous interpersonal competence instruction. This, too, may have influenced their knowledge and understanding about the semantic nature of the scales' items. Knowledge about interpersonal communication patterns and rules is important in the regulation of thoughts, feeling, and actions of others. Spitzberg and Hurt (1987) and Dawson and Spitzberg (1987) report that the CSRS, MOT, and KNO scales consist of research-based items that are consistent with competency-based communication instructions (e.g., curricula). Given the possible influence of these factors on the findings above, this study was limited in controlling for the mediational effects of past intercultural experience (PIE) and interpersonal communication competence instructions (ICCI) on the scales' obtainment of intercultural operational equivalence. Previous research (Spitzberg & Hurt, 1987) has shown that mediating variables (i.e., sex and typicality) can influence the way respondents use an instrument. Thus, future research is suggested to determine the scales' equivalence in interculture contexts using PIE (Gudykunst, Ting-Toomey, & Wiseman, 1991) and ICCI as control variables.

The extent to which the past intercultural experiences were successful or positive should also be assessed. It has been argued that past success in unique situations such as these help build confidence and a willingness to engage in similar future situations (Imahori & Lanigan, 1989). The present study did not control for types of past intercultural experiences (i.e., positive or negative).

The third hypothesis predicting the model's ability to infer competence at external levels of intercultural communication competence was also accepted. First, examination of the regression parameters for self- and other-rated impressions of communication quality indicates that identical behavior profiles were obtained for both the U.S.-German and U.S.-international populations. All of the 25 behavior items emerged as contributing to the impression of communication quality, but some items were stronger predictors than others. Behavioral items denoting vocalic characteristics (e.g., speaking rate and vocal confidence), interaction management (e.g., topic maintenance and encouragements), and expressiveness (gestures, facial expressions, and body posture) appear to be the major contributors to the self- and other-impressions obtained. In part, these results suggest that the CSRS scale, especially as a single component of competence, is capable of obtaining scalar equivalence with external measures (i.e., self- and other-rated impressions of communication quality). This finding is consistent with Hui and Triandis's (1985) argument that two different sets of test scores (e.g., U.S.-German) obtained with a single instrument (e.g., CSRS) can be similarly related to external criteria (e.g., SRC and ORC).

The finding that motivation was significantly stronger than either CSRS or KNO in predicting successful relational outcome deserves further mention. Not only is this consistent with research reported by Spitzberg and Hurt (1987), it supports also Imahori and Lanigan's (1989) claims that past intercultural experiences may have positive motivational influence on future intercultural interactions. In addition, *motivation* is here perceived as more important to relational outcome than *knowledge* for both self- and other-ratings. This presents an interesting contrast to the self- and other-rated impressions of MOT to predict communication competence for the American-international respondents over *knowledge*. This research was concerned with overall impressions of communication quality and, therefore, produced interrelationship effects that are consistent with Canary and Spitzberg's (1987) claims that integrative behaviors are seen as most successful in predicting communication quality over "specific appropriateness, general appropriateness, and effectiveness" (p. 112). These authors further noted that appropriateness was significantly more strongly associated with social and task attraction than effectiveness. Thus, the more stimulated or motivated individuals are about an episode the more appropriate will be their behaviors.

Another factor worth mentioning in the analysis of the three components to predict relational outcome is the improved amount of variance accounted for by the KNO Scale over previous reports. It is possible that both past intercultural experience and some prior interpersonal competence instruction are responsible for this increase.

Overall, the CSRS and the accompanying relational competence measures appear to have strong potential as research measures in intercultural contexts. All of the measures obtained acceptable levels of conceptual/functional, operational, and scalar equivalence. However, more research is needed that controls for the influence of PIE and ICCI on each measure to achieve equivalence. Also, research that isolates the

CSRS items more distinctly is suggested to avoid problems that result from item proximity and semantic relations. The relationship between types of intercultural experiences (e.g., positive, negative) and intercultural communication success also warrants further study.

10

Implications of Self-Disclosure on Conversational Logics, Perceived Communication Competence, and Social Attraction

A Comparison of Japanese and American Cultures

MASAYUKI NAKANISHI • *Tsuda College, Tokyo, Japan*

KENNETH M. JOHNSON • *Syracuse University*

Porter and Samovar (1976) describe intercultural communication as occurring whenever persons engaging in a communication act bring with them different experiential backgrounds that reflect a long-standing deposit of experience, knowledge, and values in their own cultures. Implied in this definition of intercultural communication is the assumption that culture is inherently manifested in individuals and their communication patterns. Hall (1961) was among the first to point out that "culture is communication," and more recently Barnlund (1989) has elaborated on this view by saying, "It is through communication that we acquire a culture; it is in our manner of communicating that we display our cultural uniqueness" (p. xiv). Indeed, differences among cultures in terms of communication patterns and in the meanings attributed to those patterns are becoming increasingly well documented, prompting some communication theorists and researchers to argue that the relationships between communication processes and culture are mutually causal (Pearce & Cronen, 1980).

As members of cultures, scholars interested in the relationship between communication and culture face the challenge of trying to describe the variations in communication without generating statements themselves so highly culture-laden as to be reduced to the status of ethnocentric editorials. At least three strategies for conducting cross-cultural empirical research that attempt to be sensitive to cultural differences yet avoid undue ethnocentrism have been identified in the communication literature (Wolfson & Pearce, 1983). First, researchers may identify particular communication acts—for example, turn-taking—and describe the frequency or contexts in which such acts occur. Second, investigators may solicit or offer meanings or accounts for particular acts to be compared across cultures. Although much of the cross-cultural research has been conducted using the first two research strategies, Kang and Pearce (1984) recently have proposed a third research strategy for scholars who view communication and culture as reciprocally causal.

Kang and Pearce (1984) identify this third strategy as the *transculture conceptual approach*. In particular, they note that if communication and culture are reciprocally causal, the relationship between them cannot be tested in a single context. Rather, researchers must propose transcultural concepts that identify processes common to both cultures, the variations in which, through testing in multicultural settings, account for the differences between cultures. In an attempt to test this research strategy in a cross-cultural study involving Chinese and North American students, Wolfson and Pearce (1983) identified the concept of logical force as transcultural. Briefly, a concept derived from the theory of the Coordinated Management of Meaning (hereafter, CMM), *logical force* refers to the strength of the conversational entailment on an act an individual performs from several aspects of that individaul's rules for meaning and action (Pearce & Cronen, 1980). CMM assumes that in conversations, persons seldom act in a random manner; instead the force that impels them to choose one act rather than another is variable and sometimes highly differentiated, such that important differences in the logic of action emerge in different episodes, relationships, or cultures. From this conceptual basis and noting research documenting cultural differences in communication patterns and in meanings attributed to those patterns, Wolfson and Pearce (1983) provided a strong argument that the concept of logical force was sufficiently sensitive for differentiating conversational logics transculturally.

The present study examined the impact of culture on the conversational implicature of self-disclosure. Two research questions were posed for the replication of previous investigations: (a) How do Japanese and Americans perceive conversations in which one conversant self-discloses at a high, medium, or low level? (b) In what ways does the act of self-disclosure influence subsequent communication for Japanese and Americans?

As an extension of previous research, two additional research questions were posed: (c) In what ways does the act of self-disclosure influence Japanese and Americans' perceptions of the communication competence of the self-discloser? (d) In what ways does the act of self-disclosure influence the perceived social attractiveness of the discloser for Japanese and Americans?

CULTURAL DIFFERENCES IN COMMUNICATION PATTERNS AND MEANINGS

If one assumes this kind of reciprocal causality between culture and communication or the inherent dialectic character of the societal phenomenon (Berger, 1979), then one would expect to find different communication patterns in different cultural contexts. Barnlund (1989) suggests two broader cultural codes that are necessary to fully understand variation in meaning across different cultures: interactional grammar and grammar of occasions. The *interactional grammar* consists of the norms that govern the structure of a conversation, including how to initiate conversation, what topics to discuss or avoid, how to shift from one type of message to another, and how to terminate conversation. The other code system, *grammar of occasions*, is used to differentiate various cultural activities such as parties, funerals, and the like with distinct meanings.

Ample evidence suggests that these often unappreciated and overlooked cultural rules of meaning exist. For example, Barnlund (1975) reported systematic differences in what Japanese and Americans characterized as public and private information. In addition, not only did Americans report more willingness to disclose in more varied social settings than did the Japanese, but both groups accurately perceived their communicative profiles to differ from each other. The Japanese perceived their communication profiles to be more formal, reserved, quiet, and private, whereas the Americans characterized their profiles as more casual, assertive, talkative, and disclosing.

By the same token, certain communicative acts common to both cultures can have different meanings. Kang and Pearce (1984), for example, found that such communicative acts as a period of silence at a meal and a direct question asked by a younger person were interpreted very differently in Korean and American cultures. There is also some empirical evidence that suggests that in the Eastern cultures where oral communication skills are not highly valued, reticence in interpersonal communication situations does not necessarily lead to negative impressions but is often interpreted as an indication of emotional strength and trustworthiness (Kang & Pearce, 1984; Klopf & Cambra, 1979). Yoshikawa (1978) concludes that for the Japanese what is not explicitly expressed is often most important.

SELF-DISCLOSURE AND CONVERSATIONAL IMPLICATURE

The communicative act the present study examines is *self-disclosure*, which is defined as revelation and communication of private information about self to another person. It seems obvious that the meaning of self-disclosure as well as its function in interpersonal communication will vary significantly in cultures possessing different value orientations. In the American cultural environment, self-disclosure is one of the most important forms of communication that helps to facilitate the development of authentic and meaningful relationships. The humanistic psychological tradition in the United States has especially emphasized the discovery, expression, and validation of the self through reciprocal self-disclosure as a means of self-actualization (Maslow, 1968; Rogers, 1970). Recent research has indicated that the very act of self-disclosure implies an interest in establishing a relationship (Gilbert & Whiteneck, 1976), and those who are unwilling to disclose information about their self-concepts will have trouble developing meaningful relationships (Zakahi, 1987).

In contrast to the strong emphasis on the self in the American culture, the major value orientations of the Japanese have been historically traced and identified by Sofue (1973) as follows: a vertical-hierarchical orientation, a group goal dedication, and a dependency-on-others orientation. Nakayama (1987) further argues that the Japanese tend to classify people they interact with into three groups: *uchi* represents a primary group of family members and close friends to whom they are emotionally attached; *soto* refers to a world of people with whom they interact based on social roles and functional needs; and *yoso* means a world of strangers whom they are most likely to ignore and with whom they rarely become intimate. As a result, Japanese people become increasingly reticent toward strangers. In fact, Ting-Toomey (1987) found that Japanese exhibited a much lower level of self-disclosure in both quality and quantity than Americans or French.

Wolfson and Pearce (1983) also reported that the Chinese subjects not only interpreted highly personal disclosure negatively, but perceived high self-disclosure as less harmonious than did the Americans. In addition, the researchers concluded that the act of self-disclosure functioned differently regarding its implicature for subsequent conversation as measured by logical force. In particular, they found that the Chinese apparently felt more obligation and less choice in making responses in the high-disclosure situation than did Americans for either situation. Their Chinese respondents also reported that the linkage between their act (response) and subsequent definitions of the relationship described in the dialogues was weaker than that for Americans in both conditions, and considerably weaker in the high-disclosure situation. Wolfson and Pearce (1983) suggested that one possible explanation of their findings is that the high-disclosure situation in particular might have been so unusual that it was perceived by Chinese as an enigmatic episode in which they could no longer figure out how to act appropriately.

COMMUNICATION COMPETENCE AND SOCIAL ATTRACTIVENESS

Although once thought to be of no importance, research on everyday conversation has demonstrated that even the most apparently simple conversations are extraordinarily complex, requiring sophisticated skills by the conversants. As ethnomethodologists studying Americans in everyday life have documented, people say less than they mean, yet expect others to have heard more than what was explicitly said. Coordinated conversations require to some extent communicatively competent participants.

CMM theory offers a conceptualization of communication competence useful as a second transcultural concept (Cronen & Shuter, 1983). Harris (1979) defines *communication competence* as the ability of participants to co-create and co-maintain the social order. This definition stresses a particular conversant's relationship to a system of meaning and action in which any particular skill may be functional or dysfunctional depending on its context-relevance for the requirements of that system. For example, being able to demonstrate active listening and paraphrasing skills may be highly commendable in a classroom context, yet may court disaster when uninvitedly demonstrated before total strangers on a crowded subway.

Harris (1979) identifies three ideal-typical levels of communication competence. *Minimal competence* exists when an individual's abilities are in some way less than required by a particular social system. *Satisfactory competence* exists when an individual is enmeshed within the system by a close fit between that individual's abilities and the social system's requirements. Finally, *optimal competence* exists when an individual's abilities are greater than and subsume the requirements of a particular social system.

In terms of communication competence, the levels outlined in CMM stress the idea that in modern Western industrialized nations, characterized as heterogeneous, complex, and reflexively self-aware of the human agency of its institutions, satisfactory competence or fitting in may be extremely difficult if not impossible. Due to heterogeneity, the enmeshment of persons in multiple systems fosters change in their self-concepts and relationships with others (Cronen & Shuter, 1983). Hall (1976) describes such cultures as *low-context*, in which communication involves providing a high amount of information explicitly in the messages for coordinating contexts.

In contrast, the Japanese culture has been characterized as being homogeneous in terms of race, language, and basic value orientations. Kunihiro (1976), for example, describes Japan as an endogamous society in which the members share a great many aspects of daily life and consciousness. In this kind of society, communication within a high-context culture is more likely to take place. According to Hall (1976), a *high-context* communication is "one in which most of the information is either in the physical context or internalized in the person, while very little is in the coded, explicit, transmitted part of the message" (p. 91). Messages exchanged between Japanese are not readily understood by those who do not share the same contextual information because characteristics of the Japanese language often reflect vagueness and indirection to those who do not understand what is going on. In the same vein, Hofstede (1980) also observes that low-context individualistic cultures (e.g., the United States) tend to use direct forms of communication, whereas high-context collectivistic cultures (e.g., Japan and China) prefer to use an indirect mode of communication.

Two skills are important for Japanese people living in a high-context collectivistic culture that emphasizes relational aspects of communication and group-oriented goals. First, Japanese communicators are expected to adjust their use of language appropriately and view their communicative acts as a whole rather than striving for complete clarity and openness. Paying special attention to nonverbal feedback and subtle situational cues, skillful communicators can move from the general to the specific and/or the opaque to the transparent with mastery. In most cases, adaptability to the situation is especially important, and being far more specific or elaborated in verbal communication than the situation demands is likely to be interpreted as a sign of incompetence, or *yabo* (insensitivity, being "uncool"). Befu (1973) summarizes it, stating that Japanese learn to "know what people mean without their saying it" (p. 6).

Another important skill for Japanese communicators involves the notion of *sasshi*, which refers to the ability to accurately discern the relationship-level of communication from its content. As Mushakoji (1976) puts it, "It is interesting to note that in Japan it is considered virtuous to 'catch on' quickly . . . to adjust to someone's position before it is logically and clearly enunciated" (p. 43).

Consequently, when properly carried out, Japanese conversation will exhibit unique characteristics. According to Barnlund (1975), "For the Japanese, conversation is a way of creating and reinforcing emotional ties that bind people together. Interpersonal attitudes are its content. Intuition is its mode. Social harmony is its aim" (p. 129).

Although one might be tempted to conclude from the above analysis that Americans strive for optimal competence whereas the Japanese strive for only satisfactory competence, we believe such a conclusion to be too simplistic, rather ethnocentric, and unwarranted. Instead, the analysis above suggests that the requirements for communication competence between the two cultures may vary. There may be occasions when Japanese conversants act in optimally competent ways, although the cultural system requires satisfactory competence. Conversely, American communicators may attempt to converse in a satisfactorily competent manner when the cultural system requires much more. Variations in the act of self-disclosure may differently influence the perceived competence and social attractiveness of the person disclosing between the cultures.

METHODS

Design

A 3 × 2 × 2 factorial design was employed in this study. Levels of self-disclosure in a conversation (high, medium, and low), culture (Japanese and American), and sex (male and female) were treated as independent variables. Dependent measures included seven aspects of logical force (Pearce & Cronen, 1980), three dimensions of episode perception, and perceived levels of communication competence and attractiveness of the discloser. In addition, perceived levels of the respondent's own communication competence were treated as a covariate, since previous CMM research found that in evaluating simulated conversations subjects' perceptions of their own competence was highly correlated to their perceptions of the other person's competence (Pearce, Cronen, Johnson, Jones, & Raymond, 1980).

Respondents

A total of 382 respondents participated in this study. Respondents from the Japanese and American samples were matched on the bases of their educational background, age, and intercultural experiences. The Japanese sample consisted of 97 males and 90 females randomly selected from students attending three large universities in Tokyo, Japan. The American sample was composed of 98 male and 97 female undergraduate volunteers enrolled in basic speech communication courses at a large Midwestern university. Mean ages for Japanese and American respondents were 19.7 (SD = 1.1) and 19.8 (SD = 2.2), respectively. The vast majority of students in both samples reported no intercultural experiences. Of those few who reported some intercultural experiences, the longest experience involved a North American student who spent three months in Mexico.

Procedures

The stimulus materials consisted of three incomplete dialogues between two college students of the same sex. A previous study employed gender-neutral names in the dialogues, but that strategy for controlling sex differences was not possible in the study. Although there are gender-neutral names in the Japanese language, linguistic styles are distinctly masculine or feminine. Both Japanese and American dialogues involved the names of two males or two females conversing. Male respondents read a dialogue between two males while females read a dialogue between two females in the present study, controlling for possible interaction between the sex of the respondent and the sex composition of the dyad in the dialogue.

The high- and low-disclosure dialogues were adopted from Wolfson and Pearce (1983). The high-disclosure dialogue described feelings of sexual inadequacy revealed by the target person, while the low-disclosure dialogue concerned attitudes toward a favorite type of music, jazz. A medium-disclosure dialogue was also created. On the basis of Barnlund's (1975) work, a number of topics were pretested, and a dialogue was chosen in which the target person disclosed personal feelings about his or her sibling who dropped out of high school. For Japanese respondents, all the dialogues were carefully translated into Japanese by a team of bilingual scholars using a parallel translation technique suggested by Hall (1985).

Line 5 of each dialogue contained the manipulated self-disclosure by the target person. Line 6 was filled out by each respondent. Respondents were instructed to make a response to the target person's self-disclosure, thinking of themselves as if they were talking to the target person in the situation.

When respondents finished reading one of the three dialogues and writing their responses down on Line 6, they were asked to fill out a questionnaire that contained several scaler items measuring the strength of each aspect of logical force, perception of the dialogue, perceived social attractiveness of the target person, perceived communication competence of the target person, and the respondents' perception of their own communicative competence.

Experimental sessions were held in classrooms, and they lasted approximately half an hour. At the conclusion of each session, respondents were thoroughly debriefed and thanked for their participation in this study.

Measures

Perceptions of the dialogue were operationalized using 20 semantic differential scales. Of the 20 scales, 5 were constructed on the basis of Rossiter and Pearce's (1975) conceptualization of self-disclosure for a manipulation check. The remaining 15 scales were subjected to a principal component analysis with Varimax rotation, yielding a three-factor solution: *valence*, *social utility*, and *openness* (see Table 10.1). Valence was comprised of: difficult, pleasant, comfortable, appropriate, predictable, and common. Social utility was defined by: productive, useful, effective, and important. Openness was composed of: intimate and open.

Perceived social attractiveness of the target person, perceived communicative competence of the target person, and perception of the respondent's own communication competence were all measured using seven-point Likert-type scales. The internal reliabilities for all scales were deemed adequate (social attractiveness: Cronbach's $\alpha = .86$; perceived communication competence: Cronbach's $\alpha = .73$; perceived self-competence: Cronbach's $\alpha = .68$).

Logical force was operationalized in terms of seven seven-point Likert-type scales based on Pearce and Cronen's (1980) measurement model for a regulative rule. These seven items were constructed to measure the strength of conversational entailment on the act performed by the respondents on Line 6 from several aspects of their rules for meaning and action. The rationale for this measurement model is that "conversants seldom act capriciously, but that the force which impels them to select one act rather than another is variable and sometimes highly differentiated, such that there are important differences in the logic of action in different episodes, cultures, relationships, etc." (Wolfson & Pearce, 1983, p. 252).

TABLE 10.1 Factor Analysis: Perceptions of the Dialogue

	Factor 1	*Factor 2*	*Factor 3*
Productive	.14	.75*	.13
Useful	.11	.85*	.10
Effective	.15	.78*	.06
Difficult	.81*	–.04	–.01
Pleasant	.69*	.38	.17
Intimate	–.29	.06	.54*
Comfortable	.84*	.07	.13
Friendly	.27	.28	.70*
Usual	.82*	.05	–.04
Appropriate	.78*	.33	.04
Predictable	.76*	.01	–.09
Important	–.16	.75*	.16
Desirable	.55	.57	.07
Open	.03	.11	.80*
Common	.81*	.03	–.13

NOTE: Factor 1 = Valence/Harmony; Factor 2 = Social Utility; Factor 3 = Openness
* denotes the items used to compute factor scores.

Logical force consists of two interrelated forces. One is called *prefigurative force*, or the extent to which the act is perceived by the actor as obligated because of its linkage to some antecedent condition prior to the act. Five items were used to measure the strength of prefigurative force felt by the respondents as they generated a response to the target person's self-disclosure: (a) perceived link between the nature of the episode and the act; (b) perceived link between the nature of the relationship and the act; (c) perceived link between their self-concept and the act; (d) perceived link between cultural norms and the act; and (e) the absence of any relationship between the act and the consequent conditions.

The second aspect of logical force is referred to as *practical force*, or the extent to which the actor perceives the act as necessary to bring about certain outcomes. Two items were used to measure the practical force within the respondent performing a particular act: (a) the linkage from the act to the relationship; and (b) the linkage from the act to the subsequent state of the relationship. Test-retest reliability coefficients for logical force items ranged from .71 to .78.

For Japanese respondents, all the items in the questionnaire as well as the instructions were carefully translated into Japanese using a parallel translation technique.

RESULTS

Data from this study were analyzed in light of the research questions that were raised. Separate analyses were performed for the perceptions of the episode, for the target person, and for logical force measures.

Manipulation Check

The validity of experimental manipulation was checked with regard to the perceived levels of self-disclosure in each of the three dialogues. The scale for the manipulation check consisted of five seven-point semantic differential items constructed using Rossiter and Pearce's (1975) conceptualization of self-disclosure (private, risky, personal, intimate, and easy to tell). Since ratings were summed, the possible range of ratings was from 5 to 35. A one-way analysis of variance revealed a significant main effect for dialogue ($p < .001$), and a Tukey HSD test showed that the three dialogues differed in the predicted direction in terms of levels of self-disclosure. The low-disclosure dialogue ($X = 12.1$, SD = 5.5), the medium-disclosure dialogue ($X = 20.3$, SD = 4.4), and the high-disclosure dialogue ($X = 23.6$, SD = 6.4) were perceived by respondents as being significantly different from one another.

Episode Perception, Social Attraction, and Communication Competence

The null hypotheses were tested using multivariate analysis of variance with three independent variables (sex, culture, and episode) and five dependent variables representing three dimensions of episode perception (valence/harmony, social utility, and openness) and two aspects of the perception of the target person (social attraction and communication competence). In addition, subjects' perceptions of their own communication competence (self-competence) was treated as covariate. Most of the significant correlations between the five dependent variables included in the analysis were moderate to high (.22 to .99), thus warranting multivariate analysis.

As expected, perceptions of the overall conversation differed. There were significant multivariate effects for sex (Wilk's $\lambda = .94$, Pillai trace = .06, $F[5/356] = 4.345$, $p < .001$), culture (Wilk's $\lambda = .83$, Pillai trace = .17, $F[5/356] = 15.0$, $p < .001$) as well as for episode (Wilk's $\lambda = .38$, Pillai trace = .73, $F[10/730] = 45.5$, $p < .001$). The analysis also revealed multivariate two-way interaction effects for sex and episode (Wilk's $\lambda = .87$, Pillai trace = .14, $F[10/730] = 5.5$, $p < .001$) as well as for culture and episode (Wilk's $\lambda = .88$, Pillai trace = .12, $F[10/730] = 4.7$,

$p < .001$). In addition, there was a significant multivariate three-way interaction among sex, culture, and episode (Wilk's $\lambda = .94$, Pillai trace = .06, $F[10/730] = 2.1$, $p < .02$). Finally, the analysis yielded a significant within cells regression for the covariate "self-competence" (Wilk's $\lambda = .89$, Pillai trace = .11, $F[5/365] = 9.2$, $p < .001$).

The significant MANOVAs were then followed by univariate analysis of variance (ANOVA) and Tukey HSD tests to more fully interpret the group differences that were found. On the perceived "valence/harmony" of the dialogue, there were significant two-way interactions found for sex and episode ($F[2/369] = 24.5$, $p < .001$, $\eta^2 = .12$) as well as for culture and episode ($F[2/369] = 13.6$, $p < .001$, $\eta^2 = .07$). Respondents generally perceived the low self-disclosure dialogue as the most positively valenced and harmonious and the moderate- or high-disclosure dialogue as less positively valenced and harmonious by comparison. Unexpectedly, Japanese respondents perceived the high self-disclosure dialogue to be less negatively valenced and disharmonious than the Americans did. Interestingly, males perceived the high-disclosure dialogue to be as harmonious as the moderate-disclosure dialogue, while females reported it to be the least harmonious of the three dialogues.

A significant main effect of episode was found for the perceived social utility of the dialogue ($F[2/369] = 36.1$, $p < .001$, $\eta^2 = .16$). Regardless of sex or culture, the high self-disclosure dialogue was perceived as the least socially useful, while the low and moderate disclosure dialogues were perceived as equally useful.

A significant three-way interaction effect among sex, culture, and episode ($F[2/369] = 3.9$, $p < .04$, $\eta^2 = .02$) emerged on the openness dimension. The multiple comparisons of means indicated some interesting patterns. Japanese males perceived the low- and high-disclosure dialogues as equally open and the medium-disclosure dialogue as least open. In contrast, Japanese females and American males exhibited a similar trend, and they rated the low-disclosure dialogue as more open than the medium- or high-disclosure dialogue. Only American females distinguished among the three levels of self-disclosure with respect to openness.

Importantly, perceptions of one's own communication competence was a statistically significant covariate in two of the three perceptual dimensions of the dialogue ($F[1/369] = 38.9$, $p < .001$, $\eta^2 = .10$ for harmony/valence; $F[1/369] = 36.1$, $p < .001$, $\eta^2 = .09$ for openness).

A number of significant effects were found in terms of the difference between Japanese and American males and females in their perceptions of the communication competence of an actor who exhibited varying degrees of self-disclosure. A culture-by-episode interaction

($F[2/369] = 13.5$, $p < .001$, $\eta^2 = .07$), a sex-by-episode interaction ($F[2/369] = 3.0$, $p < .05$, $\eta^2 = .02$), and the effect of the covariate ($F[1/369] = 5.4$, $p < .02$, $\eta^2 = .01$) achieved the level of significance. Although respondents generally rated the target person's communication competence higher in the low self-disclosure dialogue than in the medium- or high-disclosure conversation, multiple comparisons of means revealed the following patterns. First, males perceived the medium and high discloser to be equal in communication competence, but females reported that the target person's communication competence varied significantly at increasing levels of self-disclosure. Second, Japanese respondents simply perceived the low self-discloser to be more competent than the moderate and high discloser. Only American respondents perceived the dialogues to be different from one another in the level of communication competence. Furthermore, it was revealed that the Americans perceived the low discloser to be more communicatively competent than did the Japanese. No differences between cultures emerged in the moderate-disclosure dialogue, and the Americans perceived the high discloser to be less communicatively competent than did the Japanese.

The social attractiveness of the self-discloser was represented by a single factor score with four items being weighted and then summed (McCroskey & McCain, 1974). A univariate analysis of variance test revealed a sex-by-episode interaction ($F[2/369] = 5.3$, $p < .005$, $\eta^2 = .03$), a culture-by-episode interaction ($F[2/369] = 4.1$, $p < .02$, $\eta^2 = .02$), and an effect by the covariate ($F[1/369] = 19.4$, $p < .001$, $\eta^2 = .01$).

The Tukey HSD test provided results similar to the perceived communication competence findings. Comparisons across the sexes showed that social attractiveness of the discloser did not vary significantly for males, whereas females found the high self-discloser to be less attractive than the low or moderate discloser. Interestingly, Japanese respondents tended to perceive the medium discloser to be the most socially attractive. No such tendency was observed for Americans, and they perceived the high discloser to be less socially attractive than the low or medium discloser.

Logical Force

The second part of the research examined the differences between Japanese and American respondents in terms of the force of perceived oughtness (i.e., logical force) on their performance of particular acts in conversations involving varying degrees of self-disclosure. Five prefigurative force and two practical force measures, which jointly represent logical force, exhibited low to moderate positive correlations (.06 to .39).

A multivariate analysis of variance found significant effects for culture (Wilk's $\lambda = .89$, Pillai trace $= .11$, $F[7/363] = 12.7$, $p < .001$) and for episode (Wilk's $\lambda = .84$, Pillai trace $= .16$, $F[14/726] = 14.9$, $p < .001$). On the basis of Pearce and Cronen's (1980) model, prefigurative force and practical force were subsequently examined separately to further explore the differences between Japanese and Americans in terms of how they structure their systems of rules for meaning and action.

Episode-Act Linkage. A univariate analysis of variance test revealed a significant main effect for culture ($F[1/369] = 7.5$, $p < .007$, $\eta^2 = .02$). The result indicated that regardless of sex or the perceived level of self-disclosure, American respondents were significantly less concerned about the episode on their choice of a response than the Japanese counterparts.

Relationship-Act Linkage. Significant main effects for culture ($F[1/369] = 13.4$, $p < .001$, $\eta^2 = .04$) and episode ($F[2/369] = 6.7$, $p < .001$, $\eta^2 = .04$) were found on this variable. The multiple comparisons of means revealed that regardless of sex or culture, the respondents' definitions of the relationship influenced their choice of response in the high-disclosure dialogue more strongly than the low- or moderate-disclosure dialogue. Furthermore, the result indicated Japanese respondents' definitions of the relationship with the target person influenced their choice of response more strongly than the Americans.

Life-Script-Act Linkage. No effects of culture or episode were found on this variable. This result suggests that respondents' personal involvements in their responses would be generally indeterminant during initial interaction, regardless of their sex, cultural backgrounds, or the degree of self-disclosure in the conversation.

Cultural Archetype-Act Linkage. The results of a univariate analysis of variance test indicated a significant main effect for episode on this variable ($F[2/369] = 5.7$, $p < .004$, $\eta^2 = .03$). The result showed that respondents generally felt their act was derived from their cultural patterns significantly more strongly in the low-disclosure dialogue than in the medium-disclosure or high-disclosure dialogues. This result may be no surprise, because the low-disclosure dialogue reflected a highly ritualistic, ordinary interaction between two acquaintances.

Functional Autonomy. On this variable, a significant main effect was found for culture ($F[1/369] = 6.2$, $p < .01$, $\eta^2 = .02$). It follows that Japanese respondents in general reported significantly less purposive consideration of the target person's subsequent responses than the Americans.

Next, two aspects of practical force were closely examined. The results are as follows. In terms of the act-relationship linkage, the result of a univariate analysis of variance test revealed a significant effect for episode (F[2/369] = 12.1, $p < .001$, $\eta^2 = .06$). The result indicated that respondents generally felt less impact of their choice of message on their subsequent relationship with the target person in the high-disclosure conversation as opposed to the low- or medium-disclosure conversation. For act-life-script linkage significant main effects were found for culture (F[1/369] = 10.3, $p < .001$, $\eta^2 = .03$) and for episode (F[2/369] = 5.0, $p < .007$, $\eta^2 = .03$). The result showed that respondents generally felt their act in the low-disclosure conversation would better help to create and maintain a desired self-image than their act in the medium-disclosure or high-disclosure conversations. It was also found that the Americans perceived a significantly stronger link between their act and the subsequent state of their self-concept than did the Japanese.

DISCUSSION

This study was designed to make a cross-cultural comparison between Japanese and American cultures to describe the variations in the implications of self-disclosure in interpersonal encounters. The study also aimed at providing empirical support for the utility of logical force as a transcultural concept (Pearce & Cronen, 1980).

Analysis of the episode descriptors revealed some interesting patterns. It was found that Japanese males perceived the high-disclosure dialogue to be as open as the low-disclosure dialogue, while all the other groups generally felt that the high-disclosure dialogue was least open. In addition, both groups perceived the moderate and high self-disclosure dialogues as somewhat negatively valenced and disharmonious, but the Japanese less so than the American sample. Moreover, sex of the respondent had an influence on these results: American females viewed the higher-disclosing dialogues as more negatively valenced and disharmonious than did the other three groups. These findings are similar to the previous study by Wolfson and Pearce (1983) in that the Chinese found the dialogues negatively valenced and disharmonious as well.

It seems that the Americans, especially American females, are highly sensitive to the act of self-disclosure during conversation and are very critical of the person disclosing himself or herself inappropriately. In contrast, the Japanese appear to be less sensitive to the potential effects of self-disclosure. These differences may be due to (a) differences in the cultural definition of what constitutes appropriate communication behavior; (b) differences in their respective socialization processes; and (c) slight cultural differences between the Japanese and Americans concerning the topics disclosed in those dialogues. There were no cultural differences between the Japanese and American subjects concerning the social utility of the dialogues.

Logical force provides a useful descriptor of variations in the conversational implicature between Japanese and American respondents. It was found that the high-disclosure dialogue produced a greater amount of prefigurative force than did low- and medium-disclosure dialogues. Moreover, in constructing a response to different levels of self-disclosure, Japanese participants clearly felt a stronger degree of prefigurative force, or sense of obligation, in their response than did the Americans. In particular, Japanese respondents reported a stronger episode-act linkage than the Americans across the three disclosure conditions. Both Japanese males and females reported a stronger relationship-act linkage than the Americans as well as higher degrees of functional autonomy.

These results are comparable to those reported by Wolfson and Pearce (1983) and are consistent with available evidence about Japanese cultural patterns. The results suggest that the Japanese people's interpersonal communication is indeed highly context dependent, and that they tend to use information about the episode that is unfolding and the nature of the relationship between them and their partners in selecting appropriate responses in light of the situation. The rather strong functional autonomy exhibited by the Japanese sample can also explained based on the dimensions of cultural variability. According to Hofstede (1980), the Japanese people are high on uncertainty avoidance, which means they tend to resist change and have higher levels of anxiety. It is reasonable to assume that the Japanese respondents' higher degrees of functional autonomy during conversation reflects their uncertainty avoidance tendencies.

On measures of practical force, the strength of practical force decreased from low to moderate to high self-disclosure conditions for both samples. American respondents tended to feel a stronger linkage between their act and the subsequent state of affairs than did the Japanese. In addition, the Japanese felt that their responses would have less impact on who they were as individuals than did American respondents at all three levels of self-disclosure. No differences were found between the two groups on the implication of their chosen response and the meaning of the subsequent relationship. The resultant differences between American and Japanese subjects on the act-subsequent-life-script linkage were expected and consistent with the literature concerning the variable importance of self in Eastern and Western cultures. In individualistic cultures self-concept is central to one's existence, and, as Geertz (1975) observes, one's self-concept is viewed as "a bounded, unique, more or less integrated motivational and cognitive universe, a dynamic center of awareness, judgment, and action organized into a distinctive whole" (p. 48). In collectivistic cultures, people's self-esteem is linked to their relationships with those with whom they are associated, and the individual self is often overshadowed by their group identity (i.e, *messhi*, meaning denial of self-importance for the sake of the group goal).

However, the fact that no differences emerged between the two groups on the act-subsequent-relationship linkage must not be taken lightly. The result indicates that respondents felt that all three episodes had relatively strong relational consequences. Those consequences may or may not be positive and desirable. Both the Japanese and American respondents perceived that their verbal acts would impact their relationship development with the target person.

The present study also explored the possible utility of communication competence as a transcultural concept. Although a complete test of communication competence was not employed here, perceptions of the discloser's communication competence and perceptions of self-competence were used. The results appear favorable. In general, the Japanese viewed the self-discloser as less communicatively competent than did the Americans in the low-disclosure condition. Conversely, Japanese males viewed the high self-discloser as more communicatively competent than did American females. A similar pattern emerged on the perceived social attractiveness of the self-discloser in high- and low-disclosure-level conditions. The results strongly favor the claim that communication competence is an interpersonal impression of a social actor, or the actor's perceived appropriateness and effectiveness (Spitzberg & Cupach, 1984). It was also found that communication competence and social attractiveness are closely linked to each other, and communication competence and social attractiveness may not be separated in person perception. In the present study, some empirical support was also obtained for Harris's (1979) functional view of communication competence. The results suggest that the subjective context of the episode or the requirements of a particular cultural system (i.e., Japanese or American) may influence whether or not a social actor performing a certain communicative act (e.g., self-disclosure) is perceived as competent.

Of greater interest, perhaps, is the role perceptions of one's own communication competence plays in this study. Perceptions of one's own competence seem to make a difference in subjects' (a) perceptions of the episode, (b) perceptions of another's communication competence, and (c) perceptions of another's social attractiveness. These findings can be explained in terms of social comparison. When we make impressions of other people, we constantly compare ourselves with others. In fact, extensive research shows that our self-concept affects our perception of others (Baron, 1974). It is likely that people who consider themselves competent communicators will evaluate other people's communication competence more positively, and those who do not think that they are good at communicating will have a poor opinion of others. How perceptions of one's own competence influence these aspects of interpersonal communication needs to be explored further in cross-cultural contexts.

This study provided further evidence for the links between communication and culture. Both culture and gender were found to influence perceptions of self-disclosure. The results also provide additional support for the use of logical force as a transcultural concept. Finally, the study provided an initial exploration of the use of communication competence as a transcultural concept. Both perceptions of the competence of self and the other appear to have utility in understanding intercultural communication. Future research should seek to further explore these concepts.

References

Abe, H., & Wiseman, R. L. (1983). A cross-cultural confirmation of the dimensions of intercultural effectiveness. *International Journal of Intercultural Relations, 7*, 53-67.

Abelson, R. (1976). Script processing in attitude formation and decision making. In J. Carroll & J. Payne (Eds.), *Cognition and social behavior* (pp. 33-45). Hillsdale, NJ: Lawrence Erlbaum.

Adams-Webber, J. (1985). Construing self and others. In F. Epting & A. W. Landfield (Eds.), *Anticipating personal construct psychology* (pp. 58-69). Lincoln, NE: University of Nebraska.

Albert, E. (1972). Culture patterning of speech behavior in Burundi. In J. Gumperz & D. Hymes (Eds.), *Directions in sociolinguistics: The ethnography of communication* (pp. 72-105). New York: Holt, Rinehart, & Winston.

Albrecht, T. L., & Adelman, M. B. (1984). Social support and life stress. *Human Communication Research, 11*, 3-32.

Alexander, A., Cronen, V., Kang, K., Tsou, B., & Banks, B. J. (1986). Patterns of topic sequencing and information gain: A comparative study of relationship development in Chinese and American cultures. *Communication Quarterly, 34*(1), 66-78.

Altman, I., & Taylor, D. (1973). *Social penetration: The development of interpersonal relationships*. New York: Holt, Rinehart & Winston.

Altman, I., Vinsel, A., & Brown, B. (1981). Dialectical conceptions in social psychology: An application to social penetration and privacy regulation. In L. Berkowitz (Ed.), *Advances in experimental social psychology* (Vol. 14, pp. 107-160). New York: Academic Press.

Andersen, J. F., Norton, R. W., & Nussbaum, J. F. (1981). Three investigations exploring relationships between perceived teacher communication behaviors and student learning. *Communication Education, 30*, 377-392.

Andersen, P. A. (1987). The trait debate: A critical examination of the individual differences paradigm in interpersonal communication. In B. Dervin & M. J. Voight (Eds.), *Progress in communication sciences* (Vol. 8, pp. 47-82). Norwood, NJ: Ablex.

Andersen, P. A. (1991). When one cannot not communicate. *Communication Studies, 42*, 309-325.

Antonovsky, A. (1987). *Unraveling the mystery of health: How people manage stress and stay well*. San Francisco: Jossey-Bass.

Applegate, J., & Sypher, H. (1988). A constructivist theory of communication and culture. In Y. Y. Kim & W. Gudykunst (Eds.), *Theories in intercultural communication* (pp. 41-65). Newbury Park, CA: Sage.

Argyle, M. (1979). New developments in the analysis of social skills. In A. Wolfgang (Ed.), *Nonverbal behavior: Applications and cultural implications* (pp. 139-158). New York: Academic Press.

Argyle, M. (1980). Interaction skills and social competence. In P. Feldman & J. Orford (Eds.), *Psychological problems: The social context* (pp. 123-150). New York: John Wiley.

Argyle, M. (1981). The contribution of social interaction research to social skills training. In J. D. Wine & M. D. Smye (Eds.), *Social competence* (pp. 261-286). New York: Guilford.

Argyle, M., Bond, M., Lizuka, Y., & Contarello, A. (1986). Cross-cultural variations in relationship rules. *International Journal of Psychology, 21*, 287-315.

Argyle, M., Furnham, A., & Graham, J. A. (1981). *Social situations*. London: Cambridge University.

Argyle, M., & Kendon, A. (1967). The experimental analysis of social performance. *Advances in Experimental Social Psychology, 3*, 55-98.

Argyle, M., & Little, B. R. (1972). Do personality traits apply to social behavior? *Journal for the Theory of Social Behavior, 2*, 1-33.

Argyris, C. (1965). *Organization and innovation*. Homewood, IL: Dorsey.

Asante, M. K., & Gudykunst, W. B. (Eds.). (1989). *Handbook of international and intercultural communication*. Newbury Park, CA: Sage.

Asante, M. K., & Vora, E. (1983). Toward multiple philosophical approaches. In W. B. Gudykunst (Ed.), *Intercultural communication theory* (pp. 293-298). Beverly Hills, CA: Sage.

Athay, M., & Darley, J. M. (1981). Toward an interaction-centered theory of personality. In N. Cantor & J. F. Kihlstrom (Eds.), *Personality, cognition, and social interaction* (pp. 281-308). Hillsdale, NJ: Lawrence Erlbaum.

Backlund, P. (1982). A response to "Communication competence and performance: A research and pedagogical perspective." *Communication Education, 31*, 365-366.

Baldwin, A. L. (1958). The role of an "ability" construct in a theory of behavior. In D. C. McClelland, A. L. Baldwin, U. Bronfenbrenner, & F. L. Strodtbeck (Eds.), *Talent and society* (pp. 195-233). Princeton, NJ: D. Van Nostrand.

Ball-Rokeach, S. (1973). From pervasive ambiguity to definition of the situation. *Sociometry, 36*, 378-389.

Barna, L. M. (1979). Intercultural communication stumbling blocks. In R. E. Porter & L. A. Samovar (Eds.), *Intercultural communication: A reader* (2nd ed., pp. 291-298). Belmont, CA: Wadsworth.

Barnlund, D. C. (1975). *Public and private self in Japan and the United States*. Tokyo, Japan: Simul.

Barnlund, D. C. (1989). *Communicative styles of Japanese and Americans: Images and realities*. Belmont, CA: Wadsworth.

Barnlund, D., & Araki, S. (1985). Intercultural encounters: The management of compliments by Japanese and Americans. *Journal of Cross-Cultural Psychology, 16*, 9-26.

Barnlund, D., & Yoshioka, M. (1990). Apologies: Japanese and American styles. *International Journal of Intercultural Relations, 14*, 193-206.

Baron, P. (1974). Self-esteem, ingratiation, and evaluation of unknown others. *Journal of Personality and Social Psychology, 30*, 104-109.

Basso, K. (1970). To give up on words: Silence in the Western Apache culture. *Southwestern Journal of Anthropology, 26*, 213-230.

Bauman, R., & Sherzer, J. (1989). *Explorations in the ethnography of speaking* (2nd ed.). Cambridge, UK: Cambridge University Press.

Baxter, L. A. (1987). Symbols of relationship identity in relationship cultures. *Journal of Social and Personal Relationships, 4*, 261-280.

Baxter, L. A. (1988). A dialectical perspective on communication strategies in relationship development. In S. Duck, D. F. Hay, S. E. Hobfoll, W. Ickes, & B. Montgomery (Eds.), *Handbook of personal relationships* (pp. 257-273). London: Wiley.

Baxter, L. A. (1990). Dialectical contradictions in relationship development. *Journal of Social and Personal Relationships, 7*, 69-88.

Beck, A. T. (1988). *Love is never enough*. New York: Harper & Row.

Becker, E. (1971). *The birth and death of meaning* (2nd ed.). New York:Free Press.

Befu, H. (1973). *Japan and the United States: How we see each other.* Tokyo: United States-Japan Trade Council.

Belenky, M., Clinchy, B., Goldberg, N., & Tarule, J. (1986). *Women's ways of knowing: The development of self, voice, and mind*. New York: Basic Books.

Bell, R. A., & Healey, J. G. (1992). Idiomatic communication and interpersonal solidarity in friends' relational cultures. *Human Communication Research, 18*, 307-335.

Bellah, R., Madsen, R., Sullivan, W., Swidler, A., & Tipton, S. (1985). *Habits of the heart*. Berkeley: University of California Press.

Bellah, R., Madsen, R., Sullivan, W., Swidler, A., & Tipton, S. (1991). *The good society*. New York: Knopf.

Bennett, D. W. (1987, February). *The effect of relationship type, trust and different perception on judgment of interpersonal communicated competence*. Paper presented at the Western Speech Communication Association convention, Salt Lake City, UT.

Bennett, M. (1979). Overcoming the golden rule: Empathy and sympathy. In D. Nimmo (Ed.), *Communication yearbook 3* (pp. 407-422). New Brunswick, NJ: Transaction Books.

Berger, C. R. (1987). Planning and scheming: Strategies for initiating relationships. In R. Burnett, P. McGhee, & D. D. Clarke (Eds.), *Accounting for relationships: Explanation, representation and knowledge* (pp. 158-174). London: Methuen.

Berger, C. R. (1988). Planning, social affect, and social action generation. In R. Donohew, H. Sypher, & E. Higgins (Eds.), *Communication, social cognition, and affect* (pp. 93-116). Hillsdale, NJ: Lawrence Erlbaum.

Berger, C. R. (1979). Sociology of knowledge. In R. W. Budd & B. D. Ruben (Eds.), *Interdisciplinary approaches to human communication* (pp. 155-173). Rochelle Park, NJ: Hayden.

Berger, C. R., & Calabrese, R. (1975). Some explorations in initial interactions and beyond: Toward a developmental theory of interpersonal communication. *Human Communication Research, 1*, 99-112.

Berger, C. R., & Douglas, W. (1982). Thought and talk. In F. Dance (Ed.), *Human communication theory*. New York: Harper & Row.

Berger, C. R., & Gudykunst, W. B. (1991). Uncertainty and communication. In B. Dervin & M. Voigt (Eds.), *Progress in communication science* (Vol. 10, pp. 21-66). Norwood, NJ: Ablex.

Berger, C. R., Karol, S. H., & Jordan, J. M. (1989). When a lot of knowledge is a dangerous thing: The debilitating effects of plan complexity on verbal fluency. *Human Communication Research, 16*, 91-119.

Berger, J., Conner, T., & Fisek, M. (Eds.). (1974). *Expectation states: A theoretical research program*. Cambridge, MA: Winthrop.

Bernstein, B. (1981). Codes, modalities, and the process of cultural reproduction. *Language in Society, 10*, 327-363.

Berry, J. W. (1980). Introduction to methodology. In H. C. Triandis & J. W. Berry (Eds.), *Handbook of cross-cultural psychology, Vol. 2: Methodology* (pp. 1-28). Boston, MA: Allyn & Bacon.

Berscheid, E. (1985). Interpersonal attraction. In G. Lindzey & E. Aronson (Eds.), *Handbook of social psychology* (3rd ed., Vol. 2, pp. 413-484). New York: Random House.

Berscheid, E., Graziano, W., Monson, T., & Dermer, M. (1976). Outcome dependency: Attention, attribution, and attraction. *Journal of Personality and Social Psychology, 34*, 978-989.

Billig, M. (1987). *Arguing and thinking*. Cambridge, UK: Cambridge University Press.

Blalock, H. (1969). *Theory construction*. Englewood Cliffs, NJ: Prentice Hall.

Blau, P., & Schwartz, B. (1984). *Cross-cutting social circles*. New York: Academic Press.

Blum-Kulka, S., Danet, B., & Gherson, R. (1985). The language of requesting in Israeli society. In J. Forgas (Ed.), *Language and social situation* (pp. 113-141). New York: Springer Verlag.

Blum-Kulka, S., House, J., & Kasper, G. (Eds.) (1989). *Cross-cultural pragmatics: Requests and apologies*. Norwood, NJ: Ablex.

Blumer, H. (1969). *Symbolic interactionism: Perspective and method*. Englewood Cliffs, NJ: Prentice Hall.

Blumstein, P. (1991). The production of selves in personal relationships. In J. Howard & P. Callero (Eds.), *The self-society dynamic: Cognition, emotions and action* (pp. 305-322). Cambridge, UK: Cambridge University Press.

Bochner, A. P., & Kelly, C. W. (1974). Interpersonal competence: Rationale, philosophy, and implementation of a conceptual framework. *Speech Teacher, 23*, 270-301.

Boldt, E. (1978). Structural tightness and cross-cultural research. *Journal of Cross-Cultural Psychology, 10*, 221-230.

Bormann, E. (1980). *Communication theory*. New York: Holt, Rinehart & Winston.

Bormann, E. (1989). On "Communication as a practical discipline." In B. Dervin, L. Grossberg, B. J. O'Keefe, & E. Wartella (Eds.), *Rethinking communication* (Vol. 1, pp. 135-138). Newbury Park, CA: Sage.

Bostrom, R. N. (1984). *Competence in communication: A multidisciplinary approach*. Beverly Hills, CA: Sage.

Bowen, M. (1978). *Family therapy in clinical practice*. New York: Arenson.

Bradway, K. P. (1937). Social competence of exceptional children: II. The mentally subnormal. *Journal of Exceptional Children, 4*, 38-42.

Braithwaite, C. (1990). Communicative silence: A cross-cultural study of Basso's hypothesis. In D. Carbaugh (Ed.), *Cultural communication and intercultural contact* (pp. 321-328). Hillsdale, NJ: Lawrence Erlbaum.

Braithwaite, D. O. (1991a). "Just how much did that wheelchair cost?" Management of privacy boundaries by persons with disabilities. *Western Journal of Speech Communication, 55*, 254-274.

Braithwaite, D. O. (1991b). Viewing persons with disabilities as a culture. In L. Samovar & R. Porter (Eds.), *Intercultural communication: A reader* (6th ed., pp. 136-142). Belmont, CA: Wadsworth.

Brewer, M. B. (1991). The social self: On being the same and different at the same time. *Personality and Social Psychology Bulletin, 17*, 475-482.

Briggs, C. (1988). *Competence in performance*. Philadelphia: University of Pennsylvania Press.

Brislin, R. (1981). *Cross-cultural encounters: Face-to-face encounters*. New York: Pergamon.

Brislin, R. W., Lonner, W. J., & Thorndike, R. M. (1973). *Cross-cultural research methods*. New York: John Wiley.

Brown, P., & Levinson, S. (1978). Universals in language usage: Politeness phenomena. In E. N. Goody (Ed.), *Questions and politeness: Strategies in social interaction* (pp. 56-289). Cambridge, UK: Cambridge University Press.

Brown, P., & Levinson, S. (1987). *Politeness: Some universals in language usage*. Cambridge, UK: Cambridge University Press.

Burgoon, J. K. (1992). Applying a comparative approach to expectancy violation theory. In J. G. Blumler, J. M. McLeod, & K. E. Rosengren (Eds.), *Comparatively speaking: Communication and culture across space and time* (pp. 53-69). Newbury Park, CA: Sage.

Burgoon, J. K., & Hale, J. L. (1988). Validation and measurement of the fundamental themes of relational communication. *Communication Monographs*, *54*, 19-41.

Burns, D. D. (1989). *The feeling good handbook*. New York: William Morrow.

Byrne, D., & Kelley, K. (1981). *An introduction to personality* (3rd ed.). Englewood Cliffs, NJ: Prentice Hall.

Callero, P. (1991). Conclusion. In J. Howard & P. Callero (Eds.), *The self-society dynamic: Cognition, emotions and action* (pp. 323-331). Cambridge, UK: Cambridge University Press.

Canary, D. J., & Spitzberg, B. H. (1987). Appropriateness and effectiveness perceptions of conflict strategies. *Human Communication Research*, *14* (1), 93-118.

Canary, D. J., & Spitzberg, B. H. (1989). A model of competence perceptions of conflict strategies. *Human Communication Research*, *15*, 630-649.

Cantor, N., Mischel, W., & Schwartz, J. C. (1982). A prototype analysis of psychological situations. *Cognitive Psychology*, *14*, 45-77.

Carbaugh, D. (1988). *Talking American*. Norwood, NJ: Ablex.

Carbaugh, D. (1989). Fifty terms for talk: A cross-cultural study. In S. Ting-Toomey & F. Korzenny (Eds.), *Language, communication and culture: Current directions* (pp. 93-120). Newbury Park, CA: Sage.

Carbaugh, D. (Ed.). (1990a). *Cultural communication and intercultural contact*. Hillsdale, NJ: Lawrence Erlbaum.

Carbaugh, D. (1990b). Intercultural communication. In D. Carbaugh (Ed.), *Cultural communication and intercultural contact* (pp. 151-175). Hillsdale, NJ: Lawrence Erlbaum.

Carbaugh, D. (1990c). Toward a perspective on cultural communication and intercultural contact. *Semiotica*, *80*(1/2), 15-35.

Carbaugh, D. (1991). Communication and cultural interpretation. *Quarterly Journal of Speech*, *77*, 336-342.

Carbaugh, D. (in press). "Soul" and "self": Soviet and American cultures in conversation. *Quarterly Journal of Speech*.

Carbaugh, D., & Hastings, S. O. (1992). A role for communication theory in ethnography and cultural analysis. *Communication Theory*, *2*, 156-165.

Carrell, P. C., & Konneker, B. H. (1981). Politeness: Comparing native and nonnative judgments. *Language Learning*, *31*, 17-30.

Casmir, F. L., & Asuncione-Lande, N. C. (1988). Intercultural communication revisited: Conceptualization, paradigm building and methodological approaches. In M. McLaughlin (Ed.), *Communication yearbook 12* (pp. 278-309). Newbury Park, CA: Sage.

Cegala, D. J. (1981). Interaction involvement: A cognitive dimension of communicative competence. *Communication Education*, *30*, 109-121.

Cegala, D. J. (1984). Affective and cognitive manifestations of interaction involvement during unstructured and competitive interactions. *Communication Monographs*, *51*, 320-338.

Chen, G. (1989). Relationships of the dimensions of intercultural communication competence. *Communication Quarterly*, *37*, 118-133.

Chen, G. (1990). Intercultural communication competence: Some perspectives of research. *Howard Journal of Communications*, *2*, 243-261.

Chin, J. J., & Ringer, R. J. (1986, April). *What do measures of communication competence measure: A factor analytic study of three competence instruments*. Paper presented at the Central States Speech Communication Association convention, Schaumburg, IL.

Chinese Culture Connection (1987). Chinese value and search for culture-free dimensions of culture. *Journal of Cross-Cultural Psychology*, *18*, 143-164.

Chomsky, N. (1965). *Aspects of the theory of syntax*. Cambridge, MA: Massachusetts Institute of Technology Press.

Christensen, A., Sullaway, M., & King, C. E. (1983). Systematic error in behavioral reports of dyadic interaction: Egocentric bias and content effects. *Behavioral Assessment*, *5*, 129-140.

Cohen, J. (1977). *Statistical power analysis for the behavioral sciences*. New York: Academic Press.

Coker, D. A., & Burgoon, J. K. (1987). Trait versus state: A comparison of dispositional and situation measures of interpersonal communication competence. *Western Journal of Speech Communication*, *47*, 364-379.

Collier, M. J. (1988). A comparison of conversations among and between domestic culture groups: How intra- and intercultural competencies vary. *Communication Quarterly*, *36*(2), 122-144.

Collier, M. J. (1989). Cultural and intercultural communication competence: Current approaches and directions for future research. *International Journal of Intercultural Relations*, *13*, 287-302.

Collier, M. J. (1991). Conflict competence within African, Mexican, and Anglo American friendships. In S. Ting-Toomey & F. Korzenny (Eds.), *Cross-cultural interpersonal communication* (pp. 132-154). Newbury Park, CA: Sage.

Collier, M. J., Ribeau, S. A., & Hecht, M. L. (1986). Intracultural communication rules and outcomes within three domestic cultures. *Intercultural Journal of Intercultural Relations*, *10*, 439-457.

Collier, M. J., & Thomas, M. (1988). Cultural identity: An interpretive perspective. In Y. Kim & W. Gudykunst (Eds.), *Theories in intercultural communication* (pp. 99-120). Newbury Park, CA: Sage.

Colson, E. (1967). Competence and incompetence in the context of independence. *Current Anthropology*, *8*, 92-111.

Cooley, C. (1902). *Human nature and the social order*. New York: Scribner.

Cooley, R. E., & Roach, D. A. (1984). A conceptual framework. In R. N. Bostrom (Ed.), *Competence in communication: A multidisciplinary approach* (pp. 11-32). Beverly Hills, CA: Sage.

Corrigan, E. M. (1980). *Alcoholic women in treatment*. New York: Oxford University Press.

Coulmas, F. (1981). Poison to your soul: Thanks and apologies contrastively viewed. In F. Coulmas (Ed.), *Conversational routine* (pp. 69-91). The Hague, The Netherlands: Mouton.

Craig, R. T. (1989). Communication as a practical discipline. In B. Dervin, L. Grossberg, B. J. O'Keefe, & E. Wartella (Eds.), *Rethinking communication* (Vol. 1, pp. 97-124). Newbury Park, CA: Sage.

Cranley, M. J., & Brunner, C. C. (1988, April). *Physicians' interpersonal communication competence and nurses' interpersonal communication satisfaction*. Paper presented at the Central States Speech Association convention, Schaumburg, IL.

Cronen, V. E., Chen, V., & Pearce, W. B. (1988). Coordinated management of meaning: A critical theory. In Y. Y. Kim & W. B. Gudykunst (Eds.), *Theories in intercultural communication* (pp. 66-98). Beverly Hills, CA: Sage.

Cronen, V. E., & Shuter, R. (1983). Forming intercultural bonds. In W. B. Gudykunst (Ed.), *Intercultural communication theory* (pp. 89-118). Beverly Hills, CA: Sage.

Croxton, J. S., Eddy, T., & Morrow, N. (1984). Memory biases in the reconstruction of interpersonal encounters. *Journal of Social and Clinical Psychology*, *2*, 348-354.

Csikszentmihalyi, M. (1990). *Flow: The psychology of optimal experience*. New York: Harper & Row.

Cui, G. (1989, May). *Measuring intercultural effectiveness: An integrative approach.* Paper presented at the International Communication Association convention, San Francisco, CA.

Cupach, W. R., & Metts, S. (1990). Remedial processes in embarrassing predicaments. In J. A. Anderson (Ed.), *Communication yearbook 13* (pp. 323-352). Newbury Park, CA: Sage.

Cupach, W. R., & Spitzberg, B. H. (1981, February). *Relational competence: Measurement and validation*. Paper presented at the Western Speech Communication Association convention, San Jose, CA.

Cupach, W. R., & Spitzberg, B. H. (1983). Trait versus state: A comparison of dispositional and situational measures of interpersonal communication competence. *Western Speech Communication Journal*, *47*, 364-379.

Curran, J. P. (1982). A procedure for the assessment of social skills: The Simulated Social Interaction Test. In J. P. Curran & P. M. Monti (Eds.), *Social skills training* (pp. 348-398). New York: Guilford.

D'Andrade, R. G. (1981). The cultural part of cognition. *Cognitive Science*, *5*, 179-195.

D'Andrade, R. G. (1989). Culturally based reasoning. In A. Gellatly, D. Rogers, & J. A. Sloboda (Eds.), *Cognition and social worlds* (pp. 132-143). Oxford, UK: Clarendon Press.

D'Andrade, R. G., & Wish, M. (1985). Speech act theory in quantitative research on interpersonal behavior. *Discourse Processes*, *8*, 229-259.

Daikuhara, M. (1986). A study of compliments from a cross-cultural perspective: Japanese vs. American English. *Working Papers in Educational Linguistics*, *2*(2), 103-135.

Davidson, A. (1975). Cognitive differentiation and culture training. In R. Brislin & W. Lonner (Eds.), *Cross-cultural perspectives on learning* (pp. 79-94). Beverly Hills, CA: Sage.

Dawson, P. J., & Spitzberg, B. H. (1987, November). *Improving communicative competence: Validation of a social skills training workshop*. Paper presented at the Speech Communication Association convention, Boston, MA.

Descott, Y., & Latombe, J-C. (1985). Making compromises among antagonist constraints in a planner. *Artificial Intelligence*, *27*, 183-217.

Detweiler, R. (1975). On inferring the intentions of a person from another culture. *Journal of Personality*, *43*, 591-611.

Detweiler, R. (1980). Intercultural interaction and the categorization process. *International Journal of Intercultural Relations*, *4*, 275-293.

Devine, P. (1989). Stereotype and prejudice: Their automatic and controlled components. *Journal of Personality and Social Psychology*, *56*, 5-18.

DeVos, G., & Suarez-Orozco, M. (1990). *Status inequality: The self in culture*. Newbury Park, CA: Sage.

Dillard, J., & Spitzberg, B. H. (1984). Global impressions of social skills: Behavioral predictors. In R. Bostrom (Ed.), *Communication yearbook 8* (pp. 156-176). Beverly Hills, CA: Sage.

Dinges, N. (1983). Intercultural competence. In D. Landis & R. W. Brislin (Eds.), *Handbook of intercultural training* (Vol. 1, pp. 176-202). New York: Pergamon.

Dinges, N., & Duffy, L. (1979). Culture and competence. In A. J. Marsella, R. G. Tharp, & T. J. Ciborowski (Eds.), *Perspectives on cross-cultural psychology* (pp. 209-232). New York: Academic Press.

Dinges, N. G., & Lieberman, D. A. (1989). Intercultural communication competence: Coping with stressful work situations. *International Journal of Intercultural Relations, 13*, 371-385.

Dissanayake, W. (1989). Paradigm dialogues: A Europocentric universe of discourse. In B. Dervin, L. Grossberg, B. J. O'Keefe, & E. Wartella (Eds.), *Rethinking communication* (Vol. 1, pp. 166-168). Newbury Park, CA: Sage.

Doise, W. (1986). *Levels of explanation in social psychology*. Cambridge, UK: Cambridge University Press.

Doll, E. A. (1935). The measurement of social competence. *American Association on Mental Deficiency, 40*, 103-126.

Downey, H. K., Hellriegel, D., & Slocum, J. W. (1977). Individual characteristics as sources of perceived uncertainty. *Human Relations, 30*, 161-174.

Downey, H. K., & Slocum, J. W. (1979). *Uncertainty and performance*. Unpublished manuscript. Oklahoma State University.

Duck, S. (1991, May). *New lamps for old: A new theory of relationships and a fresh look at some old research*. Paper presented at the Third Conference of the International Network on Personal Relationships, Normal/Bloomington, IL.

Duck, S. W., Rutt, D. J., Hurst, M., & Strejc, H. (1991). Some evident truth about communication in everyday relationships: All communication is not created equal. *Human Communication Research, 18*, 228-267.

Duran, R. L. (1983). Communicative adaptability. *Communication Quarterly, 31*, 320-326.

Dyal, J. A., & Dyal, R. Y. (1981). Acculturation, stress, and coping. *International Journal of Intercultural Relations, 5*, 301-328.

Edelmann, R. J. (1990). Coping with embarrassment and chronic blushing. In J. A. Anderson (Ed.), *Communication yearbook 13* (pp. 353-364). Newbury Park, CA: Sage.

Eisenberg, E. (1984). Ambiguity as strategy in organizational communication. *Communication Monographs, 51*, 227-242.

Eisenberg, E, & Phillips, S. (1991). Miscommunication in organizations. In N. Coupland, H. Giles, & J. Wiemann (Eds.), *Miscommunication and problematic talk*. Newbury Park, CA: Sage.

Elliott, G. (1979). Some effects of deception and level of self-monitoring on planning and reacting to self-presentation. *Journal of Personality and Social Psychology, 37*, 1282-1292.

Ellis, D. G. (1992). Syntactic and pragmatic codes in communication. *Communication Theory, 2*, 1-23.

Epstein, S. (1976). Anxiety arousal and the self-concept. In I. Sarason & C. Spielberger (Eds.), *Stress and anxiety* (Vol. 3, pp. 185-224). New York: John Wiley.

Etzioni, A. (1990). Liberals and communitarians. *Partisan Review, 57*, 215-227.

Fisher, B. A. (1978). *Perspectives on human communication*. New York: Macmillan.

Fisher, R., & Brown, S. (1988). *Getting together*. New York: Houghton Mifflin.

Fiske, A. P. (1991). *Structures of social life: The four elementary forms of human relations*. New York: Free Press.

Foote, N. N., & Cottrell, L. S., Jr. (1955). *Identity and interpersonal competence*. Chicago: University of Chicago Press.

Forgas, J. P. (1988). Episode representation in intercultural communication. In Y. Y. Kim & W. B. Gudykunst (Eds.), *Theories in intercultural communication* (pp. 186-212). Newbury Park, CA: Sage.

Frese, M., Stewart, J., & Hannover, N. (1987). Goal orientation and planfulness: Action styles as personality concepts. *Journal of Personality and Social Psychology*, *52*(6), 1182-1194.

Gallois, C., Franklyn-Stokes, A., Giles, H., & Coupland, N. (1988). Communication accommodation in intercultural encounters. In Y. Kim & W. Gudykunst (Eds.), *Theories in intercultural communication* (pp. 157-185). Newbury Park, CA: Sage.

Gao, G., & Gudykunst, W. B. (1990). Uncertainty, anxiety, and adaptation. *International Journal of Intercultural Relations*, *14*, 301-318.

Geertz, C. (1973). *The interpretation of culture*. New York: Basic Books.

Geertz, C. (1975). On the nature of anthropological understanding. *American Scientist*, *63*, 47-53.

Gergen, K. (1985). The social constructionist movement in modern psychology. *American Psychologist*, *40*, 266-275.

Gibbs, R. (1985). Situational conventions and request. In J. Forgas (Ed.), *Language and social situations* (pp. 97-113). New York: Springer Verlag.

Giddens, A. (1979). *Central problems in social theory*. Cambridge, UK: Cambridge University Press.

Gilbert, S. J., & Whiteneck, G. G. (1976). Toward a multidimensional approach to the study of self-disclosure. *Human Communication Research*, *2*, 347-355.

Giles, H., & Byrne, J. (1982). The intergroup theory of second language acquisition. *Journal of Multilingual and Multicultural Development*, *3*, 17-40.

Giles, H., Mulac, A., Bradac, J., & Johnson, P. (1987). Speech accommodation theory. In M. McLaughlin (Ed.), *Communication yearbook 10* (pp. 13-48). Newbury Park, CA: Sage.

Giles, H., & Smith, P. (1979). Accommodation theory. In H. Giles & R. St. Clair (Eds.), *Language and social psychology* (pp. 45-65). Oxford, UK: Blackwell.

Gilligan, C. (1982). *In a different voice: Psychological theory and women's development*. Cambridge, MA: Harvard University Press.

Gilligan, C. (1988). Remapping the moral domain: New images of self in relationship. In C. Gilligan, J. Ward, & J. Taylor (Eds.), *Mapping the moral domain* (pp. 3-20). Cambridge, MA: Harvard University Press.

Gilligan, C., Ward, J., Taylor, J. (Eds.). (1988). *Mapping the moral domain*. Cambridge, MA: Harvard University Press.

Glenn, E. S., Witmeyer, D., & Stevenson, K. A. (1977). Cultural styles of persuasion. *International Journal of Intercultural Relations*, *3*, 52-65.

Goffman, E. (1967). *Interaction ritual: Essays on face to face behavior*. Garden City, NY: Anchor.

Goldsmith, D. (1990). A dialectic perspective on the expression of autonomy and connection in romantic relationships. *Western Journal of Speech Communication*, *54*, 537-556.

Gottman, J. M. (1979). *Marital interaction: Experimental investigations*. New York: Academic Press.

Greenberg, J., Pyszczynski, T., & Solomon, S. (1986). The causes and consequences of a need for self-esteem: A terror management theory. In R. Baumeister (Ed.), *Public self and private self* (pp. 189-212). New York: Springer Verlag.

Greene, J. O., & Lindsey, A. E. (1989). Encoding processes in the production of multiple-goal messages. *Human Communication Research, 16*, 120-140.

Grice, H. P. (1975). Logic and conversation. In P. Cole & J. Morgan (Eds.), *Syntax and semantics 3: Speech acts* (pp. 107-142). New York: Academic Press.

Gudykunst, W. B. (1988). Uncertainty and anxiety. In Y. Kim & W. Gudykunst (Eds.), *Theories in intercultural communication* (pp. 123-156). Newbury Park, CA: Sage.

Gudykunst, W. B. (1991). *Bridging differences: Effective intergroup communication*. Newbury Park, CA: Sage.

Gudykunst, W. B., Chua, E., & Gray, A. (1987). Cultural dissimilarities and uncertainty reduction processes. In M. McLaughlin (Ed.), *Communication yearbook 10* (pp. 456-469). Newbury Park, CA: Sage.

Gudykunst, W. B., Gao, G., Sudweeks, S., Ting-Toomey, S., & Nishida, T. (1991). Themes in opposite sex, Japanese-North American relationships. In S. Ting-Toomey & F. Korzenny (Eds.), *Cross-cultural interpersonal communication* (pp. 230-258). Newbury Park, CA: Sage.

Gudykunst, W. B., & Hall, B. J. (in press). Increasing the effectiveness of interpersonal and intergroup communication. In J. Daly & J. Wiemann (Eds.), *Communicating strategically*. Hillsdale, NJ: Lawrence Erlbaum.

Gudykunst, W. B., & Hammer, M. R. (1984). Dimensions of intercultural effectiveness: Culture specific or culture general? *International Journal of Intercultural Relations, 8*, 1-10.

Gudykunst, W. B., & Hammer, M. R. (1988). Strangers and hosts. In Y. Kim & W. Gudykunst (Eds.), *Cross-cultural adaptation* (pp. 106-139). Newbury Park, CA: Sage.

Gudykunst, W. B., & Kim, Y. Y. (1984). *Communicating with strangers: An approach to intercultural communication*. Reading, MA: Addison-Wesley.

Gudykunst, W. B., & Kim, Y. Y. (1992). *Communicating with strangers* (2nd ed.). New York: McGraw-Hill.

Gudykunst, W. B., & Nishida, T. (1989). Theoretical perspectives for studying intercultural communication. In M. Asante & W. Gudykunst (Eds.), *Handbook of international and intercultural communication* (pp. 17-46). Newbury Park, CA: Sage.

Gudykunst, W. B., Nishida, T., & Chua, E. (1987). Perceptions of social penetration in Japanese-North American dyads. *International Journal of Intercultural Relations, 11*, 171-189.

Gudykunst, W. B., Nishida, T., & Morisaki, S. (1992, May). *Expectations for interpersonal and intergroup encounters in Japan and the United States*. Paper presented at the International Communication Association convention, Miami.

Gudykunst, W. B., & Ting-Toomey, S. (1988). *Culture and interpersonal communication*. Newbury Park, CA: Sage.

Gudykunst, W. B., Ting-Toomey, S., & Wiseman, R. L. (1991). Taming the beast: Designing a course in intercultural communication. *Communication Education, 40*, 271-285.

Gumperz, J. J. (1978). The conversational analysis of interethnic communication. In E. L. Ross (Ed.), *Interethnic communication* (pp. 13-31). Athens, GA: University of Georgia Press.

Gumperz, J. J. (1982). *Discourse strategies*. Cambridge, UK: Cambridge University Press.

Gumperz, J. J., & Hymes, D. (1972). *Directions in sociolinguistics: The ethnography of communication*. New York: Holt, Rinehart, & Winston.

Guthrie, G. M., & Zektick, I. N. (1967). Predicting performance in the Peace Corps. *Journal of Social Psychology, 71*, 11-21.

Habermas, J. (1970a). On systematically distorted communication. *Inquiry, 13*, 205-218.

Habermas, J. (1970b). Towards a theory of communicative competence. *Inquiry*, *13*, 360-375.

Habermas, J. (1976). *Communication and the evolution of society* (T. McCarthy, Trans.). Boston: Beacon Press.

Hale, C. L. (1986). The impact of cognitive complexity on message structure in a face-threatening context. *Journal of Language and Social Psychology*, *5*, 135-143.

Hall, E. P. (1985). The etic-emic distinction. In B. Dervin & M. Voight (Eds.), *Progress in communication science* (Vol. 7, pp. 123-151). Norwood, NJ: Ablex.

Hall, E. T. (1961). *The silent language*. Greenwich, CT.: Fawcett.

Hall, E. T. (1976). *Beyond culture*. New York: Doubleday.

Hall, E. T. (1983). *The dance of life*. New York: Doubleday.

Hall, E. T., & Hall, M. R. (1985). *Hidden differences: Doing business with Japanese*. Garden City, NY: Anchor.

Hamill, J. F. (1990). *Ethno-logic: The anthropology of human reasoning*. Urbana, IL: University of Illinois Press.

Hamilton, D. L., Sherman, S. J., & Ruvolo, C. M. (1990). Stereotyped-based expectancies: Effects on information processing and social behavior. *Journal of Social Issues*, *46*(2), 35-60.

Hammer, M. R. (1984). Communication workshop on participants' intercultural communication competence: An exploratory study. *Communication Quarterly*, *32*, 252-262.

Hammer, M. R. (1987). Behavioral dimensions of intercultural effectiveness: A replication and extension. *International Journal of Intercultural Relations*, *11*, 65-88.

Hammer, M. R. (1989). Intercultural communication competence. In M. K. Asante & W. B. Gudykunst (Eds.), *Handbook of international and intercultural communication* (pp. 247-260). Newbury Park, CA: Sage.

Hammer, M. R., Gudykunst, W. B., & Wiseman, R. L. (1978). Dimensions of intercultural effectiveness: An exploratory study. *International Journal of Intercultural Relations*, *2*, 382-392.

Hammer, M. R., & Martin, J. N. (1992). The effects of cross-cultural training on American managers in a Japanese-American joint venture. *Journal of Applied Communication Research*, *20*, 2.

Hammer, M. R., Martin, J. N., Otani, M., & Koyama, M. (1990, March). *Analyzing intercultural competence: Evaluating communication skills of Japanese and American managers*. Paper presented to the First Annual Intercultural and International Communication Conference, California State University, Fullerton, CA.

Hanh, T. N. (1976). *The miracle of mindfulness* (rev. ed.). New York: Bantam.

Harre, R. (1984). *Personal being: A theory for individual psychology*. Cambridge, MA: Harvard University Press.

Harre, R. (Ed.) (1986). *The social construction of emotions*. Oxford, UK: Basil Blackwell.

Harris, J. G. (1975). Identification of cross-cultural talent: The empirical approach of the Peace Corps. *Topics in Culture Learning*, *3*, 66-78.

Harris, L. M. (1979). *Communication competence: Empirical tests of a systemic model*. Unpublished doctoral dissertation, University of Massachusetts, MA.

Hecht, M. L., Collier, M. J., & Ribeau, S. (1992). *African American communication*. Newbury Park, CA: Sage.

Hecht, M. L., Larkey, L. K., Johnson, J. N., & Reinard, J. C. (1991, May). *A model of interethnic effectiveness*. Paper presented at the International Communication Association convention, Chicago, IL.

Hecht, M. L., & Ribeau, S. (1984). Ethnic communication: A comparative analysis of satisfying communication. *International Journal of Intercultural Relations*, *8*, 135-151.

Hecht, M. L., & Ribeau, S. (1991). Sociocultural roots of ethnic identity: A look at black America. *Journal of Black Studies*, *21*, 501-513.

Hecht, M., Ribeau, S., & Alberts, J. (1989). An Afro-American perspective on interethnic communication. *Communication Monographs*, *56*, 385-410.

Hecht, M., Ribeau, S., & Sedano, M. (1990). A Mexican American perspective on interethnic communication. *International Journal of Intercultural Relations*, *14*, 31-55.

Hecht, M. L., & Sereno, K. K. (1985). Interpersonal communication satisfaction: Relationship to satisfaction with self and other. *Communication Research Reports*, *2*, 141-148.

Henderson, G., & Bryan, W. V. (1984). *Psychosocial aspects of disability*. Springfield, IL: Charles C Thomas.

Herman, S., & Schield, E. (1961). The stranger group in a cross-cultural situation. *Sociometry*, *24*, 165-176.

Hewitt, J., & Stokes, R. (1975). Disclaimers. *American Sociological Review*, *40*, 1-11.

Hirokawa, R. Y., & Miyahara, A. (1986). A comparison of influence strategies utilized by managers in American and Japanese organizations. *Communication Quarterly*, *34* (3), 250-265.

Ho, D. Y. F. (1976). On the concept of face. *American Journal of Sociology*, *81*, 867-884.

Hofstede, G. (1979). Value systems in forty countries. In J. Deregowski, S. Dzuirawiec, & R. Annis (Eds.), *Explications in cross-cultural psychology* (pp. 389-407). Lisse, The Netherlands: Swets & Zeitlinger.

Hofstede, G. (1980). *Culture's consequences*. Beverly Hills, CA: Sage.

Hofstede, G. (1991). *Cultures and organizations*. London: McGraw-Hill.

Hofstede, G., & Bond, M. H. (1984). Hofstede's culture dimensions. *Journal of Cross-Cultural Psychology*, *15*, 417-433.

Holland, N., & Quinn, N. (Eds.). (1987). *Cultural models in language and thought*. Cambridge, UK: Cambridge University Press.

Holtgraves, T., & Yang, J. (1990). Politeness as universal: Cross-cultural perceptions of request strategies and inferences based on their use. *Journal of Personality and Social Psychology*, *59*, 719-729.

Holtgraves, T., & Yang, J. (1992). Interpersonal underpinnings of request strategies: General principles and differences due to culture and gender. *Journal of Personality and Social Psychology*, *62*, 246-256.

Honess, T. (1976). Cognitive complexity and social prediction. *British Journal of Social and Clinical Psychology*, *15*, 22-31.

Hooker, C. A. (1987). *A realistic theory of science*. Albany, NY: State University of New York Press.

Howard, J. (1991). From changing selves toward changing society. In J. Howard & P. Callero (Eds.), *The self-society dynamic: Cognition, emotion and action*. Cambridge, UK: Cambridge University Press.

Howard, J., & Callero, P. (Eds.). (1991). *The self-society dynamic: Cognition, emotion and action* (pp. 209-237). Cambridge, UK: Cambridge University Press.

Howell, W. (1982). *The empathic communicator*. Belmont, CA: Wadsworth.

Hsu, F. L. K. (1981). *American and Chinese: Passage to difference*. Honolulu: University of Hawaii Press.

Hui, C. H. (1984). *Individualism-collectivism: Theory, measurement, and its relation to reward allocation*. Unpublished doctoral dissertation, University of Illinois at Urbana-Champaign.

Hui, C. H., & Triandis, H. C. (1985). Measurement in cross-cultural psychology. *Journal of Cross-Cultural Psychology*, *16*, 131-152.

Hui, C. H., & Triandis, H. (1986). Individualism-collectivism: A study of cross-cultural researchers. *Journal of Cross-Cultural Psychology, 17*, 225-248.

Hui, C. H., & Villareal, M. J. (1989). Individualism-collectivism and psychological needs: Their relationships in two cultures. *Journal of Cross-Cultural Psychology, 20*, 310-323.

Huspek, M. (1991). Taking aim on Habermas's critical theory: On the road toward a critical hermeneutics. *Communication Monographs, 58*, 225-233.

Hymes, D. (1972). Models of the interaction of language and social life. In J. Gumperz & D. Hymes (Eds.), *Directions in sociolinguistics: The ethnography of communication* (pp. 35-71). New York: Holt, Rinehart, & Winston.

Hymes, D. (1974). *Foundations in sociolinguistics: An ethnographic approach.* Philadelphia: University of Pennsylvania Press.

Hymes, D. (1979). On communicative competence. In J. B. Pride & J. Holmes (Eds.), *Sociolinguistics* (pp. 269-293). New York: Penguin. (Excerpts from D. Hymers, 1971, *On communicative competence*. Philadelphia: University of Pennsylvania Press.)

Imahori, T., & Lanigan, M. (1989). Relational model of intercultural communication competence. *International Journal of Intercultural Relations, 13*, 269-286.

Jackson, J. (1964). The normative regulation of authoritative behavior. In W. Grove & J. Dyson (Eds.), *The making of decisions* (pp. 213-241). New York: Free Press.

Jacobs, C. S. (1985). Language. In M. L. Knapp & G. R. Miller (Eds.), *Handbook of interpersonal communication* (pp. 313-343). Beverly Hills, CA: Sage.

Jacobson, N. S., & Moore, D. (1981). Spouses as observers of the events in their relationship. *Journal of Consulting and Clinical Pscyhology, 49*, 269-277.

Jankowski, K. (1991). On communicating with deaf people. In L. Samovar & R. Porter (Eds.), *Intercultural communication: A reader* (6th ed., pp. 142-150). Belmont, CA: Wadsworth.

Johnstone, L., & Hewstone, M. (1991). Intergroup contact. In D. Abrams & M. Hogg (Eds.), *Social identity theory* (pp. 185-210). New York: Springer Verlag.

Jöreskog, K. G. & Sörbom, D. (1984). *LISREL VI: Analysis of linear structural relationships maximum likelihood; instructional variables, and least squares methods.* Mooresville, IN: Scientific Software.

Kale, D. (1991). Ethics in intercultural communication. In L. Samovar & R. Porter (Eds.), *Intercultural communication: A reader* (6th ed., 421-426). Belmont, CA: Wadsworth.

Kang, K., & Pearce, W. B. (1984). Reticence: A transcultural analysis. *Communication, 9*, 79-96.

Katriel, T. (1986). *Talking straight: Dugri speech in Israeli Sabra culture.* Cambridge, UK: Cambridge University Press.

Kealey, D. J. (1989). A study of cross-cultural effectiveness: Theoretical issues, practical applications. *International Journal of Intercultural Relations, 13*, 397-428.

Kellermann, K. (1989). *Understanding tactical choice: Metagoals in conversation.* Department of Communication, Michigan State University.

Kellermann, K., & Kim, M. S. (1991, May). *Working within constraints: Tactical choices in the pursuit of social goals.* Paper presented at the International Communication Association convention, Chicago.

Kenny, D. A. (1990). Design issues in dyadic research. In C. Hendrick & M. S. Clark (Eds.), *Research methods in personality and social psychology* (pp. 164-184). Newbury Park, CA: Sage.

Kenny, D. A., & La Voie, L. (1985). Separating group and individual level effects. *Journal of Personality and Social Psychology, 48*, 339-348.

Keesing, R. (1974). Theories of culture. *Annual Review of Anthropology, 3*, 73-97.

Kim, J., & Mueller, C. W. (1978). Factor analysis: Statistical methods and practical issues. In E. M. Uslander (Ed.), *Series: Quantitative application in the social sciences* (pp. 34-46). Beverly Hills, CA: Sage.

Kim, Y. Y. (1991). Intercultural communication competence. In S. Ting-Toomey & F. Korzenny (Eds.), *Cross-cultural interpersonal communication* (pp. 259-275). Newbury Park, CA: Sage.

Kincaid, D. L. (1987). *Communication theory from Eastern and Western perspectives*. New York: Academic Press.

Kitayama, S., & Burnstein, E. (1988). Automaticity in conversations. *Journal of Personality and Social Psychology, 54*, 219-224.

Klopf, D., & Cambra, R. (1979). Communication apprehension among college students in America, Australia, Japan and Korea. *Journal of Psychology, 105*, 27-31.

Kluckhohn, F., & Strodtbeck, F. (1961). *Variations in value orientations*. Evanston, IL: Row, Peterson.

Knapp, M., & Vangelisti, A. (1992). *Interpersonal communication and human relationships* (2nd ed.). Boston: Allyn & Bacon.

Kobasa, S. (1979). Stressful life events, personality and health. *Journal of Personality and Social Psychology, 37*, 1-11.

Kobasa, S. (1982). The hardy personality: Toward a social psychology of stress and health. In J. Suls & G. Sanders (Eds.), *Social psychology of health and illness* (pp. 3-33). Hillsdale, NJ: Lawrence Erlbaum.

Kochman, T. (1981). *Black and white styles in conflict*. Chicago: University of Chicago Press.

Kochman, T. (1990a). Force fields in black and white communication. In D. Carbaugh (Ed.), *Cultural communication and intercultural contact* (pp. 193-218). Hillsdale, NJ: Lawrence Erlbaum.

Kochman, T. (1990b). Cultural pluralism: Black and white styles. In D. Carbaugh (Ed.), *Cultural communication and intercultural contact* (pp. 219-224). Hillsdale, NJ: Lawrence Erlbaum.

Koester, J., & Lustig, M. W. (1991). Communication curricula in the multicultural university. *Communication Education, 40*, 250-254.

Koester, J., & Olebe, M. (1988). The behavioral assessment scale for intercultural communication effectiveness. *International Journal of Intercultural Relations, 12*, 233-246.

Kreps, G. L., & Query, J. L., Jr. (1990). Health communication and interpersonal competence. In G. M. Phillips & J. T. Wood (Eds.), *Speech communication: Essays to commemorate the 75th anniversary of the Speech Communication Association* (pp. 109-126). Carbondale, IL: Southern Illinois University.

Kruglanski, A. (1989). *Lay epistemics and human knowledge*. New York: Plenum.

Kuhn, T. (1970). *The structure of scientific revolutions* (rev. ed.). Chicago: University of Chicago Press.

Kuiper, N. A., & Rogers, T. B. (1979). Encoding of personal information: Self-other differences. *Journal of Personality and Social Psychology, 37*, 499-514.

Kunihiro, M. (1976). The Japanese language and intercultural communication. In Japan Center for International Exchange (Ed.), *The silent power: Japan's identity and world role* (pp. 57-58). Tokyo: Simul.

Lakatos, I. (1970). Falsification and the methodology of scientific research programs. In I. Lakatos & A. Musgrave (Eds.), *Criticism and the growth of knowledge* (pp. 91-196). Cambridge, UK: Cambridge University Press.

Lakoff, R. (1977). What you can do with words: Politeness, pragmatics and performatives. In A. Rogers, B. Wall, & J. Murphy (Eds.), *Proceedings of the Texas conference on performatives, presuppositions and implicatures* (pp. 79-105). Arlington, VA: Center for Applied Linguistics.

Langer, E. (1978). Rethinking the role of thought in social interaction. In J. Harvey, W. Kidd, & R. Kidd (Eds.), *New directions in attribution research* (Vol. 2, pp. 35-58). Hillsdale, NJ: Lawrence Erlbaum.

Langer, E. (1989). *Mindfulness*. Reading, MA: Addison-Wesley.

Lazarus, R. (1991). *Emotion and adaptation*. New York: Oxford University Press.

Lebra, T. S. (1976). *Japanese patterns of behavior*. Honolulu: University of Hawaii Press.

Leech, G. N. (1983). *Principles of pragmatics*. New York: Longman.

Leeds-Hurwitz, W. (1990). Notes in the history of intercultural communication: The foreign service institute and the mandate for intercultural training. *The Quarterly Journal of Speech*, *76*, 262-281.

Leichty, G., & Applegate, J. L. (1991). Social-cognitive and situational influences on the use of face-saving persuasive strategies. *Human Communication Research*, *17*, 451-484.

Leung, K. (1987). Some determinants of reactions to procedural models for conflict resolution: A cross-national study. *Journal of Personality and Social Psychology*, *53*(5), 898-908.

Leung, K., & Bond, M. H. (1984). The impact of cultural collectivism on reward allocation. *Journal of Personality and Social Psychology*, *53*, 793-804.

Levine, D. (1985). *The flight from ambiguity*. Chicago: University of Chicago Press.

LeVine, R. (1982). *Culture, behavior, and personality*. New York: Aldine.

Lewis, H. B. (1971). *Shame and guilt in neurosis*. New York: International Universities Press.

Lieberson, S. (1985). *Making it count: The improvement of social research and theory*. Berkeley, CA: University of California Press.

Lim, T. (1988). *A new model of politeness in discourse*. Unpublished doctoral dissertation, Department of Communication, Michigan State University, Ann Arbor.

Lim, T., & Bowers, J. W. (1991). Facework: Solidarity, approbation, and tact. *Human Communication Research*, *17*, 415-450.

Linville, P., Fisher, G., & Salovey, P. (1989). Perceived distributions of the characteristics of in-group and out-group members. *Journal of Personality and Social Psychology*, *57*, 165-188.

Littlejohn, S. W. (1991). Deception in communication research. *Communication Reports*, *4*, 51-54.

Lonner, W. J., & Berry, J. W. (1986). Sampling and surveying. In W. J. Lonner & J. W. Berry (Eds.), *Field methods in cross-cultural research* (pp. 85-110). Beverly Hills, CA: Sage.

Luhtanen, R., & Crocker, J. (1992). A collective self-esteem scale. *Personality and Social Psychology*, *18*, 302-318.

Lustig, M. W. (1991, November). *Ecological invalidity and intercultural communication*. Paper presented at the Speech Communication Association convention, Atlanta.

Lustig, M. W., & Koester, J. (1993). *Intercultural competence: Interpersonal communication across cultures*. New York: Harper Collins.

Lutz, C. (1988). *Unnatural emotions: Everyday sentiments on a Micronesian atoll and their challenge to Western theory*. Chicago: University of Chicago Press.

Lyons, N. P. (1988). Two perspectives: On self, relationships, and morality. In C. Gilligan, J. Ward, & J. Taylor (Eds.), *Mapping the moral domain* (pp. 21-48). Cambridge, MA: Harvard University Press.

Lysgaard, S. (1955). Adjustment in a foreign society: Norwegian Fulbright grantees visiting the United States. *International Social Science Bulletin*, *7*, 45-51.

Markus, H., & Kitayama, S. (1991). Culture and the self: Implications for cognition, emotion, and motivation. *Psychological Review*, *2*, 224-253.

Marsella, A., DeVos, G., & Hsu, F. L. K. (Eds.). (1985). *Culture and self: Asian and Western perspectives*. New York: Tavistock.

Martin, J. N. (1987). The relationship between student sojourner perceptions of intercultural competencies and previous sojourn experience. *International Journal of Intercultural Relations*, *11*, 337-355.

Martin, J. N. (Ed.). (1989). Intercultural communication competence. *International Journal of Intercultural Relations*, *13*.

Martin, J. N., & Hammer, M. R. (1989). Behavioral categories of intercultural communication competence: Everyday communicators' perceptions. *International Journal of Intercultural Relations*, *13*, 303-332.

Martin, J. N., Hammer, M. R., & Bradford, L. (1992, May). *Influences of situational and cultural contexts on judgements of communicative competence*. Paper presented at the International Communication Association convention, Miami.

Martin, J. N., Hecht, M. L., & Larkey, L. K. (1992, May). *Conversational improvement strategies for interethnic communication: African American and Euroamerican perspectives*. Paper presented at the International Communication Association convention, Miami.

Maslow, A. (1968). *Toward a psychology of being* (2nd ed.). New York: Van Nostrand Reinhold.

Matsumoto, Y. (1988). Reexamination of the universality of face: Politeness phenomena in Japanese. *Journal of Pragmatics*, *12*, 403-426.

May, R. (1977). *The meaning of anxiety*. New York: Washington Square.

McCall, G., & Simmons, J. (1978). *Identities and interaction*. New York: Free Press.

McCann, C. D., & Higgins, E. T. (1988). Motivation and affect in interpersonal relations: The role of personal orientations and discrepancies. In L. Donohew, H. Sypher, & T. Higgins (Eds.), *Communication, social cognition, and affect* (pp. 53-79). Hillsdale, NJ: Lawrence Erlbaum.

McClelland, D. C. (1985). *Human motivation*. Glenview, IL: Scott, Foresman.

McLeod, J., & Chaffee, S. (1973). Interpersonal approach to communication research. *American Behavior Scientist*, *16*, 469-499.

McCroskey, J. C. (1982). Communication competence and performance: A research and pedagogical perspective. *Communication Education*, *31*, 1-8.

McCroskey, J. C., & McCain, T. (1974). The measurement of interpersonal attraction. *Speech Monographs*, *41*, 261-266.

McFall, R. M. (1982). A review and reformulation of the concept of social skills. *Behavioral Assessment*, *4*, 1-33.

McPherson, K. (1983). Opinion-related information seeking. *Personality and Social Psychology Bulletin*, *9*, 116-124.

Mead, G. H. (1934). *Mind, self, and society*. Chicago: University of Chicago Press.

Milhouse, V. H. (1986). *The effectiveness of multicultural education and skill development training: The student perspective*. Unpublished doctoral dissertation, University of Oklahoma, Norman.

Millar, F. E., & Rogers, L. E. (1976). A relational approach to interpersonal communication. In G. R. Miller (Ed.), *Explorations in interpersonal communication* (pp. 87-103). Beverly Hills, CA: Sage.

Miller, E. L. (1972). The overseas assignment: How managers determine who is to be selected. *Michigan Business Review*, *24*, 19.
Miller, G. A., Galanter, E., & Pribram, K. H. (1960). *Plans and the structure of behavior*. New York: Holt, Rinehart & Winston.
Miller, J. G. (1984). Culture and the development of everyday social explanation. *Journal of Personality and Social Psychology*, *46*, 961-978.
Mischel, W. (1965). Predicting the success of Peace Corps volunteers in Nigeria. *Journal of Personality and Social Psychology*, *1*, 510-517.
Mischel, W. (1973). Toward a cognitive social learning reconceptualization of personality. *Psychological Review*, *80*, 252-283.
Montgomery, B. (1988). Quality communication in personal relationships. In S. Duck (Ed.), *Handbook of personal relationships* (pp. 343-359). New York: John Wiley.
Moore, B. S., Sherrod, D. R., Liu, T. J., & Underwood, B. (1979). The dispositional shift in attribution over time. *Journal of Experimental Social Psychology*, *15*, 553-569.
Motley, M. (1990). On whether one cannot not communicate. *Western Journal of Speech Communication*, *54*, 1-20.
Motley, M. (1991). How one may not communicate: A reply to Andersen. *Communication Studies*, *42*, 326-339.
Mushakoji, K. (1976). The cultural premises of Japanese diplomacy. In Japan Center for International Exchange (Ed.), *The silent power: Japan's identity and world role* (pp. 35-49). Tokyo: Simul.
Naiman, N., Frohlich, M., Stern, H., & Todesco, A. (1978). *The good language learner*. Toronto: Ontario Institute for Studies in Education.
Nakanishi, M. (1986). Perceptions of self-disclosure in initial interaction: A Japanese sample. *Human Communication Research*, *13*, 167-190.
Nakayama, O. (1987). *Bokashi no Shinri* [Psychology of Ambiguity]. Tokyo: Sogensha.
Neuliep, J. W., & Hazleton, V. (1985). A cross-cultural comparison of Japanese and American persuasive strategy selection. *International Journal of Intercultural Relations*, *9*, 389-404.
Nicolson, H. (1956). *Good behavior: Being a study of certain types of civility*. New York: Doubleday.
Nishida, H. (1985). Japanese intercultural communication competence and cross-cultural adjustment. *International Journal of Intercultural Relations*, *9*, 247-269.
O'Connor, B. P., & Day, R. (1989). Could differences in the interpretation of behavior be a reason for low rating-behavior, self-peer, and peer-peer personality correlations? *Social Behavior and Personality*, *17*, 17-28.
O'Keefe, D., & Sypher, H. (1981). Cognitive complexity measures and the relationship of cognitive complexity to communication. *Human Communication Research*, *8*, 72-92.
Ochs, E. (1988). *Culture and language development*. Cambridge, UK: Cambridge University Press.
Okabe, K. (1987). Indirect speech acts of the Japanese. In D. Kincaid (Ed.), *Communication theory: Eastern and Western perspectives* (pp. 127-136). New York: Academic Press.
Olebe, M., & Koester, J. (1989). Exploring the cross-cultural equivalence of the Behavioral Assessment Scale for Intercultural Communication. *International Journal of Intercultural Relations*, *13*, 333-348.
Olson, D. H. (1981). Family typologies: Bridging family research and family therapy. In E. E. Filsinger & R. A. Lewis (Eds.), *Assessing marriage: New behavioral approaches* (pp. 74-89). Beverly Hills, CA: Sage.
Optow, S. (1990). Moral exclusion and injustice. *Journal of Social Issues*, *46*, 1-20.

Orr, E., & Westman, M. (1990). Does hardiness moderate stress, and how?: A review. In M. Rosenbaum (Ed.), *Learned resourcefulness: On coping skills, self-control and adaptive behavior* (pp. 64-94). New York: Springer.

Osgood, C. E., May, W. H., & Miron, S. (1975). *Cross-cultural universals of affective meaning*. Urbana: University of Illinois Press.

Øyen, E. (1990). The imperfection of comparisons. In E. Øyen (Ed.), *Comparative methodology: Theory and practice in international social research* (pp. 1-18). Newbury Park, CA: Sage.

Parks, M. R. (1985). Interpersonal communication and the quest for personal competence. In M. L. Knapp & G. R. Miller (Eds.), *Handbook of interpersonal communication* (pp. 171-201). Beverly Hills, CA: Sage.

Parks, M. R., & Adelman, M. (1983). Communication networks and the development of romantic relationships. *Human Communication Research, 10*, 55-80.

Parsons, T., Shils, E., & Olds, J. (1951). Categories of the orientation and organization of action. In T. Parsons & E. A. Shils (Eds.), *Toward a general theory of action* (pp. 53-109). Cambridge, MA: Harvard University Press.

Pavitt, C. (1981). Preliminaries to a theory of communication: A system for the cognitive representation of person and object based information. In M. Burgoon (Ed.), *Communication yearbook 5* (pp. 211-232). New Brunswick, NJ: Transaction Books.

Pavitt, C. (1989). Accounting for the process of communicative competence evaluation: A comparison of predictive models. *Communication Research, 16*, 405-433.

Pavitt, C. (1990). The ideal communicator as the basis for competence judgments of self and friend. *Communication Reports, 3*, 9-14.

Pavitt, C., & Haight, L. (1985). The "competent communicator" as a cognitive prototype. *Human Communication Research, 12*, 225-242.

Pavitt, C., & Haight, L. (1986). Implicit theories of communicative competence: Situational and competence level difference in judgments of prototype and target. *Communication Monographs, 53*, 221-235.

Pearce, W. B., & Cronen, V. E. (1980). *Communication, action and meaning*. New York: Praeger.

Pearce, W. B., Cronen, V. E., Johnson, K., Jones, G., & Raymond, R. (1980). The structure of communication rules and the form of conversation: An experimental simulation. *Western Journal of Speech Communication, 44*, 20-34.

Pelham, B., & Swann, W., Jr. (1989). From self-conceptions to self-worth: On the sources and structure of global self-esteem. *Journal of Personality and Social Psychology, 57*, 672-680.

Penman, R. (in press). Facework in communication: Conceptual and moral challenges. In S. Ting-Toomey (Ed.), *The challenge of facework: Cross-cultural and interpersonal variations*. Albany, NY: State University of New York Press.

Pepitone, A., & Triandis, H. C. (1987). On the universality of social psychological theories. *Journal of Cross-Cultural Psychology, 18*, 471-498.

Pettigrew, T. (1979). The ultimate attribution error. *Personality and Social Psychology Bulletin, 5*, 461-476.

Pettigrew, T. (1982). Cognitive styles and social behavior. In L. Wheeler (Ed.), *Review of personality and social psychology* (Vol. 3, pp. 199-223). Beverly Hills, CA: Sage.

Philipsen, G. (1975). Speaking "like a man" in Teamsterville: Culture patterns of role enactment in an urban neighborhood. *Quarterly Journal of Speech, 61*, 13-22.

Philipsen, G. (1986). Mayor Daley's council speech: A cultural analysis. *Quarterly Journal of Speech, 72*, 247-260.

Philipsen, G. (1989). Speech and the communal function in four cultures. In S. Ting-Toomey & F. Korzenny (Eds.), *Language, communication and culture: Current directions* (pp. 79-92). Newbury Park, CA: Sage.

Philipsen, G., & Carbaugh, D. (1986). A bibliography of fieldwork in the ethnography of communication. *Language in Society, 15*, 387-398.

Phinney, J. (1990). Ethnic identity in adolescents and adults: Review of research. *Psychological Bulletin, 108*, 499-514.

Phinney, J. (1991). Ethnic identity and self-esteem: A review and integration. *Hispanic Journal of Behavioral Sciences, 13*, 193-208.

Phinney, J., & Alipuria, C. (1990). Ethnic identity in college students from four ethnic groups. *Journal of Adolescence, 13*, 171-183.

Pike, K. (1966). *Language in relation to a unified theory of the structure of human behavior*. The Hague: Mouton.

Planalp, S., & Honeycutt, J. (1985). Events that increase uncertainty in interpersonal relationships. *Human Communication Research, 11*, 593-604.

Planalp, S., Rutherford, D., & Honeycutt, J. (1988). Events that increase uncertainty in relationships II. *Human Communication Research, 14*, 516-547.

Porter, R. E., & Samovar, L. A. (1976). Communicating interculturally. In L. A. Samovar & R. E. Porter (Eds.), *Intercultural communication: A reader* (2nd ed., pp. 4-24). Belmont, CA: Wadsworth.

Powers, W. G., & Lowry, D. N. (1984). Basic communication fidelity: A fundamental approach. In R. N. Bostrom (Ed.), *Competence in communication: A multidisciplinary approach* (pp. 57-71). Beverly Hills, CA: Sage.

Rachman, S. (1990). Learned resourcefulness as in the performance of hazardous tasks. In M. Rosenbaum (Ed.), *Learned resourcefulness: On coping skills, self-control and adaptive behavior* (pp. 165-181). New York: Springer.

Read, S. J., & Miller, L. C. (1989). Inter-personalism: Toward a goal-based theory of persons in relationships. In L. Pervin (Ed.), *Goal concepts in personality and social psychology* (pp. 413-472). New York: Lawrence Erlbaum.

Reynolds, P. D. (1971). *A primer in theory construction*. Indianapolis: Bobbs-Merrill.

Robinson, D., & Smith-Lovin, L. (1992). Selective interaction as a strategy for identity maintenance: An affect control model. *Social Psychology Quarterly, 55*, 12-28.

Robinson, E. A., & Price, M. G. (1980). Pleasurable behavior in marital interaction: An observational study. *Journal of Consulting and Clinical Psychology, 48*, 117-118.

Rogers, C. R. (1970). *On encounter groups*. New York: Harper & Row.

Rogers, E., & Kincaid, D. L. (1981). *Communication networks*. Indianapolis: Bobbs-Merrill.

Rokeach, M. (1973). *The nature of human values*. New York: Free Press.

Roloff, M. E., & Kellerman, K. (1984). Judgments of interpersonal competency: How you know, what you know, and who you know. In R. N. Bostrom (Ed.), *Competence in communication: A multidisciplinary approach* (pp. 175-218). Beverly Hills, CA: Sage.

Rosaldo, M. (1984). Toward an anthropology of self and feeling. In R. Shweder & R. LeVine (Eds.), *Culture theory: Essays on mind, self, and society* (pp. 137-157). Cambridge, UK: Cambridge University Press.

Rose, T. (1981). Cognitive and dyadic processes in intergroup contact. In D. Hamilton (Ed.), *Cognitive processes in stereotyping and intergroup behavior* (pp. 259-302). Hillsdale, NJ: Lawrence Erlbaum.

Rosenbaum, M. (1990). Role of learned resourcefulness in self-control of health behavior. In M. Rosenbaum (Ed.), *Learned resourcefulness: On coping skills, self-control and adaptive behavior* (pp. 3-30). New York: Springer.

Rossiter, C., & Pearce, W. B. (1975). *Communicating personally*. Indianapolis: Bobbs-Merrill.

Ruben, B. D. (1976). Assessing communication competency for intercultural adaptation. *Group and Organization Studies*, *1*, 334-354.

Ruben, B. D. (1977). Guidelines for cross-cultural communication effectiveness. *Group and Organization Studies*, *2*, 470-479.

Ruben, B. D. (1989). The study of cross-cultural competence: Traditions and contemporary issues. *International Journal of Intercultural Relations*, *13*, 229-240.

Ruben, B. D., & Kealey, D. (1979). Behavioral assessment of communication competency and the prediction of cross-cultural adaptation. *International Journal of Intercultural Relations*, *3*, 15-48.

Rubin, R. B., Perse, E. M., & Barbato, C. (1988). Conceptualization and measurement of interpersonal communication motives. *Human Communication Research*, *14*, 602-628.

Sandelands, L. E., & Calder, B. J. (1984). Referencing bias in social interaction. *Journal of Personality and Social Psychology*, *46*, 755-762.

Saville-Troike, M. (1982). *The ethnography of communication: An introduction*. Baltimore, MD: University Park.

Schank, R. C., & Abelson, R. P. (1977). *Scripts, plans, goals, and understanding*. Hillsdale, NJ: Lawrence Erlbaum.

Schank, R. C., & Childers, P. (1984). *The cognitive computer: On language, learning and artificial intelligence*. Reading, MA: Addison-Wesley.

Scheff, T. J. (1990). *Microsociology: Discourse, emotion, and social structure*. Chicago: University of Chicago Press.

Schieffelin, B., & Ochs, E. (Eds.). (1986). *Language socialization across cultures*. Cambridge, UK: Cambridge University Press.

Schlenker, B. R. (1980). *Impression management: The self-concept, social identity, and interpersonal relations*. Monterey, CA: Brooks/Cole.

Schlenker, B. R. (1984). Identities, identifications, and relationships. In V. J. Derlega (Ed.), *Communication, intimacy, and close relationships* (pp. 71-104). Orlando, FL: Academic Press.

Schlenker, B. R. (1986). Self-identification. In R. F. Baumeister (Ed.), *Public self and private self* (pp. 21-62). New York: Springer Verlag.

Schwartz, S. H. (1990). Individualism-collectivism: Critique and proposed refinements. *Journal of Cross-Cultural Psychology*, *21*, 139-157.

Schwartz, S. H., & Bilsky, W. (1987). Toward a universal psychological structure of human values. *Journal of Personality and Social Psychology*, *53*, 550-562.

Schwartz, S. H., & Bilsky, W. (1990). Toward a theory of the universal content and structure of values. *Journal of Personality and Social Psychology*, *58*, 878-891.

Scollon, R., & Scollon, S. (1981). *Narrative, literacy and face in interethnic communication*. Norwood, NJ: Ablex.

Scruton, R. (1979). The significance of common culture. *Philosophy*, *54*, 51-70.

Searle, J. (1969). *Speech acts*. Cambridge, UK: Cambridge University Press.

Sennett, R. (1977). *The fall of public man*. New York: Knopf.

Shimanoff, S. (1980). *Communication rules: Theory and research*. Beverly Hills, CA: Sage.

Shweder, R., & LeVine, R. (Eds.). (1984). *Culture theory: Essays on mind, self, and society*. Cambridge, UK: Cambridge University Press.

Simard, L. M., Taylor, D. M., & Giles, H. (1976). Attributional processes and interpersonal accommodation. *Language and Speech*, *19*, 374-387.

Simmel, G. (1908/1950). The stranger. In K. Wolff (Ed. & Trans.), *The sociology of Georg Simmel*. New York: Free Press.

Singer, M. (1987). *Intercultural communication: A perceptual approach*. Englewood Cliffs, NJ: Prentice-Hall.

Smith, H. (1976). *The Russians*. New York: Ballantine.

Smith, M. B. (1965). An analysis of two measures of "authoritarianism" among Peace Corps teachers. *Journal of Personality, 33*, 513-535.

Snyder, M. (1974). Self-monitoring of expressive behavior. *Journal of Personality and Social Psychology, 30*, 526-537.

Snyder, M., & Monson, T. (1975). Persons, situations, and the control of social behavior. *Journal of Personality and Social Psychology, 32*, 526-537.

Sofue, T. (1973). Continuity and change in Japanese national character. In T. Sofue (Ed.), *How have the Japanese changed?* (pp. 5-38). Tokyo: Shinbundo.

Sorrentino, R. M., & Short, J. A. (1986). Uncertainty orientation, motivation, and cognition. In R. Sorrentino & E. Higgins (Eds.), *The handbook of motivation and cognition* (pp. 379-403). New York: Guilford.

Spitzberg, B. H. (1983). Communication competence as knowledge, skill, and impression. *Communication Education, 32*, 323-329.

Spitzberg, B. H. (1987). Issues in the study of communicative competence. In B. Dervin & M. J. Voight (Eds.), *Progress in communication sciences* (Vol. 8, pp. 1-46). Norwood, NJ: Ablex.

Spitzberg, B. H. (1988). Communication competence: Measures of perceived effectiveness. In C. H. Tardy (Ed.), *A handbook for the study of human communication: Methods and instruments for observing, measuring, and assessing communication processes* (pp. 67-106). Norwood, NJ: Ablex.

Spitzberg, B. H. (1989). Issues in the development of a theory of interpersonal competence in the intercultural context. *International Journal of Intercultural Relations, 13*, 241-268.

Spitzberg, B. H. (in press). The dark side of (in)competence. In W. R. Cupach & B. H. Spitzberg (Eds.), *The dark side of interpersonal communication*. Hillsdale, NJ: Lawrence Erlbaum.

Spitzberg, B. H., Brookshire, R. G., & Brunner, C. (1990). The tactorial domain of interpersonal skills. *Social Behavior and Personality, 18*, 137-149.

Spitzberg, B., & Brunner, C. (1991). Toward a theoretical integration of context and competence inference research. *Western Journal of Speech Communication, 55*, 28-46.

Spitzberg, B. H., & Canary, D. J. (1985). Loneliness and relationally competent communication. *Journal of Social and Personal Relationships, 2*, 387-402.

Spitzberg, B. H., & Canary, D. J. (1987). Appropriateness and effectiveness perceptions of conflict strategies. *Human Communication Research, 14*, 93-118.

Spitzberg, B. H., & Cupach, W. R. (1984). *Interpersonal communication competence*. Beverly Hills, CA: Sage.

Spitzberg, B. H., & Cupach, W. R. (1989). *Handbook of interpersonal competence research*. New York: Springer Verlag.

Spitzberg, B. H., & Cupach, W. R. (1990, February). *Decision points in the assessment of competence*. Paper presented at the WSCA Conference Workshop on Assessment of Interpersonal Competence, Sacramento, CA.

Spitzberg, B. H., & Hecht, M. L. (1984). A component model of relational competence. *Human Communication Research, 10*, 575-599.

Spitzberg, B. H., & Hurt, H. T. (1987). The measurement of interpersonal skills in instructional contexts. *Communication Education, 36*, 28-45.

Spitzberg, B. H., & Phelps, L. A. (1982, February). *Conversational appropriateness and effectiveness: Validation of a criterion measure of relational competence.* Paper presented at the Western Speech Communication Association convention, Denver, CO.

Stephan, W. G. (1985). Intergroup relations. In G. Lindzey & E. Aronson (Eds.), *Handbook of social psychology* (3rd ed., Vol. 2, pp. 599-658). New York: Random House.

Stephan, W. G. (1987). The contact hypothesis in intergroup relations. In C. Hendrick (Ed.), *Group processes and intergroup relations* (pp. 13-40). Newbury Park, CA: Sage.

Stephan, W. G., & Stephan, C. (1985). Intergroup anxiety. *Journal of Social Issues, 41,* 157-166.

Stephen, T. (1986). Communication and interdependence in geographically separated relationships. *Human Communication Research, 13,* 191-210.

Stewart, E. C. (1972). *American cultural patterns: A cross-cultural perspective.* LaGrange Park, IL: Intercultural Network.

Stewart, E. C., & Bennett, M. J. (1991). *American cultural patterns: A cross-cultural perspective* (rev. ed.). Yarmouth, ME: Intercultural Press.

Street, R. L., & Cappella, J. N. (1985). Sequence and pattern in communicative behavior: A model and commentary. In R. L. Street & J. N. Cappella (Eds.), *Sequence and pattern in communicative behavior* (pp. 243-276). Baltimore, MD: Edward Arnold.

Stryker, S. (1981). Symbolic interactionism: Themes and variations. In M. Rosenberg & R. H. Turner (Eds.), *Social psychology: Sociological perspectives* (pp. 3-29). New York: Basic Books.

Stryker, S. (1987). Identity theory: Developments and extensions. In K. Yardley & T. Honess (Eds.), *Self and society: Psychosocial perspectives* (pp. 89-104). Chichester, UK: John Wiley.

Stryker, S. (1991). Exploring the relevance of social cognition for the relationship of self and society: Linking the cognitive perspective and identity theory. In J. Howard & P. Callero (Eds.), *Self-society dynamic: Emotion, cognition and action* (pp. 19-41). Cambridge, UK: Cambridge University Press.

Strzyzewski, K. D. (1987). *Development and validation of a measure of positive and negative face needs.* Unpublished master's thesis, Illinois State University, Normal.

Sudweeks, S., Gudykunst, W. B., Ting-Toomey, S., & Nishida, T. (1990). Development themes in Japanese-North American interpersonal relationships. *International Journal of Intercultural Relations, 14,* 207-233.

Sunnafrank, M. (1986). Predicted outcome value during initial interactions. *Human Communication Research, 13,* 3-33.

Swann, W. (1983). Self-verification. In J. Suls & A. Greenwald (Eds.), *Psychological perspectives on the self* (Vol. 2, pp. 33-66). Hillsdale, NJ: Lawrence Erlbaum.

Swann, W. (1986). To be adored or to be known: The interplay of self-enhancement and self-verification. In E. T. Higgins & R. Sorrentino (Eds.), *Handbook of motivation and cognition: Foundations of social behavior* (pp. 408-448). New York: Guilford.

Swann, W., Jr., Pelham, B., & Krull, D. (1989). Agreeable fancy or disagreeable truth? Reconciling self-enhancement and self-verification. *Journal of Personality and Social Psychology, 57,* 782-791.

Sypher, H. E. (1980). Illusory correlation in communication research. *Human Communication Research, 7,* 83-87.

Tajfel, H. (1978). Social categorization, social identity, and social comparisons. In H. Tajfel (Ed.), *Differentiation between social groups* (pp. 61-76). London: Academic Press.

Tajfel, H. (1981). *Human categories and social groups.* Cambridge, UK: Cambridge University Press.

Tajfel, H., & Turner, J. (1979). An integrative theory of intergroup conflict. In W. Austin & S. Worchel (Eds.), *The social psychology of intergroup relations* (pp. 33-47). Monterey, CA: Brooks/Cole.

Tannen, D. (1981). Indirectness in discourse: Ethnicity as conversational style. *Discourse Processes, 3* (4), 221-238.

Tedeschi, J., & Norman, N. (1985). Social power, self-presentation, and the self. In B. Schlenker (Ed.), *The self and social life* (pp. 293-322). New York: McGraw-Hill.

Thorndike, R. L. (1920). Intelligence and its uses. *Harpers Monthly, 140*, 227-235.

Ting-Toomey, S. (1985). Toward a theory of conflict and culture. In W. Gudykunst, L. Stewart, & S. Ting-Toomey (Eds.), *Communication, culture, and organizational processes* (pp. 71-86). Beverly Hills, CA: Sage.

Ting-Toomey, S. (1986). Interpersonal ties in intergroup communication. In W. Gudykunst (Ed.), *Intergroup communication* (pp. 114-126). London: Edward Arnold.

Ting-Toomey, S. (1987, March). *Intercultural conflicts: A face-negotiation model.* Paper presented at the Temple University Discourse Conference, Philadelphia.

Ting-Toomey, S. (1988). Intercultural conflicts: A face-negotiation theory. In Y. Kim & W. Gudykunst (Eds.), *Theories in intercultural communication* (pp. 213-238). Newbury Park, CA: Sage.

Ting-Toomey, S. (1989a). Identity and interpersonal bonding. In M. Asante & W. Gudykunst (Eds.), *Handbook of international and intercultural communication* (pp. 351-373). Newbury Park, CA: Sage.

Ting-Toomey, S. (1989b). Culture and interpersonal relationship development: Some conceptual issues. In J. Anderson (Ed.), *Communication yearbook 12* (pp. 371-382). Newbury Park, CA: Sage.

Ting-Toomey, S. (1991). Intimacy expressions in three cultures: France, Japan, and the United States. *International Journal of Intercultural Relations, 15*, 29-46.

Ting-Toomey, S. (in press a). *Intercultural communication process: Crossing boundaries.* New York: Guilford.

Ting-Toomey, S. (Ed.). (in press b). *The challenge of facework: Cross-cultural and interpersonal variations.* Albany, NY: State University of New York Press.

Ting-Toomey, S., Gao, G., Trubisky, P., Yang, Z., Kim, H. S., Lin, S.-L., Nishida, T. (1991). Culture, face maintenance, and styles of handling interpersonal conflict: A study in five cultures. *The International Journal of Conflict Management, 2*, 275-296.

Tracy, K. (1990). The many faces of facework. In H. Giles & W. P. Robinson (Eds.), *Handbook of language and social psychology* (pp. 209-226). New York: John Wiley.

Triandis, H. C. (1972). *The analysis of subjective culture.* New York: John Wiley.

Triandis, H. C. (1973). Culture training, cognitive complexity, and interpersonal attitudes. In D. Hoopes (Ed.), *Readings in intercultural communication* (Vol. 2, pp. 55-67). Pittsburgh: Regional Council for International Education.

Triandis, H. C. (1977). *Interpersonal behavior.* Monterey, CA: Brooks/Cole.

Triandis, H. C. (1983). Essentials of studying cultures. In D. Landis & R. W. Brislin (Eds.), *Handbook of intercultural training, Volume 1: Issues in theory and design* (pp. 82-117). New York: Pergamon.

Triandis, H. C. (1988). Collectivism vs. individualism. In G. Verma & C. Bagley (Eds.), *Cross-cultural studies of personality, attitudes, and cognition* (pp. 60-95). London: Macmillan.

Triandis, H. C. (1990). Cross-cultural studies of individualism and collectivism. In J. Berman (Ed.), *Nebraska symposium on motivation* (pp. 41-133). Lincoln: University of Nebraska Press.

Triandis, H. C., Bontempo, R., Betancourt, H., Bond, M., Leung, K., Brenes, A., Georgas, J., Hui, C., Marin, G., Setiadi, B., Sinha, J., Verma, J., Spangenberg, J., Touzard, H., & de Montmollin, G. (1986). The measurement of etic aspects of individualism-collectivism across cultures. *Australian Journal of Psychology, 38*, 257-267.

Triandis, H. C., Bontempo, R., Villareal, M. J., Asai, M., & Lucca, N. (1988a). Individualism and collectivism: Cross-cultural perspectives on self-ingroup relationships. *Journal of Personality and Social Psychology, 54*(2), 323-338.

Triandis, H. C., Brislin, R., & Hui, C. H. (1988b). Cross-cultural training across the individualism-collectivism divide. *International Journal of Intercultural Relations, 12*, 269-289.

Triandis, H. C., Leung, K., Villareal, M. J., & Clark, F. L. (1985). Allocentric versus idiocentric tendencies: Convergent and discriminant validation. *Journal of Research in Personality, 19*, 395-415.

Trower, P. (1982). Toward a generative model of social skills: A critique and synthesis. In J. P. Curran & P. M. Monti (Eds.), *Social skills training* (pp. 399-427). New York: Guilford.

Trower, P. (1983). Social skills and applied linguistics: Radical implications for training. In R. Ellis & D. Whittington (Eds.), *New directions in social skills training* (pp. 30-49). London: Croom Helm.

Trower, P. (1984). A radical critique and reformulation: From organism to agent. In P. Trower (Ed.), *Radical approaches to social skills training* (pp. 48-88). London: Croom Helm.

Trubisky, P., Ting-Toomey, S., & Lin, S. (1991). The influence of individualism-collectivism and self-monitoring on conflict styles. *International Journal of Intercultural Relations, 15*, 65-84.

Trungpa, C. (1973). *Cutting through spiritual materialism*. Boulder, CO: Shambala.

Turner, J. C. (1987). *Rediscovering the social group*. Oxford, UK: Basil Blackwell.

Turner, J. H. (1987). Toward a sociological theory of motivation. *American Sociological Review, 52*, 15-27.

Turner, J. H. (1988). *A theory of social interaction*. Stanford, CA: Stanford University Press.

Turner, R. H. (1968). The self-conception in social interaction. In C. Gordon & K. Gergen (Eds.), *The self in social interaction* (Vol. 1). New York: John Wiley.

Turner, R. H. (1987). Articulating self and social structure. In K. Yardley & T. Honess (Eds.), *Self and society: Psychosocial perspectives* (pp. 119-132). Chichester, UK: John Wiley.

van Dijk, T., & Kintsch, W. (1983). *Strategies of discourse comprehension*. New York: Academic Press.

Vanlear, C. A. (1991). Testing a cyclical model of communicative openness in relationship development. *Communication Monographs, 58*, 337-361.

Varenne, H. (Ed.). (1986). *Symbolizing America*. Lincoln: University of Nebraska Press.

Vassiliou, V., & Vassiliou, G. (1973). The implicative meaning of the Greek concept of philotimo. *Journal of Cross-Cultural Psychology, 4*, 326-341.

von Cranach, M., Kalbermatten, U., Indermuhle, K., & Gugler, B. (1982). *Goal-directed action*. London: Academic Press.

von Cranach, M., Machler, E., & Steiner, V. (1985). The organization of goal-directed action: A research report. In G. P. Ginsberg, M. Brenner, & M. von Cranach (Eds.), *Discovery strategies in the psychology of action* (pp. 19-62). London: Academic Press.

Waldinger, R. (1977). Achieving several goals simultaneously. In E. W. Elcock & D. Michie (Eds.), *Machine intelligence 8* (pp. 94-136). Chichester, UK: Ellis Horwood.

Watson, D. (1982). The actor and the observer: How are their perceptions of causality divergent? *Psychological Bulletin, 92*, 682-700.

Weinstein, E. A. (1969). The development of interpersonal competence. In D. A. Goslin (Ed.), *Handbook of socialization theory and research* (pp. 753-775). Chicago: Rand McNally.

Welford, A. T. (1980). The concept of skill and its application to social performance. In W. T. Singleton, P. Spurgeon, & R. B. Stammers (Eds.), *The analysis of social skill* (pp. 11-22). New York: Plenum.

Werner, H. (1957). The concept of development from a comparative and organismic point of view. In D. Harris (ed.), *The concept of development* (pp. 125-146). Minneapolis: University of Minnesota Press.

Wheeler, L., Reis, H., & Bond, M. (1989). Collectivism-individualism in everyday social life: The Middle Kingdom and the melting pot. *Journal of Personality and Social Psychology, 57*, 79-86.

Wieder, D. L., & Pratt, S. (1990). On being a recognizable Indian. In D. Carbaugh (Ed.), *Cultural communication and intercultural contact* (pp. 45-64). Hillsdale, NJ: Lawrence Erlbaum.

Wiemann, J. M. (1977). Explication and test of a model of communicative competence. *Human Communication Research, 3*, 195-213.

Wiemann, J. M., & Backlund, P. (1980). Current theory and research in communicative competence. *Review of Educational Research, 50*, 185-199.

Wiemann, J. M., & Bradac, J. J. (1985). The many guises of communicative competence. *Journal of Language and Social Psychology, 4*, 131-138.

Wiemann, J., & Bradac, J. (1989). Metatheoretical issues in the study of communicative competence. In B. Dervin (Ed.), *Progress of communication science* (Vol. 9, pp. 261-284). Norwood, NJ: Ablex.

Wiemann, J. M., & Kelly, C. W. (1981). Pragmatics of interpersonal competence. In C. Wilder-Mott & J. H. Weakland (Eds.), *Rigor and imagination: Essays from the legacy of Gregory Bateson* (pp. 283-297). New York: Praeger.

Wierzbicka, A. (1989). Soul and mind: Linguistic evidence for ethnopsychology and cultural history. *American Anthropologist, 91*, 41-58.

Wilder, D. A., & Shapiro, P. (1989). Effects of anxiety on impression formation in a group context. *Journal of Experimental Social Psychology, 25*, 481-499.

Wilensky, R. (1981). Meta-planning: Representing and using knowledge about planning in problem solving and natural language understanding. *Cognitive Science, 5*, 197-233.

Wilensky, R. (1983). *Planning and understanding: A computational approach to human reasoning*. Reading, MA: Addison-Wesley.

Wilson, S. R., & Putnam, L. L. (1990). Interaction goals in negotiation. In J. A. Anderson (Ed.), *Communication yearbook 13* (pp. 374-427). Newbury Park, CA: Sage.

Wilson, T. D., & Stone, J. I. (1985). Limitations of self-knowledge: More on telling more than we can know. In P. Shaver (Ed.), *Self, situations, and social behavior* (pp. 167-183). Beverly Hills, CA: Sage.

Wine, J. D. (1981). From defect to competence models. In J. D. Wine & M. D. Smye (Eds.), *Social competence* (pp. 3-35). New York: Guilford.

Winer, B. J. (1971). *Statistical principles in experimental design*. New York: McGraw-Hill.

Wiseman, R. L. (1980). Toward a rules perspective of intercultural communication. *Communication, 9*, 30-38.

Wiseman, R. L., & Abe, H. (1984). Finding and explaining differences: A reply to Gudykunst and Hammer. *International Journal of Intercultural Relations, 8*, 11-16.

Wiseman, R. L., & Abe, H. (1986). Cognitive complexity and intercultural effectiveness. In M. McLaughlin (Ed.), *Communication yearbook 9* (pp. 611-624). Beverly Hills, CA: Sage.

Wiseman, R. L., Hammer, M. R., & Nishida, H. (1989). Predictors of intercultural communication competence. *International Journal of Intercultural Relations, 13*, 349-370.

Wish, M., D'Andrade, R. G., & Goodnow, J. E., II (1980). Dimensions of interpersonal communication: Correspondences between structures for speech acts and bipolar scales. *Journal of Personality and Social Psychology, 39*, 848-860.

Wolfson, K., & Pearce, W. B. (1983). A cross-cultural comparison of the implications of self-disclosure on conversational logics. *Communication Quarterly, 31*, 249-256.

Wood, J. T. (1982). Communication and relational culture: Bases for the study of human relationships. *Communication Quarterly, 30*, 75-83.

Wyer, R. S., Jr., & Bodenhausen, G. V. (1985). Event memory: The effects of processing objectives and time delay on memory for action sequences. *Journal of Personality and Social Psychology, 49*, 301-316.

Yang, K. S. (1981). Social orientation and individual modernity among Chinese students in Taiwan. *Journal of Social Psychology, 113*, 159-170.

Yingling, J. M. (1986, May). *Interpersonal communication competence: Contributions of individual tendency and relational context.* Paper presented at the International Communication Association conference, Chicago.

Yoshikawa, M. (1978). Some Japanese and American cultural characteristics. In M. Prosser (Ed.), *The cultural dialogue: An introduction to intercultural communication* (pp. 220-251). Boston: Houghton Mifflin.

Yule, G., & Tarone, E. (1990). Eliciting the performance of strategic competence. In R. C. Scarcella, E. S. Andersen, & S. D. Krashen (Eds.), *Developing communicative competence in a second language* (pp. 179-194). New York: Newbury House.

Yum, J. O. (1988). The impact of Confucianism on interpersonal relationships and communication patterns in East Asia. *Communication Monographs, 55*, 374-388.

Zakahi, W. R. (1987). Gender and loneliness. In L. P. Stewart & S. Ting-Toomey (Eds.), *Communication, gender, and sex roles in diverse interaction contexts* (pp. 11-17). Norwood, NJ: Ablex.

Index

About the Editors

RICHARD L. WISEMAN is Professor of Speech Communication at California State University, Fullerton. His research interests include intercultural communication effectiveness, interpersonal persuasion, and teaching effectiveness. His work has appeared in *Communication Yearbook*, *Communication Monographs*, *Research in Higher Education*, *Communication Education*, and *International Journal of Intercultural Relations*, among others. He has served as Chairperson to the Intercultural Communication Divisions of the Speech Communication Association and the Western States Communication Association.

JOLENE KOESTER is Professor of Communication Studies and Associate Vice-President for Academic Affairs at California State University, Sacramento. Her research interests focus on intercultural communication competence and its measurement. Her work has appeared in *Communication Education*, *Communication Quarterly*, *International Journal of Intercultural Relations*, and the *Modern Language Journal*. She recently completed a textbook in intercultural communication, *Interpersonal Competence: Interpersonal Communication Across Cultures*, with coauthor Myron Lustig. She has served as Chairperson of the International and Intercultural Communication Division of the Speech Communication Association.

About the Contributors

DONAL CARBAUGH is Associate Professor of Communication at the University of Massachusetts, Amherst. His research interests concern the development of a communication theory of sociocultural interaction integrating elements of identity, forms of action, and emotional expression. His recent edited volume, *Cultural Communication and Intercultural Contact*, was given the Distinguished Scholarship Award by the Speech Communication Association's International and Intercultural Communication Division.

WILLIAM R. CUPACH (Ph.D., University of Southern California) is Professor of Communication at Illinois State University. His research interests include communication competence, relationship development and dissolution, and the management of problematic situations. He coauthored with Brian Spitzberg the *Handbook of Interpersonal Competence Research*.

WILLIAM B. GUDYKUNST is Professor of Speech Communication at California State University, Fullerton. His goal is to develop a theory of interpersonal and intergroup communication that generalizes across cultures. Recent work includes *Bridging Differences* (Sage, 1991), *Communicating with Strangers* (with Young Yun Kim), and *Communication in Japan and the United States*. In May 1992, he was elected a Fellow of the International Communication Association.

T. TODD IMAHORI (Ph.D., Ohio University) is Associate Professor of Speech and Communication Studies at San Francisco State University. His research foci are intercultural communication competence, face and problematic communication, and communication in multinational organizations. His writings have appeared in *International Journal of Intercultural Relations* and *Western Journal of Communication*.

KENNETH M. JOHNSON (Ph.D., University of Massachusetts) is Assistant Professor in the Department of Speech Communication at Syracuse University.

MIN-SUN KIM (Ph.D., Michigan State University) is Assistant Professor in the Department of Speech at the University of Hawaii at Manoa. Her research and teaching interests include intercultural message processing, the relationship between cognition and culture, and conversational styles.

MYRON W. LUSTIG (Ph.D., University of Wisconsin) is Professor of Speech Communication at San Diego State University. His research interests include intercultural and interpersonal communication theories, methods, and processes. His articles have appeared in more than a dozen national and regional scholarly journals. He is the coauthor (with Jolene Koester) of *Intercultural Competence: Interpersonal Communication Across Cultures*.

JUDITH N. MARTIN (Ph.D., Pennsylvania State University) is Associate Professor of Communication at Arizona State University. Her research interests include the situational bases of intercultural competence, cultural identity, and interethnic communication.

VIRGINIA H. MILHOUSE (Ph.D., University of Oklahoma) is Assistant Professor of Human Relations at the University of Oklahoma. Her current research interests include international/intercultural competence and international education and training.

MASAYUKI NAKANISHI (Ph.D., University of Kansas) is Associate Professor of Communication in the Department of English Language and Literature at Tsuda College, Tokyo, Japan.

JUDITH A. SANDERS (J.D., Loyola Law School) is currently Associate Professor in the Department of Communication at California State Polytechnic University, Pomona. Her research interests include intercultural communication effectiveness, instructional communication, and argumentation. She received a Distinguished Scholarship Award from the Speech Communication Association for her work on the multicultural classroom.

BRIAN H. SPITZBERG (Ph.D., University of Southern California) is Professor of Speech Communication and Director of Graduate Studies at San Diego State University. His research interests include interpersonal communication competence, relational communication and conflict management, and communication theory. He is coauthor (with

William R. Cupach) of *Interpersonal Communication Competence* and *Handbook of Interpersonal Competence Research*.

STELLA TING-TOOMEY (Ph.D., University of Washington) is Professor of Speech Communication at California State University, Fullerton. Her recent books include *The Challenge of Facework: Cross-Cultural and Interpersonal Issues*, *Culture and Interpersonal Communication* (with William Gudykunst), and *Cross-Cultural Interpersonal Communication* (with Felipe Korzenny). Her publications have appeared in *International Journal of Intercultural Relations*, *International Journal of Conflict Management*, *Human Communication Research*, *Communication Monographs*, and *Communication Education*. She has held leadership roles in major communication associations.